TRANSACTIONS

OF THE

AMERICAN PHILOSOPHICAL SOCIETY

HELD AT PHILADELPHIA

FOR PROMOTING USEFUL KNOWLEDGE

NEW SERIES—VOLUME 55, PART 1
1965

MASTER NICHOLAS OF DRESDEN THE OLD COLOR AND THE NEW

SELECTED WORKS CONTRASTING THE PRIMITIVE CHURCH AND THE ROMAN CHURCH

Edited, Annotated, and Translated by

HOWARD KAMINSKY, DEAN LOY BILDERBACK, IMRE BOBA,
and PATRICIA N. ROSENBERG

University of Washington

THE AMERICAN PHILOSOPHICAL SOCIETY

INDEPENDENCE SQUARE

PHILADELPHIA

MARCH, 1965

Copyright © 1965 by The American Philosophical Society

Library of Congress Catalog
Card Number 64–25396

FOREWORD

This edition was prepared in my seminar in medieval history at the University of Washington, in 1961. Each of the three students and myself took part of each text and carried out the work of transcription, collation, annotation, and translation; then each individual's work was checked by the seminar as a whole. Thus the actual edition is the product of our joint enterprise. The introductory essay and prefaces, however, were written by myself, and the indices were prepared by Patricia Rosenberg, who also undertook the exacting task of typing the final copy.

The cost of getting microfilms and positive copies of manuscripts, and of having the whole retyped, was paid from a grant by the Agnes H. Anderson Fund of the University of Washington, for which we are grateful. We are also indebted to Mr. Kenneth S. Allen and Miss Marie M. Gosebrink, successively in charge of Library Acquisitions, for their energetic help in securing reference works, and we are most grateful to Messrs. J. R. Todd and R. D. Monroe of the Reference Division of the Library, for allowing us to use its holdings in a convenient manner.

Finally, I should like to record the present status of the other editors: Dr. Boba is Assistant Professor at the University of Washington; D. L. Bilderback is Assistant Professor at Fresno State College; Patricia Rosenberg is humanities reference librarian at the University of Oregon.

H. K.

University of Washington

MASTER NICHOLAS OF DRESDEN: THE OLD COLOR AND THE NEW

Selected Works Contrasting the Primitive Church and the Roman Church

Edited, Annotated, and Translated by

HOWARD KAMINSKY, DEAN LOY BILDERBACK, IMRE BOBA, AND PATRICIA N. ROSENBERG

CONTENTS

	PAGE
Nicholas of Dresden and the Dresden School in Hussite Prague	5
The Works of Nicholas of Dresden	28
Tabule veteris et novi coloris	32
Preface	32
Text	38
Translation	38
Consuetudo et ritus primitive ecclesie et moderne	66
Text	66
Translation	66
Indices	86

NICHOLAS OF DRESDEN AND THE DRESDEN SCHOOL IN HUSSITE PRAGUE

Among the several components of Hussitism, one was a strong element of proto-nationalism, a combination of Slavonicism, national messianism, and anti-Germanism. The Westernization of Bohemia had been in large part the work of Germans and had taken the form of both imitation and importation of German institutions; on the other hand, the process had been successful to the point of bringing the Czech nationality up to the German—or European—level, and by the end of the fourteenth century the superior position of the Germans in many areas of social life was challenged by Czech claims to equality or pre-eminence. In some cases, most notably when Czech peasants won "German Law" status, the process hurt no one; when, however, there was a limited quantity of good things, such as offices on town councils or ecclesiastical prebends, the Czech claim to a larger share could succeed only at the expense of German interests. Nor did the objectively competitive situation fail to generate emotions of mutual ethnic hatred, with the further effect, on the Czech side, of a kind of positive ideological reflex, a feeling of Czech pride and the delusion of a special and glorious Czech destiny. As we might expect, this Czech self-consciousness found its most intensely cultivated expression among those who were professionally occupied with ideas, the Czech intelligentsia of the University of Prague.

In the last two or three decades of the fourteenth century this element had increasingly espoused the ideas of religious and moral reform, partly at least as a mode of national self-assertion, and by the beginning of the fifteenth century a good deal of the intellectual life of the University consisted of Czech-German controversies in philosophy, where the Czechs' Wyclifite realism was opposed to the Germans' nominalism, and in theology, where the Czechs' espousal of Wyclifism was met by German orthodoxy. But although much of the dynamism that would carry the Czech reform movement forward into revolt, revolution, and reformation undoubtedly derived from this fruitful struggle, the comcomitant conversion of an international community of scholars into a battleground of nationalities had unfortunate consequences. At one point in the complicated political maneuverings connected with the Schism and the Conciliar movement, King Wenceslas IV wished the University of Prague to support his withdrawal of obedience from Pope Gregory XII; the Germans refused but the Czechs agreed, and won for their reward the Kutná Hora Decree of 1409, which reversed the power relationship at the University by giving three votes to the Czech Nation, only one vote to the three German-dominated Nations combined. In consequence most of the German masters and students left Prague, some founding the University of Leipzig, others going elsewhere; henceforth Prague's University would be an instrument of the Czech reform party, a national institution. But at the same time the international matrix that had engendered and nourished the reform movement seemed to disappear, leaving the paradox of an ecumenically oriented movement that held its actual existence as a local, ethnically limited phenomenon.

And yet the universalism implicit in the idea of reform did not fail to assert itself, alongside the national element and sometimes in opposition to it. The international community of the medieval establishment, the university, was replaced by an International of heresy. Disaffected elements from far-off as well as neighboring lands began to move into Bohemia, sometimes as individuals who joined the Czechs, sometimes as groups that maintained their alien identity, but generally serving to nourish the springs of revolt and revolution with the fruits—ideas, emotions, attitudes —of generations of heretical experience. The end result was perhaps less pleasant for the Czech nation than interesting to the historian, but it is in any case probable that the greatest act of the Czech people—Hussitism—required this international concentration of ideas and energies for its realization, just as it also required a continuing international orientation to preserve itself from provincial insignificance. Nor is it surprising to find that the German nationality was well represented in the new Prague and in the reformed Bohemia that began to take shape; whatever of nationalistic prejudice the Hussites maintained, and expresesd in such phrases as "Our born enemies the Germans,"[1] was counterbalanced by the idealism that John Hus had aptly voiced when he wrote, "A good German is dearer to me than an evil brother."[2]

Thus it could happen that for a half-dozen of Hussitism's most decisive years, from 1412 to 1417, an important role in the reform movement was played by a group of Germans in Prague, known as the "Dresdeners" or the "Dresden School."[3] The history of this group in Dresden is not at all clear, but we can surmise why they left: on 18 October 1411 Bishop Rudolph of Meissen, Dresden's diocesan, issued a decree forbidding the teaching of the Bible and *Decretum* in secondary schools, and soon after that we find the Dresden School relocated in Prague, no doubt in direct consequence.[4] There is evidence that the masters of this school did indeed introduce theological and canonistic subject-matter into the curriculum of what was supposed to be simply a preparatory school teaching grammar and other basic arts; more to the point no doubt is the fact that the higher subjects were taught with a strongly anti-Roman tendency.[4a] John Drändorf, a disciple of the school who fell into the hands of the inquisition in 1425, told his examiners[5] that he had done his basic studies in Dresden, under Master Frederick and Master Peter, who had taught him, among other things, that Christ, not the Pope or even St. Peter, was the head of the Church Militant. He refused on principle to swear an oath, did not read his canonical hours, held that ordination as priest was sufficient license to preach anywhere, believed that priests should live without wealth, according to the manner of Christ, and should not exercise secular dominion, nor should the Church have accepted such dominion from the Emperor Constantine; he rejected the validity of Roman excommunications and the claims of the Roman hierarchy to obedience, and he held that it was necessary only to believe what was in the Bible. That Drändorf also confessed to a belief in utraquism—that communion should be given in both kinds to the laity—may be probably taken as an indication of what he had learnt in Hussite Prague; although there are sources that identify utraquism as among the doctrines of the Dresden School in Dresden, and indeed as a prime contribution of that School to Hussitism, these testimonies are suspect and, for the most part, late.[6] But if Drändorf's confession be taken generally and as a whole, it suggests at the very least that an extremely radical anti-Romanism was cultivated by Masters Frederick and Peter in Dresden, an anti-Romanism that

---

[1] The phrase appears in Prague's manifesto of 3 April, 1420, summoning faithful Czechs to resist the Crusade (*Archiv český*, **3** (1844), ed. Fr. Palacký, p. 212).

[2] "Výklad desatera," ed. K. J. Erben, *Mistra Jana Husi, Sebrané spisy české* (Prague, 1865), **1**: p. 156.

[3] The most important discussions of this group in the modern literature are Jan Sedlák's *Mikuláš z Dráždăn* (Brno, 1914); F. M. Bartoš's "Vznik a počátky táborství," *Husitství a cizina* (Prague, 1931), pp. 113–153; Josef Pekař's "Jakoubek a Mikuláš z Dráždăn; vznik táborství," Ch. I of *Žižka a jeho doba*, I (Prague, 1927), pp. 1–31. The first two will be referred to as "Sedlák" and "Bartoš." A sound summary of Sedlák's work, with some additional material, is offered by J. Th. Müller, "Magister Nikolaus von Dresden," *Zeitschrift für Brüdergeschichte*, **9** (1915): pp. 80–109. Less valuable, because not *au courant* of Czech scholarship, is H. Böhmer's "Magister Peter von Dresden," *Neues Archiv für Sächsische Geschichte und Altertumskunde*, **36** (1915): pp. 212–231; *cf.* Bartoš's review, *Časopis českého musea*, **91** (1917): pp. 336 f.

[4] Sedlák, p. 4; Bartoš, p. 130 f. A note at the end of one of the texts of the *Tabule*, in MS Prague Cathedral Chapter A 79/5, f. 261, reads: "Ista scripta ad hunc sensum hereticum collecta sunt redacta in hanc formam per Draznenses, qui de Drazna expulsi, plurimos seduxerunt." And an anonymous account, published by K. Höfler, *Geschichtschreiber der husitischen Bewegung in Böhmen*, III, *Fontes rerum austriacarum*, I. Abt., (Vienna, 1866), **7**: p. 156, says: "Circa annum Domini MCCCCXII in civitate draznensi, Misnensis diocesis . . . Petrus et Nicolaus puerorum eruditores in ipsius nominata civitatis draznensis schola plurimas curiosas moventes questiones illas non sunt veriti juxta capita sua contra auctoritatem sacrae scripturae et sanctorum decretorum sinistre definire. . . . Que eorum doctrina cum ad aures viri clarissimi domini Joannis episcopi . . . pervenisset, mox ipsos Petrum et Nicolaum cum eorum doctrinae faventibus excludi jussit et eliminari de episcopatu Misnensi." Bartoš shows that the account has the name of the bishop wrong, and indeed some of its other information is dubious (e.g., that Nicholas was Peter's associate in Dresden; there is no mention of Frederick Eppinge—see below). A Czech rhymed chronicle also reports that the Dresdeners had been expelled from Dresden (ed. Palacký, *Staří letopisové čeští, Scriptores rerum bohemicarum*, (Prague, 1829), **3**: p. 472).

[4a] See the anonymous account quoted in note 4. It specifies that among the "curious questions" raised by the masters in Dresden was "an laicis sit porrigenda communio duplicis speciei," a probably incorrect report (see note 6, below), and it lists the doctrines they favored in Prague as: "purgatorium post hanc vitam animarum non esse. Quod sanctorum suffragia non sunt invocanda. Quod papa sive Romanus pontifex sit antichristus cum clero sibi subjecto et quod communio eucharistie sub duplici specie laicis sit administranda, et cetere plures . . . sinistre, quas docebant, fantasie." Whether these heresies were also taught in Dresden is not stated: but compare Drändorf's confession, below.

[5] The record of his interrogation, along with four of his agitational missives, is published by J. E. Kapp, *Kleine Nachlese einiger . . . Urkunden* **3** (Leipzig, 1730): pp. 33–60. *Cf.* the discussion by H. Haupt, "Waldensertum und Inquisition im südöstlichen Deutschland," *Deutsche Zeitschrift für Geschichtswissenschaft*, **3** (1890): pp. 357 ff.

[6] The best study of this question is Bartoš's "Počátky kalicha v Čechách," *Husitství a cizina*, pp. 59–112, esp. pp. 75–80. *Cf.* Sedlák's "Počátkové kalicha," *Časopis katolického duchovenstva*, **52** (1911): p. 247 & *passim*; also Böhmer, *op. cit.*, for a systematic discussion of the main Latin sources.

reminds us of nothing so much as the doctrines of John Wyclif,[7] the very doctrines then being advocated in Prague by the more radical members of Hus's party. Pursuing this point further, we may observe that Master Peter of Dresden may have been among the Germans who had left Prague in 1409,[8] that Master Frederick—Frederick Eppinge, to give him his full name—probably had been,[9] and so, by his own statement, had been Drändorf.[10] And these are the only names that we can identify certainly with the Dresden period of the school's activity. The most reasonable supposition would be that in the decade preceding 1409 some of the German masters and students at the University of Prague agreed with the Czech reformers rather than with most of their own compatriots, that these German radicals read the works of Wyclif with the same sympathy, perhaps enthusiasm, as was displayed by Hus, and that for some reason, when the time of exile came, these men gathered at Dresden, which thus became a heretical counterpart to Leipzig as a place of refuge,[11] and a German parallel to Prague as a center of Wyclifite anti-Romanism. In any case, according to this reconstruction, the abnormal situation in Dresden lasted only for about a year and a half; when action was taken against the German radicals by Bishop Rudolph they naturally returned to Prague, which had become even more of a center of radical reform.

Once in Prague, the Dresdeners quickly formed or resumed ties of friendship with the Prague masters of Hus's party. The University's Czech Nation, dominated by this party, gave the Germans a house, "At the Black Rose," close to the Carolinum, the main University building,[12] and in a very short space of time, by July/August, 1412, Frederick Eppinge appeared as the associate of Hus, Jakoubek of Stříbro, and others in defending Wyclifism against the Czech Romanists.[13] The controversy then turned on several articles of the list of forty-five Wyclifite doctrines that had been composed in 1403 and had formed the main subject of doctrinal conflict in Prague since that date;[14] Eppinge either chose or was assigned the defense of article eleven: "No prelate should excommunicate anyone unless he know that man first to have been excommunicated by God. Otherwise, in excommunicating him, the prelate becomes a heretic or excommunicate himself." The text of the defense, "Credo communionem sanctorum," survives in several copies,[15] and, dating so soon after the move from Dresden, may be taken as further evidence of the kind of radical doctrine cultivated at the school even before it had come to Prague. The theory behind it was, in a general way, quite familiar to the Hussites: distinguishing between the "communion of the saints" and the "congregation of all believers in Christ," the former the invisible community of the just, the latter the actual church including both good and bad, Eppinge noted that exclusion by God's decree from the former communion was the effect of mortal sin and was brought on himself by the sinner, while exclusion from the actual church was the effect of judicial sentence passed by the church's judges. At best the two might coincide, and the church's excommunication would then be declaratory of God's prior judgment, but if this were not the case, if the church's sentence was erroneous, perhaps even prompted by unworthy motives, then it was negligible in its primary significance and should be feared only because of its secondary effects. Hus had developed a similar argument in his commentary on the *Sentences* (1407/1409), and most of his canonistic authorities, about a dozen, were used by Eppinge; the latter, however, was a Bachelor of Canon Law, and was able to add a great deal more canonistic documentation to his argument, which in any case did not follow that of Hus in its detailed disposition. There was undoubtedly some collaboration between the two, but most of Ep-

---

[7] Although Wyclifism shared its basic points of anti-Romanism with other reform tendencies of the time, it was especially distinguished by its emphasis on the primacy of the Bible, the *Lex dei*, on the one hand, and on the other hand, the internal contradictions in both the theory and practice of the juridical ecclesiology of the High Middle Ages. The elaborate and often penetrating use of *standard* sources—the Fathers, the scholastics, the canon law and the canonists—in an anti-Roman sense is also characteristic of Wyclifism. On all these points the Dresdeners seemed close to the Englishman's system; but much more work of textual analysis will be necessary before a more definite conclusion can be pronounced.

[8] Aeneas Sylvius Piccolomini, *Historia bohemica*, ch. xxxv: ". . . Petrus Dresdensis . . . qui cum aliis Teutonibus paulo ante [*scil.*, before 1414] Bohemiam reliquerat." To be sure, Aeneas says that Peter was infected by Waldensianism, not Wyclifism.

[9] In his *posicio* on excommunication (note 15, below) he wrote, "Ideo ex permissione matris mee, alme universitatis studii Pragensis, iuxta conclusionem eiusdem assumpsi tractandos articulos duos . . ." (p. 107).

[10] Kapp, *op. cit.*, pp. 37 f.: "Item interrogatus, anne studuit in aliquibus studiis privilegiatis. Respondit quid sic, scilicet in studio Pragensi & Lipzensi." Most of the Germans who left Prague in 1409 migrated to Leipzig. Since Drändorf was in Prague by 1412 (note 135, below), and had studied in Dresden under Frederick and Peter, who also came to Prague at that time, we cannot refer his Leipzig studies to a period after that date; since he was only eighteen years old in 1409 (*loc. cit.*), he could hardly have studied at both Prague and Leipzig in the period before that year, nor indeed was Leipzig a university before 1409.

[11] See the preceding note.

[12] Bartoš, p. 130 f.; cf. Sedlák, p. 2 ff.

[13] The best account is in V. Novotný, *M. Jan Hus, Život a dílo* (Prague, 1921), 2: pp. 123 ff.

[14] Novotný, *op. cit.* (1919) 1: pp. 103 ff.; Sedlák, *M. Jan Hus* (Prague, 1915), p. 92 ff.

[15] It is included in the *Tractatus responsivus* composed by John Hus or Jakoubek of Stříbro, and edited by S. Harrison Thomson (Prague, 1927), pp. 103–133. On the question of authorship of the *Tractatus* itself, a question turning in part on the author's relationship to Eppinge, see Bartoš, "M. J. Hussii tractatus responsivus," *ČČM*, CI (1927), pp. 23–35. See also: Bartoš, p. 131, n. 56.

pinge's work seems to be his own.[16] Furthermore, although defending a Wyclifite position, and perhaps inspired by Wyclifism, Eppinge advanced a concept of the *communio sanctorum* that differed sharply from Wyclif's—and Hus's—equivalent concept of the community of the predestined. The former was, like the latter, the invisible body constituting the true communion, but it was defined merely as a society of holy men, enjoying the communal property of spiritual goods by virtue of love (*caritas*), and individually participating in that property according to their individual spiritual qualifications, these depending on the strength of their moral characters. "One participates more than another according to the extent that he disposes himself more fully to the capacity of participating, by applying his strength with greater fervor, desire, and work." [17] Each must indeed strive to increase his own capacity for good, not only in order to share more fully, but also in order to bring something more of the good to the whole. Naturally enough, in this view, a man could fall away from the communion of the saints simply by ceasing to be good: that is, by losing the grace of *caritas* and sinning; according to predestinarian ecclesiology, however, no amount of sinning could deprive one of the predestinate of his happy status, just as no amount of "present righteousness" could change the fate of the man foreknown to damnation.[18] The differences did not matter in the case at hand, but they are sharp enough to show that Eppinge's Wyclifism was by no means unreserved; neither, for that matter, was Hus's or Jakoubek's. Each had his own mode of appropriating the common fund. Soon after Eppinge's death, which occurred at the end of 1412, John Hus wrote that he had been "a pious Christian, a great student and protagonist of the Law of Christ," [19] and Jakoubek of Stříbro wrote of him as of a "god-fearing and humble man," [20] but in 1425, testifying before the inquisition, with no reason to fear for his dead master or to hope for himself, John Drändorf said that Eppinge —"humble and devout"—"was not nor had ever been of the sect of Hussites." [21] Looking back on the matter we may say that Eppinge was as much of a Hussite as anyone could have been in 1412, that in a period when ideas were in the process of jelling into ideology he made his specific contribution to the nascent movement. Those who survived him in the Dresden school would have to find their own way of continuing his tradition.

It is precisely here that we may see the nub of the Dresdeners' problem, which has also become a problem for modern scholarship. On the one side was the world of the Czech reform movement, dominating the University, increasingly influential among the people of Prague, and very closely connected with leading members of the feudality and with the royal court.[22] It was in this world that reform, in the sense of a societal reformation, could be achieved, but at the same time the passage of reform to the sphere of political action meant its contraction, from a body of ideas to a pattern of reality, from universal formulations to concrete action. And while the Dresdeners could and did hold ideas identical to those of the Czech Hussites, they could hardly look to the same future; their mission was to preach their brand of sectarian reform to their own people, the Germans, and to continue their school as the seed-bed of such missionary activity. Peter of Dresden, as far as we know, functioned only within the school, no doubt as an inspiring teacher of evangelical reform, but not as a polemicist in the wider world: his known written work consisted chiefly of grammatical treatises.[23] John Drändorf continued his studies in Prague and later worked among the Bohemian Germans, but in time he left Bohemia for Germany and found his way to a martyr's death, in Worms.[24] Asked at his inquisition whether he believed John Hus and Jerome of Prague had been justly condemned, he replied "that he believed nothing except what Scripture taught, and that God knew if they had been justly or unjustly condemned." [25] Why did he not say that they, like Eppinge, had been humble and devout men? Quite possibly because, in 1425, he wished to make it clear that his own religious path, though parallel to theirs, was distinct: he was a Hussite in doctrine but was not a member of the Hussite movement. Such

---

[16] Thomson, *op. cit.*, p. xiii f., points to the inclusion of Hus's authorities in Eppinge's position, and suggests that Hus may have offered additional material and guidance. But this is a speculation, and nothing in Eppinge's text confirms it, nor is there the slightest reason to suppose that Eppinge, a canonist who had been accustomed to using his learning in the service of anti-Romanism, would not have produced a largely original work.

[17] Thomson's edition, p. 105.

[18] See, e.g., John Hus, *Tractatus de ecclesia,* ed. S. H. Thomson (Boulder, Colorado, 1956), pp. 17 f., 35 f.

[19] *Ibid.,* p. 216.

[20] *Tractatus responsivus,* ed. Thomson, p. 103 (I follow Bartoš in supposing Jakoubek to have been the author).

[21] Kapp, *op. cit.,* pp. 38 f.

[22] For a convenient discussion, with references to the literature, see H. Kaminsky, "Hussite Radicalism and the Origins of Tabor," *Medievalia et Humanistica* 10 (1956): *passim.*

[23] Bartoš, "Počátky kalicha," *Husitství a cizina,* p. 75. In his "Nové spisy Petra a Mikuláše z Drážďan," *Reformační sborník* 8 (1946): pp. 66 f., Bartoš has drawn attention to Peter's authorship of a short extract from Albertus Magnus's "Philosophia pauperum" ("Summa naturalium"); one manuscript names him as "M. Petrus Gerticz, quondam rector scolarum in Dresden"; a fifteenth-century catalogue of another manuscript reads: "Autor istius tractatuli mag. Petrus Gerit, mag. schole in Dressen scil. in Missna. Et sicut dicitur, tunc in ultimis suis diebus pervenit ad Boemicam pravitatem et Constancie incineratus." Bartoš observes that we must reject the last item of information in favor of the report that Peter was burned in Regensburg, 1421/1426 (Böhmer, *op. cit.,* p. 224); it should also be noted that Drändorf told his inquisitors that Peter had died in Prague (Kapp, p. 38).

[24] Kapp, *op. cit.,* pp. 3 ff. See also below.

[25] Kapp, *op. cit.,* p. 54.

indeed was the case in the 1420's. In 1412, however, it was not obviously inevitable that the Czech and German reformers should grow apart; the movement still lived for the most part in the world of ideas, and intellectuals might suppose that the ample opportunities for common action in that world constituted a sufficient basis for integration. This was in fact the belief of one leading member of the Dresden circle, Master Nicholas of Dresden, who spent the four years from 1412 through 1415 playing the double role of schoolmaster among the Germans, leading ideologue among the Czechs, and who had no hesitation in declaring his attachment to Hus's cause and, in 1415, to Hus's memory. That he too had to leave Prague and find a new career as missionary among his own people, a career that quickly ended in his martyrdom, adds the dimension of genuine tragedy to a life that more than any other embodied the hopes and failures of Hussite universalism.

Thanks to Nicholas's popularity among the Czech Hussites, his works were copied often enough to insure their survival, and it will not be too difficult to reconstruct his ideas. His biography is another matter. It is impossible to say with certainty where he was born and educated or where he spent the years before 1412, except that by his own account eleven of his adolescent years were spent in a cathedral town. This would not have been Prague, where he wrote the paragraph in question, nor Dresden, which did not have a cathedral. Perhaps it was Meissen, where Nicholas later went to preach.[26] In any case, the most important questions cannot be answered: Was Nicholas a student at the University of Prague before 1409?[27] If so, did he then leave Prague for Dresden, and if he was part of the Dresden School in that city, was it as teacher or as student?[28] Or was he rather, as F. M. Bartoš has suggested, the scion of a Prague German family, who received his epithet, "of Dresden," because of the origin of his family or because of his own association with the Dresden School in Prague?[29] If, as seems most likely, Nicholas's earliest known works date from 1412, the first year in which the Dresdeners were active in Prague,[30] the easiest inference would be that he came with the School; Bartoš, on the other hand, has explained the coincidence by conjecturing that Nicholas, as a German, could not play an active role in Hussite doctrinal development until the advent of the Dresden School made such interethnic collaboration a reality.[31] He is called a "Master," presumably of arts, and a "baccalareus decretorum": it would seem likely that he acquired these degrees at Prague's University and her Law Faculty;[32] on the other hand, he is also called a priest, but the *Libri ordinationum* of the Prague diocese do not mention him, and he may have been ordained elsewhere.[33] It is not impossible that manuscript material as yet unknown will turn up to settle some of these questions; meanwhile they must be left open, with the single conjecture, based on Nicholas's familiarity with Wyclifite ideas and with the works of the Czech reformer Matthew of Janov, that he, like other leading members of the Dresden School, had probably studied at the University of Prague before he emerged as a Hussite theoretician.[34]

Turning now to his works, we may regard the two here edited as his earliest: the "Tables of the Old and New Color" and the "Customs and Rites of the Primitive Church and of the Modern Church." The latter seems to have been a kind of sequel to the former,

---

[26] Sedlák, p. 1 f.; Bartoš, p. 129 f.

[27] For references to scholarly opinion on this question, see Bartoš, p. 127, n. 47; Sedlák, p. 2. The problem is whether the "Petrus Drozna" and "Nicolaus Drossen" mentioned in the *Liber decanorum universitatis Pragensis*—Peter received his B.A. in 1379, M.A. in 1386; Nicholas was promoted to B.A. in 1396 under Peter—are identical with our Peter and Nicholas of Dresden. Bartoš argues that the men came not from Dresden but from Drozno in the diocese of Lubusz (Lebus), in what was then Brandenburg; for the record of Peter's ordination refers to him as "Petrus Kerszner de Drosna, can. eccl. Lubuc." We are, of course, immediately struck by the possibility that "Kerszner" might have been only a variant or corruption of "Gerticz/Gerit" (above, n. 23), a hypothesis that would open the door to several others, all of them requiring much exploratory work in the manuscript sources for their verification; the possibility is mentioned here only to show that our knowledge of the Dresdeners is still in a primitive stage.

[28] The sources here are not in agreement; Sedlák, p. 2 f., examines them and concludes that Nicholas probably did not leave Prague in 1409.

[29] Bartoš, p. 125 ff. See the contrary arguments of Josef Pekař, "Nový Bartoš," *Český časopis historický* 32 (1926): pp. 364 f.; Bartoš's reply, *ibid.*, p. 680.

[30] Sedlák's dating of Nicholas's *De iuramento*, in 1408 ("Vlivy valdské," *Studie a texty* (Olomouc, 1914) 1: pp. 75 ff.) seems to have been satisfactorily refuted by Bartoš, "Studie k Husovi a jeho době. 1. Hus a valdenství," *ČČM*, 89 (1915): 2–5, where the tractate is related to the events of 1414. For the dating of Nicholas's other works, see below.

[31] Bartoš, p. 130 (note 54 on this page has evidently been omitted by mistake; what is now numbered 54 should be numbered 55, and so on through what is now 59).

[32] Sedlák, p. 2, n. 1, gives some of the references; Bartoš, p. 127, n. 47, doubts that Nicholas was ever an M.A.

[33] Bartoš, p. 130, n. 53.

[34] Sedlák, p. 35, cites some of Nicholas's references to Matthew of Janov; see also Sedlák, "Počátkové kalicha," *Časopis katolického duchovenstva* 52 (1911), 788, for a more decisive identification with Matthew's cause. And see the extensive proofs offered by Jana Nechutová, "Traktát Mikuláše z Drážďan 'De imaginibus' a jeho vztah k Matěji z Janova," *Sborník prací filosofické fakulty Brněnské university,* E 9 (1964): pp. 149–161. Bartoš, p. 143, stresses the influence of Wyclif on Nicholas, but without particular documentation. I do not know that Nicholas ever cites Wyclif by name, and although convinced of Wyclif's influence (see note 37 below), I can see no way to explore the matter except by the painstaking comparison of Nicholas's authorities with those of Wyclif, a work that can be efficiently undertaken only after Nicholas's treatises have been published. It may also be observed, in support of the opinion that Nicholas's intellectual formation was acquired in Prague, that he cites various works of Prague German reformers, such as Matthew of Krakow and the (anonymous) *Speculum Aureum* (see below).

which was far more popular, surviving in twelve known manuscript copies, as against only one for the other.³⁵ Both are composed almost entirely of citations, arranged to show that the current system of the Roman Church was the opposite of the system of the Primitive Church: the Decretals and the glosses on the canon law provide most of the documentation for Romanism, while the Primitive system is presented chiefly through quotations from the New Testament, as well as the Fathers and certain selected post-patristic writers, with the *Decretum* serving as a great repertory of source material. Perhaps by 1412 the antitheses of the "Tables" were illustrated, and the picture-text combinations that resulted gave the work its present form, which preserves the texts as they were grouped in the pictures.³⁶ While the "Customs and Rites," as well as the similarly constructed "Puncta" composed perhaps in 1413, have a somewhat discursive, even exploratory character, the "Tables" are sharp and propagandistic, hard-hitting and fast-moving: it may be conjectured that all three originated as topical collections of authorities for future use—medieval codices are full of such informal repertories—but that the "Tables" evolved further, with the help of the pictures, into a genuine polemic.

The doctrines expressed in these works do not go beyond those of contemporary radical Hussitism, and if there is one influence that seems most important it is that of Wyclif, who, we may suppose, provided not only the idea behind the "Tables" but much of the documentation for both works.³⁷ The "Tables" begin with a picture of Christ on his cross, opposed to one of the Pope riding a horse and decked out with the insignia of the papal office, a contrast which contains the theme of the whole work.³⁸ Christ was poor and humble, he suffered without complaint, but the Pope is wealthy and pompous, and he rigorously punishes disobedience. Peter, the prototype of the follower of Christ, followed his master in poverty and martyrdom, but the Pope, who claims to be Peter's successor, leads an entirely different life. The whole apparatus of the Roman Church's hierarchy, authority, and legal system stands in contrast to the inspired freedom of the Primitive Church. The simony and fornication prevalent among the Roman clergy are held up to attack with appropriate citations, some of which, in this case, come from the Church's orthodox reform tradition. The rags in which the infant Jesus was clothed are contrasted with the gorgeous vestments of the Roman prelates. Then the picture of Jesus washing the feet of the disciples is opposed to the picture of the Pope having his feet kissed, and finally the Pope appears as Antichrist surrounded by whores. Through these contrasts the original point, the dissimilarity between the *conversacio* of Christ and of the Pope, is amplified into a contrast between the Church of Christ—the Primitive Church—and the Church of Rome, and is then lifted to an eschatological level of meaning with the identification of the Pope as the Antichrist who will come in the last days to seduce the faithful. Jakoubek of Stříbro had expressed similar ideas, including the last one,³⁹ but in the "Tables" we see something new, not a new doctrine but a new mode of thought, one that projects in sharp and positive form what is implicit, dispersed, or attenuated by qualifications in the works of Wyclif, Matthew of Janov, and even of Jakoubek. In this mode of thought all the standard criticisms of the Roman Church are presented as parts of a single concept of that church as the mystical body of Antichrist, and the counter-image of the Primitive Church appears not as an ideal to guide criticism but as a real system, capable of being reborn among men. Earlier criticisms of the Roman system expressed the point of view of men *within* a church that had been taken over by the minions of Antichrist; Nicholas's point of view is that of one who stands outside the criticized institution.

The "Customs and Rites" carries a similar message, in three main parts.⁴⁰ It begins with texts documenting the nature of the Primitive Church as a fellowship of the Holy Spirit, without a formally defined sacrament of ordination. Hence, one infers, clergy was a function rather than an office. In this church all things were common, but the modern doctors have

---

³⁵ See the bibliography of Nicholas's works, below.

³⁶ See the Preface to the edition, below.

³⁷ Wyclif developed the antithesis between Christ and the Pope in his *De Christo et suo adversario Antichristo*, ed. R. Buddensieg (Gotha, 1880), pp. 47–58; *Exposicio textus Matthei xxiv*, in *Opera minora*, ed. J. Loserth (London, 1913), p. 361 f.; *De ordine christiana*, *Op. min.*, pp. 131, 136 f. One passage in the *De Christo et . . . Antichristo*, p. 50, may even be read as a kind of command to compose the *Tabule*: ". . . videat homo scripta apostolorum, que ex fide sunt scripta domini Iesu Christi, et scripta papalia, cuiusmodi sunt bulle et decretales epistole, et potest percipere, quomodo in sentencia non concordant, cum scripta papalia dicunt mundanam excellenciam, scripta autem ewangelica insinuant humilem fugam mundi." Of the texts in the *Tabule*, the following, cited by Table and note-number from the present edition, may be found in the *De Christo . . .* of Wyclif: Gal. i, 8–9 (V, 29); Luc. ix, 55–56 (III, 4); II Thes. ii, 4 (IX, 17); Mat. viii, 20 (I, 8); Mat. xix, 27 (II, 7); Mat. x, 8 (V, 11). Furthermore the texts of Table III, § 3 are clearly referred to by Wyclif, p. 57, and the antithesis between Christ washing the disciples' feet and the pope having his feet kissed is also in Wyclif, p. 57. Another antithesis, between Christ riding an ass and the pope riding splendidly on a horse (Wyclif, p. 56), was used by the Dresdeners (see Preface, p. 35), but appears in a different form in the *Tabule* (Table I, §§ 1–2). However these particular correspondences are only illustrative; the *Tabule* consists almost entirely of authorities, while Wyclif's discussion uses authorities only to support generalizations, and it would require a reading of both texts to appreciate the way in which the *Tabule* seems *obviously* to be a working out of Wyclif's general thesis.

³⁸ Here and elsewhere in this discussion of the *Tabule* the reader is referred, generally, to the printed text.

³⁹ In his *Posicio de Antichristo* of January 1412; most of it has been published by V. Kybal, "M. Matěj z Janova a M. Jakoubek ze Stříbra," *ČČH* 11 (1905): pp. 22–37.

⁴⁰ See, generally, the printed text below.

glossed this provision away, and the Roman Church, with its distinction between bishops, priests, and monks, has restricted the originally universal communism to a single group, the monastic order. The early church had been a band of preachers wandering throughout the world, without hierarchic offices, but the Roman Church has a legally defined system of parishes and dioceses, a fixed and privileged hierarchy, and a legal code that takes cognizance of differences in wealth. In the Primitive Church all were brothers, but the Pope does not allow any but the bishops to call him brother. In Part Two the Roman Church's theory and practice of excommunication is on the one hand contrasted with the Primitive Church's, and on the other hand exposed to doubt by judicious citation of the canonistic texts defining the precise conditions under which a sentence of excommunication is valid or not. In Part Three the argument turns against the monastic orders—their clothing and settled way of life, their immoral actions, their withdrawal from work among the people, their renunciation of individual responsibility, their refusal to earn their keep, their hypocrisy. The final text of Part Three seems out of place: it is a passage from St. Jerome, suggesting that priests have as much power as bishops. Indeed the whole work suffers from diffuseness. It is probably not an accident that it survives in only one copy; nonetheless it amplifies the idea of the "Tables" by carrying the critique of the Roman Church into a wider field and by presenting an even more detailed portrait of the Primitive Church. Later in 1412 Nicholas wrote a more specialized tractate, *De quadruplici missione*—"The Four Kinds of Mission"—defending freedom of preaching against the restrictions of the canon law; it uses a sizable amount of material from the "Tables" to attack the "doctors" of the opposing side, and its argument, that preaching is licit for all, even laymen and women, if they have the call from God, fits into the framework of ideas we have just been considering.[41]

A fourth major work of this early period was the *Puncta* ("Points"), again a collection of authorities against the Roman system, but even looser in structure than the "Customs and Rites."[42] It is noteworthy for its extensive use of the *Speculum aureum,* an antisimoniac work written in 1404, perhaps by Matthew of Cracow,[43] and for the historical material it draws from the chronicle *Flores temporum*.[44] It attacks or casts doubt upon the endowment of the church with property, upon compulsory tithes, the sacramental acts of simoniac and otherwise sinful priests, the elaborately developed Roman liturgy, the necessity of auricular confession, and the power of the keys in its Roman form.[45] The fundamental attitude of the "Tables" and "Customs and Rites" is given more extensive expression, and there is a perhaps more urgent insistence on the idea of the Church as a community based on virtue rather than on laws and offices, but the most striking feature of the *Puncta* is its use of history to fill out the contrast between the two churches by showing how the unwholesome practices of the Roman system came into being through papal legislation and human custom. Some of this had been shown before, but not as thoroughly as in the *Puncta,* which supplements the basic historical scheme, centering around the Donation of Constantine, with material showing when the various elements of the Roman liturgy were adopted, when the various monastic orders were founded, and the like.[46] Thus the Roman system, already seen to be the contradiction of the Primitive Church, now appears as a conglomeration of historical innovations; the formal antithesis is seen as a real one that has developed through time, and the psychology of reform is thereby set on more solid foundations.

In 1414 and 1415 the ideas and attitudes expressed in these works were focused on a new issue, that of the lay chalice. The cult of the Eucharist had received much attention in the works of Matthew of Janov, who believed that due reverence for that sacrament and its frequent, even daily, reception by the laity would serve to unify and reform the church from the inside out. Matthew of Cracow had also championed frequent communion, and the Hussites absorbed this sort of eucharistic piety along with other ideas of their teachers, including John Wyclif's rejection of transsubstantiation. The more conservative Hussites were conservative in these matters also, and it is probable that not even John Hus was willing to go all the way with Wyclif, but the radicals, especially Jakoubek of Stříbro not only accepted Wyclifite remanence but also took over Matthew of Janov's intensely emotional exaltation of the eucharistic cult.[47] Unlike Matthew, however, Jakoubek pushed

---

[41] See the bibliography of Nicholas's works, below.

[42] *Ibid.*

[43] See the discussion in J. Haller, *Papsttum und Kirchenreform* (Berlin, 1903), pp. 483–524; cf. Bartoš, "*Speculum aureum,*" *Věstník české akademie* **53** (1944): pp. 11–20.

[44] See Bartoš, "Německá kronika (Flores temporum) v duchovní výzbroji Táborů," *Jihočeský sborník historický* **12** (1939): pp. 82–85.

[45] See Sedlák's summary discussion, pp. 18–24.

[46] In the text of the *Puncta* in MS. Univ. Prag. IV G 15, these historical references may be found on f. 30'–31 (Donation of Constantine), f. 31 (introduction of various orders), f. 36' (introduction of parts of the liturgy). On f. 6' there is a reference to "Cestrensis"—i.e., Ranulph Higden's *Polychronicon,* which the Hussites knew only from Wyclif's use of it.

[47] For the Eucharistic doctrine of Wyclif and Hus, see Paul de Vooght's "Huss a-t-il enseigné la *remanentia panis post consecrationem?*" & "La présence réelle dans la doctrine eucharistique de Wiclif," both in *Hussiana* (Louvain, 1960), pp. 263 ff., 292 ff. The influence of Matthew of Janov's eucharistic fervor is stressed by V. Kybal, *M. Matěj z Janova* (Prague, 1905), pp. 310 ff., and by Sedlák, "Počátkové kalicha," *ČKD* **52** (1911): pp. 497 ff.; Sedlák shows how Jakoubek, arguing for communion in both kinds, used Matthew of Janov's argument for frequent communion. For an appreciation and critique of Kybal's and Sedlák's position, see Bartoš, "Počátky kalicha," *Husitství a cizina,* p. 61 ff.

this cult to the point of insisting that the layman receive not only the consecrated bread but the consecrated wine as well—the Blood of God, which the Roman rite withheld from the laity for allegedly practical reasons.[48] It is possible that Wyclif's remanence played a role here. According to Roman doctrine, the Body of God in the species of bread also contained the Blood; thus the layman was not really denied anything. But if one followed Wyclif in supposing that the substance of the bread was not annihilated—as transsubstantiation had it —but rather remained, as the only proper support for the accidents of the bread, then one might be less inclined to accept the bread alone as equivalent to the bread-wine combination. But even if this guess be rejected there are obvious reasons to suppose that utraquism, the doctrine and practice of giving communion to the laity in both kinds, may have emerged as the product of previous ideas held by the Hussite Left: on the one hand, the tradition of eucharistic piety that tended to center the *positive* religious reform around the sacrament of holy communion; on the other hand the anti-Romanism that not only regarded the Roman Church as the church of Antichrist but also viewed the former as the result of a historical process of perversion. All that was necessary was the realization that communion in both kinds had been given in the Primitive Church and that this practice, like so many other features of that Church, had been changed after the Donation of Constantine. It would of course have been possible to infer this fact from a simple comparison of current practice with the practice attested in the New Testament; such comparisons were indeed made, and they would certainly have encouraged a literal interpretation of what became the classic text of utraquist polemic: John 6: 53: "Except ye eat the flesh of the Son of man and drink his blood, ye have no life in you." But as Professor Bartoš has shown, all of this came relatively late in utraquist literature; in Jakoubek's first utraquist formulations we find not the text of John 6: 53 but rather the canon "Comperimus" of Pope Gelasius I, commanding that communion in the second species not be omitted.[49] It is Bartoš's suggestion that Nicholas of Dresden may have discovered this text— that is, realized its import—in the course of his canonistic research, perhaps indeed while composing the *Puncta*,[50] and that Nicholas may have drawn Jakoubek's attention to it. Although Bartoš seems to reject this possibility in favor of another—that Jakoubek became aware of the original practice of utraquist communion when he heard Jerome of Prague's report on the Orthodox rite [51]—it still seems most attractive.

The problem is in fact more complex than the above discussion would indicate. Among the many theories that have been proposed to explain the origins of utraquism, one, resting on the explicit testimony of several sources, credits the Dresdeners with the innovation: utraquism was taught by the Dresden masters in Dresden, and when they came to Prague they brought their doctrine to the attention of the radical Master John Jičín, who in turn persuaded Jakoubek and others; it was then Jakoubek who actually introduced the practice in Hussite Prague.[52] The Dresdener mentioned in these accounts is not, as we might expect, Nicholas, but Peter, who indeed must have been the senior member of the school after the death of Frederick Eppinge at the end of 1412.[53] Unfortunately, there is no direct literary evidence to support this account: we know of no utraquist work clearly attributable to Peter of Dresden, no mention of his name in the polemics of utraquists and anti-utraquists. Moreover the sources on which the account rests are for the most part late, tendentious, and interrelated.[54] In any case, the Dresden theory in this form would simply move the problem of origins back one stage. Again it is Bartoš who suggests a way out: rejecting the testimonies for Peter of Dresden, he observes that *Nicholas* of Dresden was demonstrably close to Jakoubek in this period, that Nicholas's research was precisely the sort that could have led him to an appreciation of "Comperimus," and that Nicholas did in fact distinguish himself as an ardent and effective polemicist in favor of the lay chalice.[55] At the very least we may say—and this is also the opinion of Sedlák [56]—that on the basis of Nicholas's early and active collaboration with Jakoubek, his membership in the leading circle of utraquist pioneers,[57] he is entitled to rank as the co-originator of the lay chalice. Perhaps indeed, as Bartoš guesses, Nicholas's prominence in this work was the foundation for the later stories that attributed the innovation itself to the Dresden circle.

These possibilities, indefinite as they are, have the great value of leading us to Nicholas's utraquist work

---

[48] The issues at stake in the controversy are excellently analyzed by Emile Amann, "Jacobel et les débuts de la controverse utraquiste," *Miscellanea Francesco Ehrle* (Rome, 1924) 1: pp. 375-387.

[49] Bartoš, "Počátky kalicha, "*Husitství a cizina,* p. 62 f.

[50] *Ibid.,* pp. 68–70.

[51] *Ibid.,* pp. 71–74.

[52] *Ibid.,* pp. 75–80—a discussion, with references to the sources and to the modern literature. *Cf.* H. Böhmer, *op. cit.,* pp. 213–220.

[53] The only teachers of the school mentioned by Drändorf as having functioned in Dresden were Frederick and Peter (Kapp, *op. cit.,* p. 38; see also Bartoš, *op. cit.,* p. 79 f.).

[54] Bartoš, *op. cit.,* pp. 75–80. Sedlák identified one utraquist tractate as the work of Peter of Dresden ("Počátkové kalicha," *ČKD* 54 (1913): pp. 708–711), but Bartoš's arguments in favor of Peter Payne's authorship seem convincing (*op. cit.,* p. 103 f.), although they did not convince Josef Pekař ("Nový Bartoš," *ČČH,* 32 (1926): p. 363; *Žižka a jeho doba* 1: p. 205).

[55] Bartoš, *op. cit.,* pp. 68–70 & *passim.*

[56] Sedlák, pp. 5–7.

[57] Sedlák, "Počátkové kalicha," *ČKD* 54 (1913): p. 407, cites the following passage from Nicholas's *Apologia* (ed. Von der Hardt, *Concilium Constantiense* 3 (1698): col. 614): "Non pro nostro libito incepimus porrigere, sed secundum primitivam institutionem filii dei, longa et matura super hoc praehabita deliberatione cum magistris et aliis legem Christi diligentibus."

by the proper path, that is *via* his extremely radical anti-Romanism, and its counterpart, his cult of the Primitive Church. The lay chalice epitomized both lines of thought and carried them a step further, by raising a question of absolute and universal urgency, with the utmost clarity and in the form of an overt act. The Primitive Church had been poor, the Roman Church was rich, but it was not perfectly clear that riches by themselves would send a cleric to Hell, nor was it obviously true that the riches corrupting the Roman Church deprived her of the power to administer valid sacraments. In the matter of utraquism, however, everything was evident: Jesus himself had instituted the sacrament of the Eucharist in both kinds and had commanded all to eat the Body and drink the Blood if they would have life in them; the church that he himself had founded did in fact obey his command; it was only the modern Roman Church that had deprived the laity of God's Blood and hence of an indispensable prerequisite for salvation. Taken together and in all of their implications, these ideas could contain the whole burden of radical Hussite reformism, and in fact we find that Nicholas's utraquist works teem with authorities developed in his earlier treatises and pointing to a general condemnation of the Roman Church's *conversacio;* the denial of the chalice to the laity was merely one modern abuse among many. In the *Tabule* Nicholas had established the fundamental opposition between the Primitive and modern churches; he had developed the point in more detail in the *Consuetudo et Ritus,* and in the *De quadruplici missione* had bolstered his argument in favor of free preaching by branding the Roman hierarchy and its doctors as minions of Antichrist, servants of Babylon—simoniacs, fornicators, usurers.[58] Now he pursued the same line in defense of the lay chalice, which was condemned by the doctors of the Council of Constance on the grounds that although Jesus had in fact given communion in both kinds, and so had the Primitive Church—the doctors conceded this—the custom of the Roman Church was against it.[59] Nicholas had only to unleash his gift for plastic imagery to find the most striking formulation of the issue:[60]

Suppose as a possibility that Christ and his Primitive Church, with their apostolic life and evangelical practice, were to come into the midst of the Council of Constance, and were to say to the multitudes there, as he said and taught at Capernaum: "Except ye eat the flesh of the Son of Man and drink his blood, etc." And suppose that he wished to perform the sacrament as he had instituted it. Do you think that he would be listened to and would have an opportunity for this, things being as they now are? It would go hard with him. Indeed those at the Council would probably not withdraw from him scandalized, as did those at Capernaum, but would hereticate and condemn him, according to their condemnation [of the lay chalice], saying that this was not their custom.

---

[58] See the text, published by Sedlák, *Studie a texty* 1: pp. 103-111.
[59] The text in Von der Hardt, III, col. 586 f.
[60] *Ibid.,* col. 624 f.

Nor did Nicholas fail to include in the same treatise—the "Apologia"—a substantial section showing that the church whose custom was cited against Christ was in fact Antichristian—here the dossier developed in the *Tabule* was pressed into service along with a long passage from the *Speculum aureum* detailing the venality of the Roman Curia.[61] We are on familiar ground.

The actual point at issue, if we disregard the technical battle of "authorities" that filled up most of the polemical literature for and against the chalice, was whether or not Jesus, by giving communion in both kinds and saying "do this in my memory," had instituted such communion as a binding practice for the future.[62] Much depended on the meaning of "this." As always in theological debates, each side could find plenty of arguments to support its own view; but even more depended on the concept of the Church that the several writers had in mind. For Nicholas, of course, the perfect form of the true Church Militant was the Primitive Church, which was nowhere more perfectly represented than at the Last Supper, where Christ figured the priest, the disciples the laity (the Romanist argument was that Christ represented the future bishops, the disciples the future priests). On this basis, Nicholas could plausibly develop his argument that Christ's "do this in my memory" meant that priests should give both bread and wine to the laity; the point is made in his first utraquist work, a sermon on the text, "Nisi manducaveritis," and appears in the others, as well as in the works of Jakoubek.[63] But more revealing than the arguments proper are the extra-logical criticisms of the opposing side, criticisms designed to show *why* the doctors have set themselves against Christ's command. Something has already been said of Nicholas's accusations of simony, fornication, and the like, but there is more to his polemic than mere abuse. On the one hand, there is the question of what is the true church, what constitutes valid authority, valid

---

[61] *Ibid.,* coll. 608-617.
[62] Although the doctors of the Council of Constance actually conceded that Jesus had instituted communion in both kinds (*ibid.,* col. 586), they did not attach the same force to the idea of institution as the Hussites did, to whom the Council's admission seemed almost to end the matter. Thus Nicholas of Dresden's *Apologia* (Von der Hardt, 3: col. 509): "Ecce, nunc audivimus ab ore ipsorum, Christi esse institutionem, sicut est in primitiva ecclesia tentum. Hoc est fundamentum, super quo aedificamus." Of all the polemical tracts on the subject that I have read, only Jean Gerson's defines the issue with precision (Von der Hardt, 3: coll. 765-780, esp. col. 773 f.). Cf. Amann, *op. cit.,* p. 386, n. 3 & n. 4, for examples of doctrinal confusion on the Roman side.
[63] "Nisi manducaveritis," MS. Univ. Prag. IV G 15, f. 198', f. 203, f. 209'; cf. *Apologia,* Hardt, 3: col. 638. See also Jakoubek's reply to Andrew of Brod, Hardt, 3: col. 443 ("Apostoli tunc suscipientes sacramentum sub utraque specie habuerunt se per modum gregis spiritualis, et non per modum pastoris sive sacerdotis"); also his "Posicio pro informacione monachi M. Petri," written in 1417, MS Vienna Nationalbibliothek 4488, f. 97'-98. For the Romanist position see, e.g., the anonymous antiutraquist tractate in Hardt, 3: coll. 705-708.

custom, valid priesthood. The community based on office, the church of the Pope and the cardinals, is not only marked by evident corruption, and hence entitled to little respect, but is *per se* inadequate to stand for the real church, which is a community of faith, the *congregacio fidelium*, which of course can have no custom contrary to reason or natural law—"and natural law is understood as the divine law," the Bible.[64] The prelates and doctors of the Roman institution are not interested in imitating Christ's way of life but in preserving their own; it is for this reason that they always interpret Scripture falsely: "they follow modern realities rather than the Law of Christ, which for the most part they adapt to current realities and the customs of men, with their glosses and additions."[65] The prime case is what they have done to the many texts forbidding simony, the worst of all heresies,[66] which the doctors count as nothing and cover up by glossing all texts against it in line with their "cupidinous custom."[67] And yet it may be doubted whether those who have paid money for their holy orders are really capable of valid consecrations.[68] But all of this points to another consideration: the members of the Roman institution simply do not care about the inner essence of the Christian faith; they are perfunctory, lacking love and enthusiasm. Naturally they have no interest in promoting fervid communion, and the same motives that prompted the clergy a generation earlier to oppose frequent communion and persecute Matthew of Janov, its great proponent, now move them to neglect giving the chalice to their congregations.[69] Utraquism thus emerges in its true shape—it is not primarily a matter of technical theological debate, but a sign and component of the true Christian religiosity that seeks in all things to come as close to Christ as it can. This virtue is indeed claimed by Nicholas for his side. Its doctors, who support the lay chalice, are the learned, faithful, and humble masters of the University of Prague. Here the texts first used in the *Tabule* to mark out the arrogant, pompous, fat, and swollen prelates of the Church of Antichrist are cited again, with the observation that the members of the University are not of this sort. Rather they resemble the early teachers of the Church, and study God's Law in the Church of God; some of them have indeed sacrificed their lives for the Blood of the Lamb.[70] And it was with the counsel of these men that the chalice was reinstituted for the laity.[71]

Like Nicholas's other contrasts between the good and bad churches, this one is worked out in an apocalyptic spirit that distinguishes his program of return to the Primitive Church from any merely moral "philosophy of Christ." The mystical body of Antichrist existed, it was a complete union of total evil, striving to destroy Christ's Law and in the present case threatening to invoke the secular arm against Christ's followers.[72] The revivification of the Primitive Church in Hussite Bohemia meant above all that the Church Christ had led in person would exist again, the band of the elect that would suffer in his cause in the last days of cosmic cataclysm. And in the most immediate sense the conflict over the lay chalice was polarized by the antithesis between Heaven and Hell, eternal bliss and

---

[64] *Apologia*, Hardt, 3: pp. 610 ff. "Et sumitur jus naturale pro jure divino, quod continetur in lege et evangelio" (col. 612). Cf. *Decretum*, I. dist. § *Humanum* and c. 1.

[65] *Ibid.*, col. 602; the full text reads: "Doctores moderni temporis magis sequuntur facta, seu consuetudines, vel potius corruptelas modernas, quas plus apprecientur et ponderant cum constitutionibus humanis, quam legem Christi. Cum ut plurimum legem Christi cum glossis eorum et additionibus trahunt secundum facta currentia, et ad hominum consuetudines, simul aliquando corruptelas excusando."

[66] *Ibid.*, col. 604; *cf.* on this subject P. de Vooght, "La 'Simoniaca haeresis' de Saint Thomas d' Aquin à Jean Huss," *Hussiana*, pp. 379–399, where it is shown that the old concept of simony as a heresy, modified by the major scholastics (in favor of simony as a sin), was *revived* by Wyclif and other reformers; thus the late-medieval struggle for reform included a controversy over the meaning of simony (see the next two notes).

[67] *Apologia*, Von der Hardt, 3: p. 604: "simoniaca haeresis . . . ab haereticis simoniacis nihil reputatur, imo omnem scripturam id peccatum et vitium scilicet simoniae improbantem glossant, et ad suam cupidinosam trahunt consuetudinem. Sic potest dici de usura, fornicatione, etc." The same passage appears in the sermon on "Nisi manducaveritis," MS IV G 15, f. 210'.

[68] "Nisi manducaveritis," MS. IV G 15, f. 202': "Et quid sit de symoniacis, qui lepram recipiunt in ordinacione et maledicionem, secundum Ambrosium [*Decretum*, I.q.i, c. 14], an conficiant vel non, relinquo iudicio superiorum meorum, sed utique nichil dat quod non habet. De hiis alibi dixi." The last phrase no doubt refers to the *Tabule* and to the *Puncta*, MS. Univ. Prag. IV G 15, f. 17 sqq., a collection of texts from the *Decretum* showing, in general, that virtue, not office, makes a priest. Technically, to be sure, the point would have to be put differently: a priest in mortal sin should not perform his priestly functions and if he does he should be shunned (LXXXI. Di., c. 15 (Gregory VII)); an evil cleric is not really a cleric at all (II. q. vii, c. 29 (Jerome); XL Di. c. 12 (Chrysostome): "malus sacerdos de sacerdotio suo crimen acquirit, non dignitatem"). As for the simoniac, the text from Ambrose makes it clear that if he has bought his ordination he has not received a true ordination at all, and hence is no priest. All of this is practically equivalent to Donatism, if not formally identical with it, but the authorities are those of the tradition.

[69] "Nisi manducaveritis," MS. IV G 15, f. 203: "Et sunt hii qui magis diligunt ocium hic quam laborare pro ewangelii implecione et gracie proximi augmentacione, qui forsan vel raro minimam scintillam divine gracie que in hoc sacramento tribuitur habuerunt; sed quadam indulta conswetudine et quasi perfunctorie res agatur, ad illud accedent et sic inanes et sine gracia recedent, non ut accedant sed ut recedant festinantes, non ex affectu devocionis sed ex defectu divini fervoris, et ideo fideles laicos, qui ex fervore divine caritatis cupientes [*sic*] accedere, repellunt, et ipsis totum ac perfectum sacramentum denegant." The passage on frequent communion is on f. 212: "Et rogo, nonne in magnam diswetudinem fuit deducta communio frequens seu cottidiana, et adhuc aput multos propter pigriciam ipsorum est odibilis et scandalosa! . . ."

[70] *Apologia*, Von der Hardt, III, coll. 621 f.

[71] *Ibid.*, col. 617.

[72] *Ibid.*, coll. 626 f.; *cf.* 624: "Ecce, ab initio Christi secta est persecuta et haereticata. . . ."

eternal damnation; thus the *Apologia,* composed for the most part of intricate patterns of scriptural, patristic, and canonistic authorities, ends on a note of emotional prophecy, with a fine bit of hysteria cited at length from Heinrich Suso's *Horologia sapiencie,* spelling out the torments awaiting the doctors of the Council; but blessedness is in store for the Hussites.[73]

In the light of what has been said thus far, it is not surprising that Nicholas of Dresden eventually turned out to be too radical for even the radicals of the Prague University reform party. In July or August of 1415 Nicholas had taken on the task of defending utraquism against the Council of Constance, and, in his *Apologia,* had shown himself to be one of the inner circle of reform leaders;[74] a scant month or two later we find him developing a highly sectarian program, embracing ideas of a Waldensian character, and in consequence setting himself in opposition to Jakoubek of Stříbro. So sharp was the break between Nicholas and his erstwhile allies that he left Prague, evidently in early 1416, and set out to preach reform in neighboring parts of Germany; it was probably in that same year that he met his death at the hands of the Inquisition, in Meissen.[75] It is not easy to arrive at a satisfactory explanation of exactly what happened during this period; retrospectively the break seems inevitable, given Nicholas's extreme and turbulent radicalism, which always had a sectarian character, but the retrospect always suggests that what did happen had to happen, and this view begs the question of whether an accommodation might not have been possible. The period is in any case remarkably obscure, for there is little direct testimony about the detailed course of events, and we must depend on inferences from the tractate literature, most of which remains unpublished. The difficulty of working with source material in this condition is well known; in the present case it is proven by the very divergent interpretations of the two main connoisseurs, Jan Sedlák and F. M. Bartoš. The former regards Nicholas of Dresden as, simply, a Waldensian, from the first, and he points to the Waldensian character of Nicholas's most important doctrines: that everyone has the right to preach, that all priests are equal, that singing and praying should not be carried on in churches, but in the soul, that confession should be made directly to God, that no oaths may be sworn, that there is no justification for any killing by Christians, that there is no Purgatory, and that the foundation of Christian life is the observance of the "six minimal commandments"—not to anger, not to lust, not to divorce one's wife, not to swear oaths, not to resist evil-doers, to pray for and help one's enemies.[76] It was on the basis of Sedlák's opinion that Josef Pekař developed what has become the most influential explanation of the relationship between Nicholas and Jakoubek: the former played a key role as the more radical in temperament and doctrine, working always to draw his Czech colleague to the left, further to the left, indeed, than Jakoubek would otherwise have gone; eventually Jakoubek sobered down and Nicholas stood alone, although his Waldensian ideas, fostered in the favorable environment created by his own work and by Jakoubek's temporary extremism, were soon taken up by the most radical Hussites, who would in a few years emerge as the Taborite party.[77]

Bartoš's reconstruction is more complex.[78] At first, in 1412–1413, Nicholas was merely one of the radical Hussite theoreticians, intellectually an apprentice of the Czech reformers, and heavily influenced by Hus and Jakoubek, as well as by the works of Wyclif. He was not a Waldensian at this time, and his special contribution to Hussite ideology lay in his mastery of the canonistic material. But in 1414 Peter Payne, the prominent Wycliffite, came to Prague, bringing with him reports of the condition of the German Waldensians whom he had visited; at the same time, by refusing to swear the oath required for admission to the University of Prague, he raised the question of oath-taking to the forefront of Hussite concern. Nicholas took Payne's side in rejecting all oaths, and, himself a German, began to entertain the idea of uniting the Hussite movement with the Waldensians of Germany. Thus in 1414–1415 he developed a theoretical foundation for positions of a Waldensian cast; his guide, however, was not any actual schooling among the heretics, but the Pseudo-Chrysostom's *Opus imperfectum in Matthaeum,* to which the works of Wyclif had introduced him. Jakoubek, however, would not follow Nicholas on this path, but defined his own contrary position on point after point; hence the break between the two and Nicholas's decision to leave Prague. Bartoš's hypothesis that Nicholas was a Prague German, first recruited to the cause of reform by the Hussite movement, rather than a fully formed reformer of the original Dresden School, fits in with his other ideas about Nicholas's doctrine and career.

Some of the points at issue in these two conflicting interpretations can be settled more or less conclusively. Thus Bartoš has shown that Nicholas's *De quadruplici missione* was not a source for Hus's defense of Wyclif's article on free preaching, as Sedlák had argued, but

---

[73] *Ibid.,* coll. 653–657.

[74] Above, n. 57.

[75] Bartoš, p. 141 f. None of Nicholas's works seem to date from after the end of 1415; a refutation of his *De purgatorio* referred, in 1417, to his having been martyred; in 1419 John Želivský mentioned a "Nicholas, priest of Christ" who had been martyred in Meissen. Bartoš also observes that one of Nicholas's works, a defense of utraquism addressed to a schoolmaster in Wildungen, formerly in Corbach, points towards an interest in carrying on Hussite propaganda in Germany.

[76] Sedlák, p. 51 f.

[77] Pekař, *Žižka* 1: ch. i.

[78] Bartoš, pp. 142–146 & *passim.* Cf. Pekař's critical note, *Žižka* 4: p. 191. It must be said that although Bartoš's study is extremely valuable, its argument is not perfectly unified, nor are its major points adequately demonstrated by detailed analysis of texts.

rather came later, and in fact drew on Hus's work.[79] Again, Sedlák supposed that Nicholas's treatise on Purgatory was a source for parts of Hus's sermon on the text, "Dixit Martha"; since the sermon was preached in 1411 and the *De purgatorio* was written in 1415, Sedlák had to conjecture that Hus used an earlier draft of Nicholas's work, now lost.[80] But his arguments in favor of Nicholas's originality in this case are quite unconvincing, and an examination of both works suggests that, as we might suppose from the dates, Nicholas drew on Hus.[81] As for Jakoubek, there is really no reason to regard his radicalism as inspired by Nicholas, for the Czech had already reached some of his most extreme positions before Nicholas's appearance on the Prague literary scene; Jakoubek had been among those reformers who, more radical than Hus, had adopted Wyclif's doctrine of remanence, and he had not shown any noticeable caution in his appeals to the secular power to take over the church's property, in his attacks on the corrupt clergy as the Whore of Babylon, or in his identification of the Pope as the Great Antichrist.[82] As early as 1410 Jakoubek was ready to reject the authority of the Roman institution because its way of life was in contradiction to evangelical poverty [83]—and this attitude was perhaps the most fundamental element of the body of doctrine that Nicholas of Dresden was to begin developing two years later. In fact Jakoubek's two main sources, Wyclif and Matthew of Janov, are enough to account for every radical position he ever took, if we allow for the stimulating and crystallizing effect of political involvements, and it is impossible to demonstrate that Nicholas of Dresden's influence was decisive at any particular point. In certain issues, such as the condemnation of usury and of the cult of holy images, the literary work of the two was closely related, and their ideas were on the whole identical; in regard to the distinction between civil and evangelical possession, Nicholas's discussion was much the same as Jakoubek's, to whose work Nicholas referred his readers for additional authorities.[84] All of this suggests that it would be wrong to see Nicholas of Dresden as uniquely radical or uniquely original: he was one of many Hussite intellectuals, formed by the movement itself, and if he in fact went further to the left than anyone else around him, this development must itself be explained in terms of the history of Hussitism. Thus on the whole, Bartoš's view seems sounder than Sedlák's.

What then are we to say about Nicholas's alleged Waldensianism? Again, we must agree with Bartoš

---

[79] Bartoš, "Studie k Husovi a jeho době. 1. Hus a valdenství," *ČČM* 89 (1915): pp. 5 f.

[80] Sedlák, pp. 46–48.

[81] This is Novotný's conclusion (*M. Jan. Hus, život a dílo* (Prague, 1921) 2: p. 20 n. 2, p. 22 n. 2), but he offers no demonstration to back it up. Some of the evidence for Nicholas's dependence on Hus, rather than *vice versa,* is brought out in the discussion of the *De purgatorio* below, and a few more items may be offered here, although a full-scale demonstration would require much more space than can be afforded in a footnote. First of all, it may be fairly said that Sedlák's *literary* arguments, turning on the alleged unity of Nicholas's work as opposed to alleged incongruities in Hus, are simply not convincing; but even if they were, it would not follow that the more unified work was the original—quite the opposite! Then there is the fact that Hus used his Lectures on the Sentences as a source. Thus the passage in Hus's sermon from ". . . oportet, ut purgandi hominis capacitas procedat ex propria dignitate" to ". . . que hic pro ipsis ab aliis fiunt" ("Dixit Martha," ed. A. Schmidtová, *Iohannes Hus . . . Positiones, recommendationes, sermones* (Prague, 1958), p. 165) is taken almost verbatim from his Lectures on the Sentences (*Super IV Sententiarum,* ed. V. Flajšhans (Prague, 1904), p. 716 f.; *cf.* Novotný, *op. cit.,* p. 496), which were composed in 1407–1409, well before Nicholas began his literary career. But parts of this passage are in Nicholas's *De purgatorio,* MS. Univ. Prag., III G 8, f. 36′. Finally, along with the passages compared in the text below, the following comparison may be adduced:

Hus, p. 159

Secundo nocent recipientibus sacerdotibus, quia propterea magis avaricie intendunt et simonie, *et crapulosius pascuntur sicut corvi de cadaveribus. Et hinc dicitur: "De morbo medicus gaudet, de morte sacerdos,"* quia medicum morbus et sacerdotem cadaver pascit, suple occasionaliter.

Nicholas, f. 43′

Secundo nocent sacerdotibus recipientibus, quia propterea magis avaricie intendunt et symonie, sicut corvi, quia medicum morbus et sacerdotem cadaver pascit, suple occasionaliter.

Here Nicholas's text is obviously defective because of the omission of the italicized words; the verse in quotation marks appears in Nicholas on f. 42, and perhaps was therefore left out here, but in any case it cannot be supposed that Hus took his passage from Nicholas.

[82] Reference is to the works listed in Bartoš's *Literární činnost M. Jakoubka ze Stříbra* (Prague, 1925), Nos. 1, 2, 19, 25; the last was composed in January 1412, the others earlier.

[83] *Ibid.,* No. 22.

[84] Nicholas of Dresden's *De usura* is "evidently a continuation of the similar tractate by Jakoubek," according to Bartoš, p. 137. Nicholas's discussion of evangelical possession and the like in the "Querite primum regnum dei," MS. IV G 15, f. 120–121, puts forth the same theory that we find in Jakoubek's works, and ends with: "Cetera et aliorum sanctorum dicta de ista materia vide in actu Magistri Jacobi quem fecit super isto articulo, utrum decime sunt pure elemosine"; ironically, this only reference to Jakoubek in Nicholas's work is incorrect, the article in question having been defended by Hus (Sedlák, p. 35 n. 1; of course we should not exclude the possibility that Nicholas was right and that Hus used as his own a work written by Jakoubek). Finally, on the question of images, Nicholas's position (in the "Querite," f. 129 sqq., and in his *De imaginibus* (see bibliography)) and Jakoubek's (*Činnost Jakoubka,* Nos. 58, 69) were not only close to each other in doctrine but were capable of being combined in a single work. MS. Prague Cathedral Chapter B 81, f. 175–263′, contains an anonymous anti-Hussite treatise refuting an also anonymous radical-Hussite attack on the cult of images, the use of the kiss-of-peace plaque, and aspersion; fortunately large portions of the Hussite work are quoted, and the section on images contains whole passages identical with sections of Nicholas's and Jakoubek's works cited above. I would guess that the anonymous Hussite work was in fact written by Jakoubek, to guide the priests who were taking over churches from the Catholics in 1415/1417, and that he drew not only on his own material but on Nicholas's as well.

that this was a later development, although it would be wrong to draw any very clear lines between earlier and later stages. Bartoš's hypothesis assigning a decisive role to the advent of Peter Payne seems too external, for even before 1414, Nicholas had developed positions pointing toward Waldensianist heresy—the right of inspired laymen and women to preach, the invalidity of sacraments performed by simoniacs, etc.[85] Above all he had from the first worked out a conception of the antithesis between the Church of Christ and the Synagogue of Satan that set these two in opposition not as polar positions in theory but as actual bodies competing for men's allegiance; Hus and Jakoubek approached this point of view very nearly in the implicit presuppositions of their anti-Roman agitation, but they never went all the way—for them the Roman Church, however corrupted, was the body to be reformed, not a union of mere evil to be destroyed. But in at least one place Nicholas too takes this more conservative position— "recedere non intendo a romana ecclesia, inter cuius viscera nutritus sum" [86]—backing it up by a reference to the *Decretum,* the canon "Non decet." The passage is of course to be understood in the light of the canonistic tradition that defined the Roman Church not as the corporation of offices and jurisdictions, but as the congregation of the faithful, a body perfect by definition.[87] But still we may observe that here as in his other canonistic constructions, Nicholas displayed a mode of thought that was in itself alien from that of the Waldensian heretics, who would hardly have thought it worth the trouble to build up a body of reform doctrine by manipulating the authorities of the Roman Church's law and tradition. Nor indeed would a Waldensian theoretician have called for the secular power to reform the church by taking away her property and disciplining her priests, as Nicholas did in the *Puncta* and *Querite;* to the Waldensians the secular power was part of the whole alien apparatus of corruption that they were opposed to.[88] If then we bear in mind Nicholas's consistently and characteristically intellectual style of thought, and if we remember that the work of Wyclif and Matthew of Janov contained ideas of reform identical with many of the doctrines of the Waldensians, we will not find very much of that heresy in Nicholas's early work except possibly as one influence among many others; on the other hand, we can say that the direction of Nicholas's thought pointed towards an outright sectarianism that the pressure of conflict would inevitably bring to realization. Here—anticipating what will be said below—we may suppose that the decisive factor was Nicholas's role as an ideologue unfettered by the political responsibilities that kept his Czech colleagues from pushing reform beyond the point at which it ceased to be compatible with a church established in society.

At any rate the case for Nicholas's Waldensianism does not rest on his early works, which, without the later ones, would hardly have prompted scholars to make such a case at all. But with the treatises composed by Nicholas in the second half of 1415, his radicalism took on a shape that, as we have seen, even Professor Bartoš has labeled Waldensian. The absolute condemnation of all oath-taking, all killing, and of the doctrine of Purgatory—these are radical ideas not easily derivable from Wyclif or Matthew of Janov, and they function as a kind of tracer group, allowing us to distinguish the extreme points of University radicalism from sectarian heresy still further to the left; all are Waldensian tenets, so characteristically indeed that those refusing to swear oaths were regarded as Waldensians *ipso facto,* while the denial of Purgatory was frequently branded in the same way, as one of *the* Waldensian errors.[89] And yet even here the case is not so simple: Jakoubek matched Nicholas's condemnation of oath-taking with a condemnation of his own, from which he exempted only what were not properly oaths at all but mere promises of future good behavior, like

---

[85] In the *De quadruplici missione,* the *Puncta,* and the Fifth Table of the *Tabule.*

[86] Sermon on "Nisi manducaveritis," MS. IV G 15, f. 199'.

[87] See the discussion by Brian Tierney, *Foundations of the Conciliar Theory* (Cambridge, 1955), pp. 36-46.

[88] *Puncta,* MS. IV G 15, f. 15' sq. *Cf.* also the *Querite,* MS, IV G 15, f. 111'-112 (canonistic texts to show that the laity and the secular powers can reject or depose priests in mortal sin); and f. 123' sq.: after citing the texts that show simony to be a heresy, Nicholas writes, "Et ideo domini temporales iuste et catholice auferrant et auferrent ab huius[modi] anticristis et maximis hereticis possessiones temporales, et in usus pauperum et defensionem legis dei converterent." The formulation here points us towards one of the forty-five articles of Wyclif: "Domini temporales possunt ad arbitrium suum auferre bona temporalia ab ecclesiasticis habitualiter delinquentibus" (Palacký, *Documenta Mag. Joannis Hus . . .* (Prague, 1869), p. 329). The Waldensians might conceivably have supported such a position, but their whole mode of thought pointed in another direction, towards an absolute alienation from the state power: see, e.g., the "Errores haereticorum Waldensium," ed. J. Döllinger, *Beiträge zur Sektengeschichte des Mittelalters* (Munich, 1890) 2: p. 338: "Item dicunt, papam esse caput omnium heresiarcharum et ex eo ipso cardinales, archiepiscopos, episcopos, imperatorem, reges, principes, duces et omnes iudices, tam spirituales quam seculares una cum omnibus presbyteris, esse damnandos."

[89] John Hus, defending a priest who in 1408 refused to swear an oath, observed, "Ecce vos vultis istum sacerdotem condemnare, dicentes eum tenere errorem Waldensium" (*Documenta,* p. 185; cited by Sedlák, *Studie a texty* 1: p. 75). The Prague Hussite chronicler, Master Laurence of Březová, referring to the Taborite rejection of Purgatory, wrote, "Item purgatorium animarum esse post hanc vitam cum Valdensibus negabant . . ." ("Kronika husitská," ed. J. Goll, *Fontes rerum bohemicarum* (Prague, 1893) 5: p. 411). These are only two examples, immediately pertinent to the present context; others could be added not only from the sources for Hussitism but from the anti-Waldensian sources generally: see, e.g., the discussion of the canonistic texts prescribing that those refusing to swear an oath were to be regarded as *ipso facto* heretical, in Nicholas of Dresden's *De iuramento,* ed. Sedlák, *Studie a texty* 1: p. 91.

marriage vows and vows of feudal fidelity.[90] Moreover, although Jakoubek was eventually to sanction Hussite warfare, he did so with the greatest reluctance, as a concession to the needs of the time—the true Christian path was that of suffering, of non-resistance even to mortal enemies—and in his discussion of whether Christian magistrates might inflict the death-penalty, he at one point came very close to an outright negative—only a special revelation could justify such killing.[91] Thus even Jakoubek took more or less Waldensian positions on these key questions, and we are not unduly surprised to find him referring at this time to the Waldensians as holy people, "fideles Christi," nor will we refuse to believe Peter Chelčický's later testimony, that Jakoubek's belief in Purgatory went hand in hand with a refusal to declare such belief obligatory as an article of faith.[92] If then we find that Nicholas of Dresden's movement towards a Waldensian position in the second half of 1415 caused a break between himself and Jakoubek, we shall not suppose that this break was essentially a difference of opinion about this or that doctrine, or that it represented some sort of psychological difference between a true radical and a crypto-conservative.

Here the controversy over the doctrine of Purgatory is most instructive. Bartoš has argued that Jakoubek opposed Nicholas on the matter of Purgatory because of a conviction that the early church had believed in it; but if Jakoubek had wanted to come to the opposite conviction, he could have found plenty of texts to back him up there too [93]—no one who has worked his way through any good amount of medieval theological polemic will suppose that basic positions were arrived at through the agency of pure, disinterested reason. That the two former allies found themselves in opposition on the question of Purgatory shows us that this question involved issues that could not be suppressed; such issues must have touched the very heart of the reform movement. To define exactly what the issues were, we shall have to study the pertinent sources, above all Nicholas's *De purgatorio*, in which we shall find very little further information about the question of Waldensianism, but a great deal about the meaning of Hussitism. Whether Nicholas took his views from the Waldensians, whether he in fact was one, or whether he simply picked up heresies that were in the air and supplied his own argumentation, these possibilities cannot be clarified in the present condition of the sources, and it may very well be that his doctrine should be called not Waldensian but Waldensianist—similar in kind to but not necessarily derived from the actual heretical movement. What is clear is that heretical configurations have an inner logical consistency, and that a given point of view will, if worked out in sufficient amplitude, necessarily produce doctrinal positions characteristic of itself. Thus the controversy between Nicholas and Jakoubek over the "Waldensian" doctrines can be read as a struggle over basic points of view about the meaning of evangelical reform: as we shall see, the issue was one of sociology rather than, in essence, doctrine.

Perhaps the most striking feature of Nicholas of Dresden's *Dialogus de purgatorio* is its deliberately Hussite formulation, in which the rejection of Purgatory appears as nothing but the inevitable consequence of positions long and solidly established by Hus and his associates. Nicholas was above all a reformer, not a speculative theologian, and if he addressed himself to the question of dogma, does Purgatory exist? he was primarily interested in the practical issue: are prayers for the dead of any use? The work opens with a

---

[90] Jakoubek, *De iuramento*, MS. Vienna Nationalbibliothek 4936, f. 185: "... iuramentum primo modo dicitur analogice confessio promissi ad aliquid bonum prosequendum fugiendumve malum"—such as baptismal oaths, vows of marriage or chastity, "aut dum inferiores subditi suis superioribus, officiales dominis suis, et omogiales regibus spondent fidelitatem"; "hoc modo iuramentum sumendo . . . non est prohibendum." The second kind of oath, also licit, was that sanctioned by special revelation or divine inspiration. The third kind was prohibited (f. 185 sq.): "Aliud est iuramentum tercio modo sumptum quo iam utuntur cristiani communiter in iudiciis vel in quibuscumque factis aliis. Et est invocacio dei vel creature in testimonium alicuius cum supraposicione in crucifixo, ewangelio, vel gladio duorum digittorum et observancia forme, ac verbis ad hoc in iuramento institutis. . . . De isto iuramento . . . pono conclusionem istam: In policia bene recta non est licitum iurare."

[91] For Jakoubek's attitude to warfare in 1420 see my "Chiliasm and the Hussite Revolution, *Church History* (1957) 26: p. 48 ff. His strictures on the death-penalty are quoted by Bartoš, "Jakoubkův Výklad Desatera," *Věstnik české akademie* (1942) 51: p. 94. In his "Studie o Žižkovi a jeho době," *ČČM* (1925) 99: pp. 18–22, Bartoš publishes a tract "De bellis" which he assigns to Jakoubek and dates in June 1414 (see his *Činnost Jakoubka*, No. 52); it is a scholastic set-piece, defining the conditions under which Christians might legitimately fight, and showing none of the hesitation of Jakoubek's later discussions—if it was really written by him, in 1414, it would have to be taken as evidence that he had not yet begun to think seriously about the problem. Inded, in 1414, the issue of whether a *Hussite* might fight, for God's cause, had not yet been raised.

[92] Bartoš, p. 138 n. 75; p. 140 n. 80.

[93] Bartoš's opinion is put forth on p. 140 n. 79. But in Jakoubek's sermon on Purgatory (below, n. 126) there are more biblical and patristic texts quoted for the negative position than for the positive, and of the Fathers, Cyprian, Chrysostome, and Jerome were older than Augustine and Gregory, quoted in favor of Purgatory. Nor can it be said that the former group were less directly to the point than the latter. It is a great merit of the scholastic form of argument that it reveals the true character of every theological determination, as an act of the will; this is particularly evident in the clean-up section, where the authorities *in oppositum* are taken care of. In Jakoubek's sermon the only argument used for this purpose consists of a long quotation of almost the whole of ch. 26, Bk. xxi, of Augustine's *The City of God*, where several interpretations of the fire that proves men's works (I Cor. iii, 12–16) are canvassed: of the interpretation corresponding to Purgatory, Augustine says only, "this I do not contradict, because possibly it is true." He attaches no such reservation to the interpretations—the fire of suffering and persecution in this world, the fire of the day of tribulation—that Nicholas of Dresden was to follow.

passage devoted to this latter question, and the immediately following explicit rejection of Purgatory is merely part of the argument for a negative answer—the house of Christ has only three storeys, Hell, Earth, and Heaven, and those who have died are either in Hell, where prayers will not help them, or in Heaven, where they have no need of prayers. The authority here is Pseudo-Chrysostom,[94] one of Nicholas's favorites, but even this doctor must yield in importance to the Gospels, and the real theme of the tractate is contained in the following passage, still on the first page:[95]

Neither the prophets, nor Christ with his apostles, nor the saints who immediately followed them, taught explicitly that we should pray for the dead, but rather carefully taught the people to live without sin and to be holy. Wherefore the Savior in his Sermon on the Mount taught his disciples and others of the crowd . . . about the strait gate and the broad way, saying (Mat. 7: 13–14): "Enter ye in at the strait gate: for wide is the gate, and broad is the way, that leadeth to destruction, and many there be which go in thereat. How strait is the gate, and narrow the way, which leadeth unto life, and few there be that find it." Whence the saints had great confidence of being immediately saved, because they led a holy life in the present world; and so, undoubtedly, if men were to live well in the manner of the saints, they would reach the Fatherland [*patriam*: Heaven] immediately after death. For who does not know that the most secure way to life is to live as Christ and his apostles taught?

These are sentiments that animate virtually the whole corpus of Nicholas's work, but they are not peculiarly his: in fact all the elements of the above paragraph, except for the scriptural reference, appear in various parts of John Hus's sermon on the text, "Dixit Martha ad Iesum," preached on 3 November 1411.[96] Hus accepted the doctrine of Purgatory and of works for the dead presumed to be there, but he was concerned to show that a truly evangelical faith would not make much of such works, and he sharply attacked various superstitions and greedy practices involved in them, especially in funeral ceremonies, chantries, and the contracts for thirty masses for the dead. What Nicholas did was to take over Hus's criticisms, sometimes in large chunks, sometimes in fragmentary lines; passages in which Hus acknowledged the existence of Purgatory were by-passed or excised from the borrowed material.[97]

In the paragraph just quoted, four separate passages from different parts of Hus's sermon are put together to make up Nicholas's mosaic; elsewhere the pattern is even more intricate, and these cases suggest that we have here something more than just ordinary medieval borrowing: Nicholas took what must have been a good deal of trouble in order to use Hus, even though he certainly realized that the very work he was using contradicted his own.

His *modus operandi* becomes even more curious later on in the treatise. The borrowing from Hus in the first part is made without acknowledgment, and what must have been perfectly obvious to Hussite contemporaries has had to be rediscovered by modern scholarship, but elsewhere the appeal to Hussite consensus is more explicit. In a rather contrived fashion the demand for scriptural proofs of Purgatory is compared with the University of Prague's demand, in 1412, for similar proofs before it would agree to condemn the Forty-five Articles of John Wyclif; and the account of this episode is given in the very words used by John Huss, three years earlier.[98] Then, towards the end of the dialogue, when the orthodox protagonist, M, has chosen a procurator to carry on the argument, Nicholas's spokesman, V,[98a] chooses a procurator of his own —Master John Hus! In fact, Hus's attack on John XXIII's indulgences is quoted, this time with due acknowledgment, to refute a point of the opposite side, and this passage leads into the most extraordinary twist of all: M's procurator, now at a loss for arguments, resorts to a judicial process—he is indeed an inquisitor—and has Hus cited to the Council of Constance.[99] There follows a brief account of what happened to Hus there, including his martyrdom, which is thus presented, literally, as consequent on his defense of V, in whose central position Hus did not in fact believe. Furthermore, the whole procedure in the tractate is tied in with the cause of utraquism: V chooses his procurator because he himself has no more time to argue—he is needed back home to give communion in both kinds and to administer other sacraments. Then, reflecting on Hus's death, V says that he is not surprised that the Council has done this to a saint of God, when it did not fear to condemn what it itself

---

[94] *Opus imperfectum in Matthaeum,* ed. Migne, *Patrologia graeca* 56: col. 817. Nicholas's attachment to this work is discussed by Bartoš, p. 143 ff.

[95] MS. Prague Univ. III G 8, f. 36.

[96] Ed. A. Schmidtová (above, n. 81), pp. 172, 177, 177, 169, in that order.

[97] An example is offered in the text, below, *ad* n. 106. Many others could be cited, but none as charming as the following (Hus, p. 170; Nicholas, f. 39; the text is quoted from Hus, passages deleted by Nicholas are in italics): "O utinam sic faceremus nos sacerdotes, tunc enim non *solum* triginta missas propter pecuniam, sed quottidianas propter vitam eternam, spernentes mundum et sic mundi pecuniam in purgacionem omnium *defunctorum* fidelium missaremus, denique non pactacio symoniaca nos percuteret. . . , doceret autem nos caritas et mentis sinceritas annunciare populo, quod quelibet missa [Nicholas inserts: que] agitur *pro defunctis, a qua eciam nullus in purgatorio excluditur, sed quod* tantum sibi [Nicholas: cuilibet] proficit, quantum meruit hic in via [Nicholas: meruit et se disposuit]."

[98] MS. III G 8, f. 47'; see Novotný, *M. Jan Hus* 2: p. 125, n. 3.

[98a] Sedlák, p. 40, understands V and M as "Viklefista" and "Machometista," and he cites a contemporary writer who interpreted the initials similarly; Bartoš, p. 139, opts for "Veritas" and "Mendacium" (in n. 77 he erroneously gives Sedlák's conjecture as "Vita" and "Mors"). There is no reason why both Sedlák and Bartoš cannot be right, although in favor of the latter it may be observed that "Viklefista" was usually used as a term of abuse by the Catholics, not as a confession of allegiance by the Hussites.

[99] MS. III G 8, f. 64 sq.

recognized as Christ's own institution, the lay chalice. And he goes on to prophesy that the people will do God's will not only in this matter of utraquism but "in every truth inspired by the Spirit of God."[100] Thus, hardly a half-year after Hus's death, the martyr replaced the actual man, the symbol of evangelical anti-Romanism suppressed the living teacher, and the man who had steadfastly refused to embrace doctrinal extremities that would have separated him from the Roman Church was transmuted into the patron saint of endless sectarian innovations. In fact, at about the same time that Nicholas was composing his *Dialogus de purgatorio,* the Waldensianist extremism that he stood for was being put into practice by Hussites in South Bohemia and elsewhere, who rejected all works for the dead, along with other standard orthodox practices, and who drew the line between good and bad priests according to the attitude taken to Master John Hus.[101]

But if the foregoing paragraphs have suggested that Nicholas was a perhaps excessively cunning artist, they also show that he had good material to work with. The Benedictine monk, Paul de Vooght, has recently submitted Hus's "Dixit Martha" to careful scrutiny and has concluded that it is perfectly orthodox,[102] but if we read it along with Nicholas's *Dialogus de purgatorio,* marking out the common passages, we are less impressed by its conservatism than by its radicalism. Thus Nicholas could begin the dialogue between *V* and *M*[103] by having *V* say, in Hus's words:[104]

I wonder why it is that men of modern times are so concerned with suffrages for the dead, when in the whole of canonical Scripture the Spirit of the Lord has not expressly taught these things.

M replies with II Maccabees 12:43, the story of Judah's offering of money for the dead, but *V* counters, again using Hus, that this book is of the Apocrypha; since, of course, this fact is more important to *V* than to Hus, who had no objection to such offerings in principle, *V* must develop the point further by stipulating that the apocryphal books are not binding, only useful, and that anyway the passage in question refers not to the dead in Purgatory but to the dead in the limbo of the Fathers, which was subsequently emptied by Jesus. But *V* then goes on, with a mosaic from Hus:[105]

I cannot see any other cause why men of modern times are so concerned with suffrages for the dead, than men's evil life and, as a result, their lack of confidence. For this is why men have little confidence that they will enter the Fatherland immediately after death—because they live evilly in their present life. And the cause of this is seduction by the priests, which stems from avarice: the priests do not imitate the prophets, Christ, and the apostles, and carefully teach the people to live well, but they teach them to make abundant offerings, and set before them the hope of blessedness and speedy liberation from Purgatory.

What immediately follows this passage provides an excellent illustration of Nicholas's method: a few pages before the last-quoted sentence, Hus had argued that the best work in aid of the *ecclesia dormiens*—those in Purgatory—was the purification of the *ecclesia militans,* above all through preaching of the Gospel; for this reason Satan sought to suppress such preaching. Nicholas quotes the passage, with a few necessary changes, and makes it refer, simply, to what *V* has just said about living well; the passage is so exemplary that it may be quoted in the original:[106]

Hus: Ex quo videtur, quod ewangelizacio sancta, sic—ut dicitur—disponens militantem ecclesiam, multum prestat suffragium ecclesie dormienti. Istud autem Sathan considerans maxime nititur ewangelizacionem extingwere et sophisticans tam sacerdotes quam simplices ducit utrosque in caribdim: clericos in avariciam per vendicionem triginta missarum de requiem et laycos in presumptuosam confidenciam et empcionem symoniacam earumdem.

Nicholas: Istud ergo Sathan considerans, maxime nititur extingwere euwangelizacionem verbi dei, que militantem ecclesiam disponit et multum suffragium prestat, et sophisticans tam sacerdotes quam simplices ducit utrosque in caribdim, clericos in avariciam per vendicionem triginta missarum de requiem, et laycos in presumptuosam confidenciam et empcionem symoniacam earumdem.

And yet, with all his sharp practice, Nicholas remains true to what is obviously Hus's main point. Conceding the existence of Purgatory, Hus has absolutely no interest in developing its cultic implications; quite the reverse, he wishes to reduce the prayers and works predicated on Purgatory's existence to a minimum, in order to foster a religious life based on the imitation of Christ. In pursuit of this aim he not only delivers the most savage attack on the institution of contractual masses for the dead—the thirty masses—but even skirts the edge of heresy by declaring that the masses of a sinful priest, although "valid," will not be pleasing to God and hence will hardly liberate souls from Purgatory.[107] He insists that Christ's sacrifice is the basis of all redemption and is perfectly sufficient to redeem all those needing purgation; in any case, no soul can receive more help after death than it has earned in

---

[100] *Ibid.,* f. 65'.

[101] *Documenta,* pp. 636–638; see my "Hussite Radicalism" (above, n. 22), p. 109 ff.

[102] P. De Vooght, "La doctrine et les sources du sermon *Dixit Martha ad Jesum," Hussiana,* pp. 365–378; the verdict is pronounced on p. 377.

[103] The dialogue begins on f. 38, after three pages of preliminaries setting up the difference of opinion about Purgatory in terms of the "three-storey house" vs. the "four-storey house" (see above). V is introduced thus: "Aggrediatur aliquis ex parte tristege domus, et sit gracia exempli 'V', adversarium suum de quatristega domo, et sit 'M', in hac forma...."

[104] MS. III G 8, f. 38; Hus, p. 171 f.

[105] F. 38'; Hus, pp. 177, 172.

[106] F. 38'; Hus, p. 169.

[107] Hus, pp. 172, 174 f; *cf.* De Vooght, *op. cit.,* p. 376 f., where it is shown that Hus did not embrace the donatist heresy. Nicholas has the passage on f. 39' sq.

life.[108] Nicholas picks up these strains, at length and usually *ad verbum;* he leaves out all references to Purgatory, but in the end it does not matter: given the overriding interest in evangelical *conversacio* shared by Hus and Nicholas, the former's belief in Purgatory is just so much excess baggage that the latter is well rid of. Theologically this statement may be monstrous, historically and practically it is true, and it may be said that in terms of the logic of the Hussite reformation, considered in itself, Nicholas has betrayed Hus in order to reveal Hus's truth.

At the same time Nicholas's tractate is entirely in line with his own body of work and thought, and all of the key themes that we have examined in the previous discussion make their appearance here, often with references to this or that earlier work. Although much space is devoted to the mechanics of theological argument, with citations from Scriptures and the Fathers given, expounded, and where necessary distorted into the desired meaning, all according to scholastic ritual, we are never allowed to forget that the real point is the confrontation between the two churches and their respective spokesmen. *M* is indeed described as:[109]

> one of the plump priests and fat canons who had daily commemorations of the dead, for which indeed he visited churches . . ., said masses, and received much money, to support his carnal, luxurious life, his idle household, his horses and dogs . . . —to say nothing of his cooks, his mistresses, and his children.

He is surrounded by a crowd of others like him, all of them afraid that their snouts will be plucked from the trough by *V*'s teachings—"Non enim gratis facta est mencio de memoria defunctorum in canone misse!" Hence "from that day on, they planned to kill him": "Such a destroyer of the holy church deserves death, let us condemn him to death most foul!" [Sap. 2: 20]. *V* is duly impressed, in fact he is scared, but he comforts himself with evangelical precepts and remembers that Christ had to face just such a gang of simoniacs, fornicators, and brigands, whom indeed he threw out of the Temple. "They are not the Holy Church but the Congregation of Babylon and the Synagogue of Satan." For further details on the difference between the two, we are referred to the *Apologia*. If then we are told that masses for the dead were not the institution of Christ or the Primitive Church, but of the popes —the historical material is drawn from the *Flores temporum,* which Nicholas had studied and used in his *Puncta*—we have no doubt about what inference should be drawn from this. Later on,[110] when *M*'s procurator, an inquisitor belonging to one of the mendicant orders, observes that prayers for the dead are a "praiseworthy custom of the Church," *V* responds by calling the friar a "doctor of custom and present practice" rather than a doctor of law. We are here referred to the *Apologia* again, and we perforce recall its contrast between the Primitive Church, which observed the commands of Christ, and the modern Church, represented by the doctors of the Council of Constance, who explicitly exalted their own custom over those commands.

But all of these considerations—in fact the whole critique of works for the dead and of the clergy who hold to them—are in form an *accessus* to the theological issue, which is broached when *M* "plainly says" that to deny Purgatory and hold that souls after death either go straight to Heaven or straight to Hell is an error, including three others.[111] These are: (1) that no venial sin remains after this life; (2) that *pena* is remitted along with *culpa;* (3) that the suffrages of the Church are of no help to the dead. *V*'s responses serve to define what Nicholas has to say about the matter at hand and, in the process, to set forth his general and basic religious attitudes with a profundity he does not elsewhere attain; here, for the first time, he appears to us not as a mere critic of abuses, or as a mere partisan of a sloganized *ecclesia primitiva,* but as the preacher of a genuinely reformed religion. Even *V*'s preliminary remarks about the meaning of "error" have an interesting charge of deeper significance; he insists that nothing is an error, with regard to the faith, except what is against Holy Scripture, and he proposes that this be taken as judge: "Igitur iudicium eligamus nobis"[112]—the very formula that would appear twenty years later in the negotiations between the Hussites and the Council of Basel, and which would preside over the whole intra-Hussite debate in which Tabor developed its theology against Prague. There could indeed be no human judge in these ultimate issues, only a mortal struggle between two truths. It is at this point that Nicholas makes his only reference in the treatise to the Waldensians, a complaint that because of the false belief that Purgatory was a matter of the faith, "many have been burnt to death as unbelievers."[113] The same

---

[108] Hus, p. 165 f.; the passages are also in his commentary on the Sentences, ed. Flajšhans, *op. cit.,* pp. 716 f, 715; they are in Nicholas's work on f. 36', minus the one about the sufficiency of Christ's sacrifice (*cf.* f. 51' for an equivalent).

[109] F. 43 sq. Earlier *V* had refuted one of *M*'s arguments and added an apology: "Maneat michi reverencia tua salva et amicicia ab antiquo contenta . . ." (f. 42); but it is not clear what the significance of the last phrase is, unless we suppose that Nicholas had once been a friend of someone who either was or became a prosperous prebendary, and that *V* and *M* were intended to designate Nicholas and his old friend, respectively. But there is no other reason to think this.

[110] F. 59' sq.

[111] F. 47.

[112] F. 47.

[113] F. 47': ". . . in presenti materia purgatorii sicut comuniter de eo loquuntur homines nonnulli et fere omnes, credulitatem dicunt esse necessariam et ponunt quasi fidem—quin ymo ut constat, multi voragini ignis ut increduli traditi sunt. . . ." In the *De iuramento,* ed. Sedlák, *Studie a texty* 1: p. 92, there is a similar reference, in regard to swearing oaths: "In primitiva enim ecclesia communiter fideles ruebant in gladio [Dan. xi, 33; *cf.* Table Nine, § 8], sicut patet de martiribus; postea autem et maxime post dotacionem Constantini incipiebant ruere in flamma ignis, et multi, quia nolebant iurare vel quia ex toto

fate was in store for Nicholas, whose theology actually pointed to the stake.

We see this particularly in *V*'s discussion of the second alleged error. (The first, attacked by *M* with a single passage from Gregory the Great, has been easily refuted by analysis of the passage and by the position that Scripture is to be preferred to the works of any posterior doctor.[114]) Here *M* has stated the key Romanist doctrine that while confession and penance can win absolution from every *culpa*, the obligation to discharge the *pena* will in most cases be unfulfilled in this life: hence the need for Purgatory, which is proven in this context by I Corinthians 3:13, "... and the fire shall try every man's work of what sort it is." *V*'s reply is that the fire in question is that of trial and tribulation here on earth: the true Christians will inevitably be tried by such fire as they seek to follow the path of Christ, and if they persevere their purgation by fire is behind them—"the elect are punished in this world that they may not be punished in the next."[115] Again relying on the Pseudo-Chrysostom, *V* devotes several pages to an excursus on this theme, showing that the church is never free of tribulation, that life in this world is never free of sin, and that all adversity afflicting the just may be understood as a baptism of fire. As for the alleged residue of *pena* to be worked off by the *salvandus* after death, *V* insists that even though *pena* is not ordinarily remitted in full and at once, as is *culpa*, still it may happen so "because of the penitent's fervor or even through the pure generosity of God";[116] and if it does not, then the man must pursue his repentance, always hoping for full remission of *pena*, either through his own merits or through God's grace and the merit of Christ's passion. But none of this implies future remission in Purgatory. And when *M* insists on the difficulties presented by cases of incomplete penance, *V* in turn insists on the position that the merits of the penitent are not a determining factor. "Sufficiency is based not only in our merits ... , but in the merits of Christ and of God, who is merciful and capable of supplying all our defects [*cf.* II Cor. 3:5]." As Nicholas of Lyra has pointed out, God favors one and not the other. It is not a matter of justice but of God's generosity and grace.[117] Earlier *M* had argued that God would not be a just judge if at the end both the man who had been good all his life and the man who had been bad but repented at the last minute went straight to Heaven.[118] *V* had then answered by referring to the parable of the laborers in the vineyard—all got the same pay, although some had been working from the first, others only for a short time—and in observing that anyway there were different degrees of beatitude in Heaven, since some enjoyed the *summum bonum* more than others. Now *V* adds a more fully developed statement of the divine mystery: "Man cannot fully understand even the least of God's works, as for example the leaf of a tree—why is it of just such a size and shape, etc.?—and still less can he understand His greatest works, among which are election and reprobation."[119] Indeed the trouble with the Romanists is that they want "to assimilate God and his works to human works and to creatures."[120] In any case, if *M* wishes to invent hypothetical examples, *V* can play the game too: what if a man who has been good all his life falls into mortal sin just before he dies, while a man who has been bad all his life repents just before he dies? If divine justice can be preserved only by postulating a middle place of temporary torment on the second man's way to Heaven, then must we not also postulate a middle place of temporary bliss for the first man, before he descends into eternal Hell? Or if it be said that differential retribution in Hell is provided for by different degrees of suffering, then the converse can be said about Heaven; if on the other hand it be urged that the sinner who has done some good is rewarded here on earth, then why not say that the *salvandus* who has sinned is punished here on earth?[120a] These are rationalistic trivialities, necessitated by the actual argument; both text and context show that they are less important in Nicholas's concept of the issue than his basic understanding of what it means to be a follower of Christ. Indeed a long digression pins this point down: Nicholas re-emphasizes the central place of Christ's teaching about the two paths, and the harsh corollary, that "more will perish than will be saved."[121]

Are prayers for the dead then of no use? Since the Roman Church includes everyone, and hence consists for the most part of those who will be damned, its prayers—that is, its institutional actions—are of du-

---

corde volebant deum diligere et ipsi soli servire. . . ." Jakoubek wrote similar passages at this time (Bartoš, p. 138 n. 75).

[114] F. 48 sq. "Quis enim nesciat, sanctam scripturam canonicam tam novi quam veteris testamenti certis suis terminis contineri eamque posterioribus omnibus episcoporum literis ita preponi, ut de illa omnino dubitari et disceptari non possit, utrum verum vel utrum rectum sit quidquid in ea scriptum constiterit esse?"

[115] F. 48' sq.; there follows a long passage from Pseudo-Chrysostom on f. 49–50.

[116] F. 51 sq.

[117] F. 52 sqq.

[118] F. 46'.

[119] F. 53.

[120] F. 58': "Contra illos enim volentes deum in factis suis assimilare operibus humanis et creaturis. . . ."

[120a] F. 54 sq.

[121] F. 54'–58. "Plures sunt qui pereunt quam qui salvabuntur" (f. 57'). The digression ends with a summary: "Ex quibus iam dictis considerare volenti plane potest patere de igne purgatorio et quomodo diversis modis purgantur salvandi, qui et valde pauci comparacione aliorum. Et de duabus viis et tristega domo, et de purgacione quarte partis terre. Ante hominem enim, bonum et malum, aqua et ignis, vita et mors, dextrum et sinistrum, album et nigrum—quod voluerit dabitur ei. Non ergo restat aliud nisi quod dicit beatus Bernhardus: Via tua est vita tua. . . ." The theory of the *imitacio Christi* here receives its most violent form, with an explicitly sectarian inspiration—there is no provision for the great majority.

bious value; *V* can here cite no less an authority than Innocent III.¹²² And the presupposition of such prayers, the existence of the *ecclesia dormiencium* in Purgatory, need not be accepted, as already shown. On the other hand, the true Church, the congregation of the faithful, does form a unity and the prayers of one part enrich the whole. Moreover the prayers of Jesus Christ, the sole mediator, are supremely effective.

The whole argument of Nicholas against Purgatory, with all of its "authorities," really rests on this concept of the Church as a spiritual body, the small band of those who follow the evangelical commandments in their full rigor, and whose whole life constitutes their purgation. Those outside this group may exhibit varying degrees of goodness and badness, but salvation is not for them; since the function of Purgatory was precisely to provide for those who were neither very good nor very bad, the middle class,¹²³ the evangelical ideologue naturally refused to believe in it. This attitude exactly corresponded to that of the Waldensians, who also held to the scheme of the two paths, one leading straight to Hell, the other straight to Heaven,¹²⁴ and it may be labeled a sectarian attitude, expressing the ideology of a small group within the large mass. Nicholas had first envisaged this group as the historical Primitive Church, and if he shared this idea with other Hussites, he nevertheless had a peculiarly lively awareness of it. In the *Tabule* he had provided for a pictorial actualization of the Primitive Church; in the *Apologia* he had gone so far as to summon up the image of that Church, led by Christ, coming into the Council of Constance to practice utraquist communion; in his sermon on the text, "Querite primum regnum dei," composed about the same time as the *De purgatorio,* he went even further: tracing the development from the frequent communion of the Primitive Church to the yearly communion of the modern one, he commented, "If then a man feels himself to be in the estate of the Primitive Church, he should take communion frequently."¹²⁵ We may reasonably regard the *De purgatorio,* as well as the other works composed in the second part of 1415, as formulations of the reformed faith of those few who felt themselves to be in the estate of the Primitive Church, and we may see in the doctrines of these works, with their emphasis on implementing the counsels of perfection—this is the gist above all of the "Querite"—and with their renunciation of the religiosity that sought to capture the workings of God with nets of human rationalization, the specific religious outlook of such a sect. Since, however, the sect would be a minority in Hussite Bohemia as well as in Romanist Europe, the effect of Nicholas's "Waldensianist" works was to face the whole movement with a crisis of its own being: would evangelical reform be limited by existing ecclesiastical and societal realities, or would it become the program of a sect, or, finally, would it become the point of departure for some sort of fundamental reconstruction of the existing order?

From 1415 on, the internal history of the Hussite movement can be read as a response to this problem, and we will not be far wrong if we understand Jakoubek of Stříbro's break with Nicholas of Dresden in 1415 as the first step on the road that would lead him to become the bitter opponent of the Taborites—whose teacher he had once been. On 29 November 1415, the anniversary of the death of Charles IV, Jakoubek preached a sermon on the question of Purgatory, in which he responded to Nicholas's arguments and defined his own, orthodox position; one has only to read this sermon to see how hard it must have been to write, and how weak in fact was its own argument.¹²⁶ Beginning with the authorities against Purgatory—most

---

¹²² F. 61'; the reference is to the decretal "Cum Marthae" (III, xli, 6), of which the last few lines are quoted: ". . . defunctorum alii sunt valde boni, alii sunt valde mali, alii mediocriter boni, alii mediocriter mali"; prayers for the first group are superfluous, for the second useless, and as for the last two, the addressee of the letter is to think about the matter—"tua discretio investiget." Nicholas then cites the gloss (*in verbum,* "investiget"), in which the problem of distinguishing between the *mediocriter boni* and the *mediocriter mali* is discussed, but not clearly resolved. He then comments: "Ecce quomodo dubitando et quasi in incertum loquuntur, quasi super arenam fundati. . . ."

¹²³ Innocent III's distinction, cited in the previous note, was a modification of a simpler, tripartite distinction made by Augustine in his *Enchiridion;* the passage is included in the Sentences, IV, xlv, 2, and in the *Decretum,* XIII. q. ii, c. 23, whence (no doubt) Hus quotes it in his *Dixit Martha,* p. 164. Augustine talks of the very good and the very bad, and defines the third class as the "non valde mali"; Hus picks this up as defining "quibus defunctis prosunt suffragia ad celeriorem liberacionem a penis"—"non valde boni nec valde mali, sed medii"—it is for these that Purgatory, a "statum [*sic*] medium," must be posited.

¹²⁴ See, e.g., the "Errores . . . Waldensium," Döllinger, II, 338: "Etiam negant purgatorium post hanc vitam, dicentes solum esse duas vias, scilicet immediate ad vitam aeternam, et malorum immediate ad mortem aeternam."

¹²⁵ MS. IV G 15, f. 131: "Si igitur homo sentit in statu primitive ecclesie, communicet frequenter."

¹²⁶ The sermon is listed in Bartoš's *Činnost Jakoubka,* No. 63; I have used MS. Vienna Nationalbibliothek 4524, f. 39–45, and have compared 4749, f. 160–169', and 4937, f. 177–186. A treatise *De purgatorio* was also written by Jakoubek, according to Bartoš soon after the sermon (*Činnost,* No. 64); it has been published by C. Walch, *Monimenta medii aevi* (Göttingen, 1759) 3: pp. 3–25. Unfortunately there is no way to date it with precision, since it consists almost entirely of "authorities"; it differs from the sermon chiefly in taking a much less tentative line, citing a great many more authorities for Purgatory, and citing none for the other side. The opponents are indeed defined rather insultingly as those who "nec scriptura solida adiuti, nec ratione aliqua suffulti deductiva, rubore omni semoto, in contemtum magnorum primitivae ecclesiae sanctorum. . . , dicere audent et asserere, quod ignis purgatorius post hanc vitam non existat quodque pro animabus fidelium de mundo hoc exeuntium non sit orandum" (pp. 3–4). On the basis of these traits, I would guess that the tractate was written not against Nicholas but against the extremists of 1416–1417, some of whom indeed did not meet scholastic standards of erudition (see note 145 below).

of them the same as Nicholas's—and putting the negative case quite strongly, even to the point of noting that there are only two paths, and that Purgatory after death would seem superfluous for those who have followed the strait path of suffering on earth,[127] Jakoubek nevertheless rejects this case in favor of one built on the premise that some of the *salvandi* might not be fully purged before their death.[128] The authorities he cites are not particularly powerful—certainly not superior to those cited for the other side—and the real point is obviously that Jakoubek refused to agree with Nicholas, that the *salvandi* would be purged in this life, if not by their sufferings then by God's grace. In short, Jakoubek preferred to follow the Romanists in defining the body of the *salvandi* broadly enough to accommodate the mediocrities. But he then went on to say that even though Purgatory existed, the faithful should, so to speak, behave as if it did not, placing no emphasis on works for the dead, and trying themselves to lead the virtuous lives that would make it unnecessary for them to pass through Purgatory at all.[129] Thus although he, like Nicholas, believed in the evangelical principle of the strait way, he preferred to apply this principle within the framework of a sociology based on the existing order; for him the Primitive Church was a historical concept, not, as with Nicholas, a sociological one. Some years later, during the defense of Prague against the anti-Hussite crusade, Jakoubek told Peter Chelčický that he could not condemn all killing because such a condemnation would dishonor the knightly estate:[130] here we have another "Waldensianist" point, on which Nicholas had taken the "pure" position, and we may perhaps be justified in using this datum to illuminate the struggle of 1415. Jakoubek simply refused to take sectarian positions that would have made establishment of the reform in alliance with the existing powers impossible. We need not suppose that he always made conscious choices between the counsels of perfection and of prudence, but we can infer that his political program, looking towards establishment of the reform by the nobility and the burghers, functioned as a limiting factor in his thinking. And to wrap the matter up, we may observe that there is some evidence attesting the duplicity that would inevitably have stemmed from such an attitude. Peter Chelčický tells us that Jakoubek once admitted, under questioning, that a Christian was not bound by faith to believe in Purgatory as in other articles of faith; on another occasion, again under questioning, Jakoubek defined Purgatory not as palpable torment but as the soul's shame at recognition of its stains.[131] The first position is identical with Nicholas's, the second is reconcilable with it, and yet Jakoubek insisted on defending Purgatory against both Nicholas and the Taborites who later took up the cause of the two paths. Finally, no less an authority than Master John Rokycana, Jakoubek's disciple and successor, revealed that when his master was on his death bed, he said to those attending him: "You should have two sets of books, one set for your own contemplation—and do not take these to the people—and another set for the information of the people."[132] This is better advice for politicians than for evangelical reformers; but Jakoubek was neither the first nor the last to prove unequal to the task of reconciling the faith of the Gospels with an actual order of society.

Next to the *Dialogus de purgatorio* the most considerable work of Nicholas's last, Waldensian period was his set of sermons on the text, "Querite primum regnum dei," which picked up all the old themes of the earlier works and added others. Like the *Puncta* it ranged far and wide, with little pretense to thematic unity, but unlike the earlier work it argued for its author's positions instead of merely allowing them to emerge from the grouping of authorities. Thus on point after point—rejection of images, condemnation of all killing, refusal to swear oaths, condemnation of traditions, rituals, hierarchical authority, usury, various forms of simony, etc. etc.—we have both theory and documentation; as Sedlák has observed, it contains the whole reform program, presented in unrivaled depth and breadth.[133] Those who had learned their radicalism from Nicholas or who had been influenced by him were thus well provided for, against the master's absence, and, although it is not at present possible to trace a direct literary line from the "Querite" to the extremists of 1416/1419 who would advocate its doctrines, the linkage could hardly have been absent.

---

[127] MS. 4524, f. 40: "Item secundum ewangelium, Mat. vii [13–14], tantum due ponuntur vie in hac vita, 'una arta et angusta, que ducit ad vitam, et pauci sunt qui inveniunt ea; alia est lata et spaciosa via que ducit ad perdicionem et multi sunt qui intrant per eam,' que quidem vie solum hic in hac vita ponuntur et non in futura. In futuro autem ponuntur solum duo termini illarum ante precedencium viarum; scilicet vita eterna et perdicio eterna. Cum ergo omnes qui pie volunt vivere in Cristo persecucionem pacientur, per artam viam transeuntes, hic ante terminum vie tribulacionibus purgantur, videtur superfluum talibus post hanc vitam igne aliquo purgatorii tribulari."

[128] The case against Purgatory occupies f. 39–40′; the case for it, f. 40′–42, and it consists of II Macc. xii, 42–44; Di. XXV, c. 4 (Gregory I); XIII. q. ii, c. 21 (Gregory I); XIII. q. ii, c. 23 (Augustine); Mat. v, 25–26; plus a few rational arguments, of which one is the familiar "stat per valde possibile quod aliquis salvandus tam graviter peccet contra deum, et ita diu, quod ante mortem non perfecte peniteat . . ." etc. (f. 42).

[129] This is the sense of the refutation of the opposing position (f. 42 sqq.) and of the concluding section, on how to help those in Purgatory (f. 44 sqq.).

[130] See the account in Peter Brock, *The Political and Social Doctrines of the Unity of Czech Brethren* (The Hague, Mouton, 1957), p. 32.

[131] Bartoš, p. 140 n. 80.

[132] *Liber diurnus Petri Žatecensis*, ed. F. Palacký, *Monumenta conciliorum generalium saec. decimi quinti* (Vienna, 1857) 1: p. 298; cf. Pekař's comments, *Žižka* 1: p. 111.

[133] Sedlák, p. 38 f.

For one thing, the Dresden School continued to function, with Peter of Dresden now joined by the English Wycliffite Peter Payne.[134] Apart from one manuscript text, a set of glosses on a copy of Nicholas of Lyra's postil on the New Testament,[135] we have no evidence of the School's scholarly activity, but we know that its members played a role in Hussite agitation in this period—carrying the antithetical posters of the *Tabule*[136]—and we may presume that the very continuity of Nicholas's manuscript tradition, including codices that may be described as collected editions of the master's works, attests to the continued action of his German disciples.[137] Nor can it have been an accident that some of the latter would appear side by side with Czech radicals in one of the crucial episodes of the development of the Hussite reformation: on 6 March 1417 a large number of radical leaders were ordained priests by titular Bishop Herman of Nicopolis, held prisoner for the purpose in Lord Čeněk of Vartemberk's castle of Lipnic. This event was the result of a deliberate program through which the University masters and the Hussite nobility sought to stabilize the reform, by securing ordinations and parochial livings for the younger Hussite clerics, who for the past two years had been making trouble as leaders of extremist movements in the provinces and as partisans of extremism in Prague; as it turned out, most of those who passed through Herman's hands emerged a few years later as leaders of Tabor.[138] It is therefore most interesting to learn that when candidates for ordination were being rounded up, some of the students at the Dresden School were included; two of these, John Drändorf and Bartholomew Rautenstock, eventually fell into the hands of the Inquisition and their confessions provide us with our only detailed, particular knowledge of the Lipnic affair. In the present context the most noteworthy bit of information is that although the candidates were asked to swear the usual ordinee's oath, neither John nor Bartholomew did so: the latter simply said that he had refused, the former that he had uttered not a *iuramentum* but only a *votum*, of poverty and chastity.[139] It is indeed otherwise clear from their confessions that they held to a radical doctrine similar to that of Nicholas. Bartholomew, who named Nicholas and Peter as his teachers, confessed to not believing in Purgatory (he held to the doctrine of the Two Paths) or in the cult of saints or in the use of holy images; he was a utraquist and attacked the secular dominion and simony of the hierarchy.[140] Drändorf did not name Nicholas, only Frederick and Peter, as his teachers, and his doctrine, as preserved in his (fragmentary) confession, seems somewhat milder: his protest was more against the jurisdictional aspects of the Church—its property, dominion, excommunications, hierarchical authority, etc.—than its doctrines, although he did refuse to swear an oath and he did declare his belief in utraquism.[141]

---

[134] The only direct source is a rhymed chronicle that names the masters at the Dresden School as "Mistr Petr, mistr Mikuláš,/ Engliš, a Nikolaus Loripes" (*Staří letopisové čeští*, ed. F. Palacký, *Scriptores rerum Bohemicarum* (Prague, 1829) 3: p. 472); Sedlák, p. 3 n. 1, observes that the verses are best understood as referring not to four men but to two, the second line being in apposition to the first. At the same time, Sedlák supposes that the chronicler had made a mistake, naming Peter "English"—i.e., Payne—where he should have named Peter of Dresden. Bartoš, p. 134, accepts the source's evidence, which is indeed bolstered by what seems to be a relationship between Payne and Nicholas of Dresden, manifested in Payne's *De iuramento* (Bartoš, p. 136). To this I would add the following curious bit: a manuscript codex now in the Herrnhut Unitätsarchiv, No. 220, contains some items associated with the Dresden School (Müller, *op. cit.*, p. 85 n. 13), including what is either an early draft of the *Tabule* or excerpts from it (f. 93'-97); the next leaf (f. 97') has three paragraphs concerning the election of a Holy Roman Emperor, his coronation, and, finally, the oath that he must swear—all according to texts in the Decretals and Clementines; the last paragraph, on the oath, ends with, "Ad idem est discipulus M. Joh. W[iklef] in suis oracionibus tangens Iuramentum tale." If anyone in Bohemia was known as Wyclif's disciple it was Peter Payne, who indeed functioned as a prime expert in Wyclifism for the Hussite Left (see Bartoš, *Literární činnost . . . M. Petra Payna* (Prague, 1928), Nos. 3, 4, 5, 7, 9, etc.). Thus we have another link between him and the Dresden School, although due appreciation of the value of this evidence is impossible without full examination of the codex (I have used photographs of only a few pages).

[135] A Neumann, "Glossy v Drändorfově postile," *Hlídka* 41 (1924): pp. 457–465, with texts on pp. 460–465. The postil itself was copied by John Drändorf, and Konrad Stoeklin, members of the Dresden School, in 1412; the glosses, which reflect a doctrine identical with Nicholas of Dresden's, were written sometime after 1414 but before 1417.

[136] *Chronicon Procopii notarii pragensis*, ed. K. Höfler, *Geschichtschreiber der husitischen Bewegung in Böhmen*, I. *Fontes rerum austriacarum* (Vienna, 1856) I. Abt., 2: p. 72. The context seems to refer to events of 1415/1417.

[137] Such codices are: Kraków, Jagiellon Library, 2148; Prague University Library, IV G 15; Mikulov, II. 123; Bautzen, VIII 8; the now-lost original of Basel University Library MS. A X 66. Each of these codices also has material not by Nicholas, but each also groups enough of his work so that we can infer a conscious effort of collection.

[138] See my "Hussite Radicalism and the Origins of Tabor 1415–1418," pp. 117–125.

[139] Kapp, *op cit.*, p. 56: "Item queritur, an Studio Pragensi rectori suo fecerat juramentum, Respondet quod non, sed solam promissionem, et dicit se nunquam jurasse, nec eciam in promotione ordinis sacerdotalis, sed tunc solum votum castitatis et paupertatis emisit." *Cf.* Jakoubek's formulation, above, n. 90, for similar distinctions; these did not vitiate the principle, at least in Drändorf's mind, for he went on to declare (*loc. cit.*), "quod iurare est contra deum et ecclesiam catholicam."

[140] See his confession, ed. Döllinger, *op. cit.* 2: pp. 626–629.

[141] Uniquely valuable are the items of propaganda composed by Drändorf and included in the inquisitional record: (1) a letter attacking *excommunicatio frivola, obedientia ceca*, and *dominatio secularis, lege evangelica sacerdotibus interdicta* (Kapp, pp. 41–46); (2) a letter to the aldermen of Weinberg, urging them to pay no attention to the Church's ban and to the clergy's jurisdiction in secular affairs (pp. 48–51); (3) two other letters to the same addressees, pursuing the issue and arranging to carry on agitation in Weinberg (pp. 51–53). (Items 2 and 3 are in German.) Of course these texts show only what points initially came to the fore when Drändorf was

But these confessions also tell us something else, that despite the close association of the Dresden School with the Hussite movement, from 1412 through 1417, the matter of nationality eventually claimed its due importance, leading the Germans onto their own, separate path. It was not a matter of ethnic hatred or dislike, but of something much more ordinary and infinitely more important: when reform of the Church was envisaged not in terms of institutional or moral reform of the clergy, but as a reform of the whole body politic, as a process of evangelization that inevitably had its center of gravity in the laity, then the passage from reform to reformation necessarily excluded whatever could not be useful in the new societal organism. The year 1417 was in fact a crucial one in this process, and the Lipnic ordinations, along with other events of the same period, inform us that henceforth the theoretical elaboration of a reform program would be less important than the realization of reform among the people. The Dresden School is not heard from after that year, nor did Drändorf or Rautenstock return to the School from Lipnic; both were assigned jobs as priests among the Germans in Bohemia, the former in South Bohemian Jindřichův Hradec (Neuhaus) and in Prague, the latter in Prague. Presumably a similar path was followed by other Germans consecrated by Bishop Herman. But this disposition was not a stable one, for reasons that are not clear; after one year Rautenstock set out to preach in Germany, and Drändorf followed him two years later. Henceforth the Dresdeners are known to us only as they fall into the hands of the Inquisition, and their school may justly be called, in the phrase of Heinrich Böhmer, a "School for Martyrs." [142]

Turning now from the Germans to the Czechs, we can trace the enduring effects of Nicholas's program only by hypotheses and combinations, some more convincing than others. Anchoring the whole structure will be two facts: (1) When Nicholas of Pelhřimov, Bishop of Tabor, wished to defend his rejection of Purgatory against the Prague masters in 1431, he dipped into Nicholas of Dresden's *De purgatorio* for arguments and even whole passages.[143] (2) John Želivský, the radical preacher of Prague's New Town, referred to Nicholas of Dresden, in 1419, as a martyr.[144] To these we may add an assumption: when, after 1415, we find evidence of *intellectual* activity promoting Nicholas's program—the combination of general radical Hussite positions with the specifically "Waldensian" points—we may assume that the Dresdener's influence was at work, either through the effect of his oral teaching or through the circulation of his tractates. That the program existed as a significant element on the Hussite Left is beyond question. We find it in 1415/1416 in South Bohemia, by the end of 1416 in the area around Plzeň, and in 1418 as a set of doctrines to be rejected by the Hussite Synod of St. Wenceslas's Day (28 September); unfortunately it cannot be said with any certainty that these cases represented Nicholas's influence, since it is at least possible, in one case probable, that the influences at work stemmed from popular Waldensian sectaries in the provinces—"unlearned men and women," as they are called by one text.[145] But a few hitherto unused literary sources show the same program on the theoretical level. One is a parody of a confession that a heretic might have made to an inquisitor. Such confessions were indeed sought during this period, at the order of the Council of Constance, and it was no doubt in reaction to this sort of thing that the anonymous author composed his list, the style of which will be obvious from the following examples: [146]

First, I confess that I have said confession in the belief that the priest could absolve me of sins. *Item,* I have sinned because I have taken on the penance that the priest imposed, and I have done everything that the priest commanded, even though I was not bound or obligated to do so. *Item,* I have sinned because I have received the communion of the Eucharist in only one kind, which was not complete communion.... *Item,* I have sinned because I have paid over tithes, cheeses, eggs, etc., and the priest lived sumptuously from these and spent them on concubines. *Item,* I have sinned because I have attended the masses of concubinaries, knowing that they were concubinaries.

Some of the points were even more extreme:

I have sinned because I have said prayers for the dead, but this is neither necessary nor worth anything; each must do satisfaction for himself. I have sinned because I have given candles and a groschen, that the priest might name the names of my predecessors. I have sinned because I have believed that there was a Purgatory, but there is none, except to do well here—after my death no one will do good for me.... I have sinned because I have given money for church buildings and ornaments, thinking that it was for the temple of God—but prayers should be said everywhere and anywhere. I have sinned because I have believed that confession should be said to priests, but confession should not be said to anyone but God, for only God absolves of sins, so that after death the soul at once rises to Heaven or goes to hell.... I have sinned because I have done reverence to images, bending the knee or lighting candles before them, I have sinned because I have believed that in the mass singing and other such things were necessary, but

---

carrying on propaganda; they do not exhaust his ideology. *Cf.* H. Haupt, "Waldensertum und Inquisition im sudöstlichen Deutschland," *Deutsche Zeitschrift für Geschichtwissenschaft* **3** (1890): 358 f., where Drändorf's (and the Dresdeners') heresy is explained as an original Waldensianism, influenced by Wycliffite and Taborite elements; emphasis is here placed on Drändorf's ideal of *paupertas Cristi*.

[142] Böhmer, *op. cit.*, p. 228.

[143] The fact was first noted by Sedlák, p. 45 (see n. 152 below).

[144] Jan Želivský, *Dochovaná kázáni z roku 1419*, I, ed. Amadeo Molnár (Prague, 1953), 126 f. See Bartoš, p. 141 n. 83, for evidence that in 1417 Nicholas was remembered as a martyr for Christ.

[145] For all this see my "Hussite Radicalism," p. 109 ff., p. 119 f., p. 125 ff.

[146] The best text is that of MS. Vienna Nationalbibliothek 4314, f. 134′–135, entitled, "Sequitur confessio heretica et falsa que concordat cum valdensibus." See also the next note.

the only thing necessary is the consecration of the body and blood of Christ. I have sinned because I have believed that one priest may not ordain another, although he can indeed. I have sinned because I have believed that the pope's authority is superior, although it is not greater than that of another priest.

There are also other articles of the same tendency, forming a full conspectus of the most extreme sectarian heresy; the whole list is dated in 1418 in one codex, where the scribe names himself as a Czech, and indeed it would be impossible to date the work elsewhere than in the period after the introduction of utraquism and before the founding of the Taborite movement (1419).[147] Closely associated with the ideas and language of provincial extremism in this period,[148] the list also reminds us strongly of the works of Nicholas of Dresden, and thus suggests that the latter were not without their effect upon the emergence of the radical, Taborite reformation.

But this suggestion would not be worth very much in the present argument if it were not reinforced by other evidence of a more certain sort. Sometime around 1418, certainly before the rise of Tabor, a Catholic author addressed himself to the problem of refuting Nicholas of Dresden's *Tabule veteris et novi coloris* and the doctrines that seemed to have inspired it; he composed his work in the form of two treatises, the first refuting twenty-one errors of a sectarian Hussite stamp, the second proceeding to the refutation of the arguments of the *Tabule* itself.[149] Here the first treatise is of primary concern; it is directed against the following positions:

1. The Roman Church is not the one universal church founded by Christ. 2a. The Roman Church became corrupted from the time of the Emperor Constantine. 2b. Spiritual persons should not possess temporal goods. 3. The church does not include evil people but only the good. 4. Denial of the church's power of the keys and of binding and loosing. 5. Rejection of holy orders. 6. Denial that only priests may consecrate the Eucharist, offer sacrifice, etc. 7. Opposition to the constitutions of the church and the holy canons. 8. Because of the sins of prelates and priests, their ministration is worthless. 9. Evil prelates have no power to excommunicate. 10. The church cannot excommunicate the good, and unless sin excommunicate a man, the church's excommunication is nothing. 11. The prelates of the church should not excommunicate, persecute, or shun the evil, but should commit punishment to God alone. 12. It is not licit in the church of God to kill heretics physically and to remove the evil from amongst the good. 13. The miracles performed in the church are not of God. 14. Rejection of indulgences and assertion that offerings given for them are venal. 15. Opposition to material churches and their dedications. 16. Destruction of images of Christ and the saints in the church. 17. Denial that Purgatory exists and that suffrages for the dead are of any use. 18. Confession should not be made to priests but only to God. 19. The bread and wine remain in the Eucharist after consecration. 20. Communion to be given to newly born children. 21. Communion to be given to the laity in both kinds. [The last two chapters are directed against not just the theory but the actual practice of such communion.]

These are quite clearly the same heresies as those animating the author of the parody confession; they are also very much in the spirit of the Dresden School, and they are explicitly associated with the *Tabule*. Unfortunately the author composed his treatise as a collection of excerpts from the enormous anti-heretical work of Benedict d'Alignan, Bishop of Marseilles (1229–1267), but since he selected so little out of so much, and since he did include original elements, we are entitled to read the treatise as a refutation of actual heresies rather than a mere exercise in polemical ritual.[150] That the heretics under attack were Czech Hussites is apparent from the inclusion of both the practice and doctrine of infant communion in the list. This was a novelty emerging at about the beginning of 1417, among the Czechs;[151] in any case, by the time the treatise was written, the Dresden School had prob-

---

[147] The text in MS. Univ. Prag. XII F 30, f. 40′–41′, begins well but then drops the ironical elements and ends up as a list of heretical doctrines. It is entitled: "articuli hereticorum videlicet Wyklephistarum, anno domini MCCCCXVIII conscriptorum [sic]"; at the end the scribe has written: "Ego Magister Jacobus dictus Hnyewek. Y budess sye hnyewaty o tho, peczye zadne nemyey, przydeth tha hodyna genz wsseczko spolu zaplatyss. Conclusio" ("I am Master James, called Hněvek. And you will indeed be angry [hněvati], don't worry, when the time comes that you'll have to pay for all this! The end."). In favor of accepting the date given for this text, are the following considerations: (1) the *terminus a quo* would be the end of 1415, when the extreme radical doctrines of the "confession" emerged as actualities (denial of Purgatory, rejection of images and of the Roman liturgy, etc.); (2) the *terminus ante quem* would be 1419, when the emergence of the Taborite movement caused intra-Hussite polemic to replace anti-Romanism as the subject of Hussite literary endeavors.

[148] See, e.g., the report of extremism around Ústí in 1415/1416, Documenta, pp. 636–638; the summary in my "Hussite Radicalism," p. 111, may be compared with the translated excerpts from the "Confession" in the text above.

[149] The first part is entitled "Collecta et excerpta de summa Benedicti Abbatis Marsilie super capitulo Firmiter credimus . . ."; it begins, "Una est fidelium universalis ecclesia." I use the text in MS. British Museum, Arundel 458, f. 107–147′, MS. Prague Cathedral Chapter D 119, f. 4–107, MS. Rome, Vatican Library, Ottob. Lat. 350, f. 209′–236. In all of these the second part, refuting the *Tabule* follows the first; each part, however, also exists alone, in other manuscripts. The second part has been published, badly and incompletely, by K. Chytil, *Antikrist v naukách a umění středověku* (Prague, 1918), pp. 237–247, with an attribution to Stephen of Páleč; cf. Bartoš, ČČH (1913) 19: p. 507, where the work is attributed to Páleč and Stanislav of Znojmo, but without argumentation.

[150] For Benedict see the *Dictionaire de droit canonique* 2 (1937): pp. 761–765. I have looked at the text of his *Tractatus fidei* in MS. Univ. Prag. VII B 6, and have compared some passages with the *Collecta et excerpta*. Systematic comparison would be desirable, but without printed editions it would take more time than it was worth. Benedict's treatise really should be edited, if not for its intrinsic interest—which is often very great—then as a document; it was quite popular in the later Middle Ages, as a glance at the major manuscript catalogues will show.

[151] See my "Hussite Radicalism," p. 119 f.; Bartoš, "Roztržka v husitské straně r. 1417, "*Sborník příspěvků k dějinám Prahy* 5 (1932): pp. 548 f.

ably lost its importance as an actual grouping on the Left. Finally, it may be guessed that the form of the treatise, a highly technical canonistic and theological discussion, is evidence that the heresies it refutes were maintained on the theoretical level, not merely among popular sectarians.

Thus when we find that in 1419 John Želivský declared his sympathy with Nicholas of Dresden and that at the same time both Želivský and the Taborites were maintaining doctrines similar to those of Nicholas, we shall hardly go far wrong if we suppose that the Dresden master's works and teachings were prime factors in the history of the period 1415–1418. That Nicholas of Pelhřimov, Bishop of Tabor, later used Nicholas of Dresden's works is merely a clinching argument.[152] Tabor did not go all the way to sectarianism and hence did not pick up all of Nicholas's ideas, but the sociological pattern of Taboritism—the congregational community—could embody much that was too radical for the national Hussite Church centered in Prague; perhaps indeed if Nicholas of Dresden had held on for a few years longer he would not have had to leave Bohemia at all. Here, however, we come up against what must be called the mystery of the Dresden School —Tabor, which realized extreme reform in a manner that could hardly have been dreamed of in 1415, yet failed to provide a home for such Dresdeners as Drändorf and Rautenstock; then later in the 1420's, when Tabor was intensely interested in spreading Hussitism to Germany, she did not as far as we know enjoy the collaboration of those Germans, the Dresdeners, who were uniquely qualified to bridge the gap between the Czech and German nationalities. Fortunately the source material for this whole subject is so largely unexplored that we are entitled to hope for much more knowledge in the future.

THE WORKS OF NICHOLAS OF DRESDEN

The following list is based on the work of Jan Sedlák and F. M. Bartoš. Only one item (No. 1) has been added, and nothing new has been offered in the way of dating or attribution, except in so far as a choice between conflicting hypotheses may be regarded as a novelty. In any case, until more of Nicholas's works are published, no catalogue can be more than a provisional checklist.

Manuscript codices of the three major collections can be identified by their style of numbering, as follows:

—Prague National and University Library: [e.g.] IV G 15
—Prague Cathedral Chapter Library: N 7
—Vienna Nationalbibliothek: 4343.

The provenience of other codices is indicated explicitly.

The two basic works discussing Nicholas of Dresden and his literary activity are Jan Sedlák's *Mikuláš z Drážďan* (Brno, 1914), and F. M. Bartoš's "Vzník a počátky táborství," *Husitství a cizina* (Prague, 1931), pp. 113–153. They are cited as "Sedlák" and "Bartoš." Nicholas's utraquist apologetics are discussed in Sedlák's "Počátkové kalicha," *Časopis katolického duchovenstva* **52** (1911), **54** (1913), **55** (1914); this article is cited as *"ČKD,"* with appropriate references.

The arrangement of the works in this list follows a roughly chronological scheme in Part I—works certainly or probably by Nicholas; the listings in Part II —*dubia* of various degrees—are more or less haphazard. Bartoš's division of the whole corpus into works influenced by Wyclif and works influenced by Peter Payne and Waldensianism is not followed, since it does not seem to be more than hypothetical.

Part I: Works Certainly or Probably by Nicholas

1. (De iure et eius divisione)

Inc. Color duplex novus et vetus. . . . Ius quot duplex est. . . .

Expl. . . . nisi papa cum cardinalibus, etc.

MS: III G 16, f. 127′–128.

Subject: Brief instructions for students: the nature of the law, its divisions, how to remember them, how to cite them.

Date: Uncertain: 1412/1416.

Authorship: Its association with the Dresden School is indicated by the combination of subject and attitude (e.g., the Clementines are called "liber . . . venenosus et laqueis plenus"). The first paragraph, defining the two "colors," points to the *Tabule,* and some of the citations adduced for illustration are the same as some in the *Tabule.*

2. Cortina de anticristo, *or* Tabule novi et veteris coloris

Inc. (Cristus portans crucem dicit,) Novissimus virorum. . . .

---
[152] See note 143, above. It is possible, perhaps likely, that Nicholas of Pelhřimov drew directly on Nicholas of Dresden for other things besides just the refutation of belief in Purgatory. Thus, e.g., in his defense of Tabor's simplified liturgy, Nicholas of Pelhřimov wrote (*Chronicon Thaboritarum,* in Höfler, *op. cit.,* II, *FRA,* I. Abt. (Vienna, 1865) **6**: p. 491: ". . . si sacerdotes Dei et Christi sumus, non invenimus, quem magis sequi, quam Christum et suos apostolos debeamus"—a phrase that he may well have picked up from Nicholas of Dresden's *Apologia* (Hardt **3**: p. 594): "Si sacerdotes Dei et Christi sumus, non invenio, quem magis sequi debeamus, quam Christum." But a systematic comparison of texts remains to be carried through.

Expl. . . . arma sunt cristiani. Hec Ambrosius in libro de officiis.

MSS:
1. IV G 15, f. 232–240
2. VG 15, f. 84–92
3. A 79/5, f. 256–261
4. N 7, f. 30'–35
5. O 50, f. 127–132'
6. 4343, f. 181–188 (incomplete)
7. 4875,* f. 29–34
8. 4902, f. 181–186 (incomplete)
9. 4488, f. 64–67'
10. Kraków, Jagiellon Library, 2148, f. 111'–118
11. Basel, University Library, A X 66, f. 296–304
12. Karlsruhe, Badische Landesbibliothek, 346, f. 120–127
13. Herrnhut, Unitätsarchiv, 220, f. 93'–97 (variant redaction)
14. I D 9, f. 137'–138' (excerpts)

Subject: Quotations arranged to contrast Christ and the Pope, the Primitive Church and the modern Roman Church.

Date: ca. 1412. See the preface to the present edition.

Authorship: Certain, from Nicholas's own references to the work in his other compositions.

Editions: 1. The text of MS. 6 has been published by Johann Loserth, "Ein kirchenpolitischer Dialog aus der Blütezeit des Taboritentums," *Mittheilungen des Vereins für Geschichte der Deutschen in Böhmen* **46** (1908): pp. 114–121. The text is only a fragment, and the edition is not good.

2. In the present volume.

Literature: Sedlák, pp. 8–14; Bartoš, pp. 131 f., 147; K. Chytil, *Antikrist v naukách a umění středověku a husitské obrazné antithese* (Prague, 1918), pp. 139–172 & *passim*; H. Preuss, *Die Vorstellungen vom Antichrist im späteren Mittelalter* . . . (Leipzig, 1906). A contemporary refutation of the *Tabule* has survived in a number of manuscripts; one text is published incompletely and badly by Chytil, pp. 237–247.

3. Consuetudo et ritus primitive ecclesie et moderne seu derivative.

Inc. Primus. Et cum complerentur dies penthecosti. . . .

Expl. . . . ut sitis dominantes in clero. Amen. (Anno domini 1417.)

MS: IV G 15, f. 240–249

Subject: Same as that of No. 2, but different themes are taken up and developed at greater length.

Date: Perhaps 1412.

Authorship: The work is very much like the *Tabule* and has many of the same citations; it follows the *Tabule* directly in the manuscript.

Edition: In the present volume.

Literature: Sedlák, p. 15; Bartoš, p. 147.

4. De libera verbi dei predicacione

Inc. Ve michi, quia tacui . . . Is. vi. Quia vergente mundi vespere. . . .

Expl. . . . coronam, quam dignetur.

MS: D 52, f. 227–234, 173–174.

Subject: Same as that of No. 5.

Date: 1412/1414

Authorship: Probable, because of style.

Literature: Bartoš, p. 148.

5. De quadruplici missione

Inc. Viri eciam perfecti et iusti. . . .

Expl. . . . inter filios eius se non computet.

MSS:
1. IV G 15, f. 85'–96'
2. X F 8, f. 136–143'
3. D. 19, f. 217–224
4. 4673, f. 1–8
5. Bautzen, VIII 8, f. 166–183
6. Mikulov (Nikolsburg), II 123, f. 88'–99' (*Inc.* Quidam iurista ponit. . . .)
7. XXIII F 204

Subject: The four ways in which one may have a mission to preach; ecclesiastical authorization is only one way.

Date: 1412, perhaps in the Autumn (according to Bartoš, "Studie k Husovi a jeho době," *Časopis českého musea* **89** (1915): 5 f., where it is argued that the work is a reply to a sermon of Štěpán of Páleč, delivered on 4 September 1412.). Sedlák dates it earlier.

Authorship: Nicholas cites it as his in later works.

Edition: by J. Sedlák, *Studie a texty* (1914) 1: pp. 95–117 (from MS. 1, collated with MS. 4).

Translation: into Provençal, by the Waldensians; *cf.* Bartoš, p. 148.

Literature: Sedlák, p. 16; Bartoš, p. 148; Sedlák, *Studie a texty* 1: pp. 79–85; Bartoš, *ČČM* (*supra*).

6. Puncta

Inc. Pax fratribus et caritas. . . .

Expl. . . . Et tantum de isto triplici iudicio.

MSS:
1. III G 28, f. 140–163' (incomplete)
2. IV G 15, f. 1–43'
3. X D 10, f. 80–82', 201–208', 208'–211' (excerpts)
4. Kraków, Jagiellon Library, 2148, f. 120–157'
5. Bautzen, VIII 8, f. 35–90'
6. Basel, University Library, A X 66, 306–319 (incomplete).

Subject: Various Roman doctrines and practices are refuted or called into question by various quoted authorities; the work is not a unity.

Date: Sedlák: not before end of 1414, although parts may have been composed earlier. Bartoš: written very early (1413?), but in its present form probably put together after Nicholas's death.

Authorship: Certain: it cites Nicholas's works and is cited by them.

Literature: Sedlák, pp. 18–24; Bartoš, pp. 132–134, 148; Bartoš, "Počátky kalicha v Čechách," *Husitství a cizina,* pp. 68–70.

7. Sermo ad clerum de materia sanguinis

Inc. Nisi manducaveritis. . . .Hec Joh. vi sunt intitulata.

Expl. . . . angelis dei in vita eterna. (In MSS. 1, 2, 6, & 8 there follow authorities for the chalice.)

MSS: 1. III G 28, f. 165–179'
2. IV G 15, f. 198–213'
3. XI D 9, f. 221–235
4. V F 22, f. 1 (fragment)
5. V G 19, f. 251 (fragment)
6. A 163, f. 225–231'
7. 4940, f. 255–271
8. Basel, University Library, A X 66, f. 320–336'

Subject: An argument that the lay chalice is necessary for salvation.

Date: (Shortly) before 12 November, 1414, date when the sermon was copied (Bartoš).

Authorship: Attributed to Nicholas in MS. No. 5; style and content also stamp it as his.

Literature: Sedlák, *ČKD* **52** (1911): pp. 786–789; Bartoš, pp. 135, 151; Sedlák, p. 17 f.

8. Sermon on text, "Quod fuit ab inicio"

MS: Kraków, Jagiellon Library, 2148, f. 34'–39'

Subject: Necessity of communion in both kinds.

Date: Neither Sedlák nor Bartoš suggests a date; the text (I Joh. i, 1) is a lesson for the Sunday of Ascension Week, and perhaps the sermon should be dated 12 May, 1415.

Authorship: Sedlák & Bartoš: probable.

Literature: Sedlák, p. 50; Bartoš, p. 153.

9. Contra Gallum

Inc. Nisi manducaveritis. . . . Secundum Thomam. . . .

Expl. . . . quam prestare dignetur unus et trinus optimus pater et filius et spiritus s. Amen.

MSS: 1. IV G 15, f. 142–157'
2. VII E 6, f. 107–111' (incomplete)

Subject: Argument that communion is necessary *ex mandato Christi,* and not, as the preacher Havlík had written, just *ex statuto ecclesie.*

Date: July/August, 1415.

Authorship: Apparent from style and references to earlier works by Nicholas.

Literature: Sedlák, p. 29 f.; Sedlák, *ČKD* **54** (1913): pp. 468–470; Bartoš, p. 151.

10. De iuramento (Extant in two redactions, the second a reworking of the first.)

I. *Inc.* Iuramentum secundum iura canonica. . . .

Expl. . . . ut supra non condempnant.

MS: X F 8, f. 144–147'

Subject: Argument that oaths may not be sworn at all.

Date: Sedlák: 1408; Bartoš: 1415 (this seems preferable).

Authorship: Clear from style and from citations (in the second redaction) of Nicholas's works.

Edition: By J. Sedlák, *Studie a texty* **1**: pp. 86–94.

Literature: Ibid., pp. 75–79; Sedlák, p. 39 f.; Bartoš, pp. 135–137, 151; Bartoš, "Studie k Husovi a jeho době," *ČČM* **89** (1915): pp. 1–5.

II. *Inc.* Nota: Jurando vane. . . .

Expl. . . . dissolvi et esse tecum.

MS: C 116, f. 159'–169' (subsequent pages have more material against oaths)

Date: Second half of 1415.

Authorship: It cites earlier works by Nicholas.

Literature: As above.

11. De usura

Inc. Species usure sunt due. . . .

Expl. . . . in casto proposito audacius loqui. Hec (autem) ad presens dicta sufficiant.

MSS: 1. III G 9, f. 99–142'
2. X D 10, f. 220'–228
3. VIII F 3, f. 127–153 (incomplete)

Subject: Absolute condemnation of interest, against canonistic arguments allowing it in certain cases.

Date: June, 1415: Nicholas refers to the deposition of John XXIII (25 May, 1415), and he cites from this work in his *Apologia,* written at the end of June.

Authorship: MS. No. 1 is a collection of Nicholas's works, and a note at the end of the text names him as author.

Literature: Sedlák, pp. 24–28; Bartoš, p. 151; Bartoš, *Literární činnost M. Jakoubka ze Stříbra* (Prague, 1925), No. 60 (Nicholas's tractate may be a continuation and defense of Jakoubek's on the same subject).

12. (Reply to Rector of schools in Corbach and Wildungen)

Inc. Dominus Jesus, deus et homo, cuius perfecta sunt opera. . . .

Expl. . . . apostolus. . . .

MS: D 118, f. 1–51' (incomplete).

Subject: Refutation of anti-utraquist arguments of the rector, who was himself refuting a utraquist letter that Nicholas had sent him.

Date: ca. 1415.

Authorship: Sedlák judges the style to be that of Nicholas.

Literature: Sedlák, p. 30; *cf.* Bartoš, p. 153.

13. Apologia (*or:* De conclusionibus doctorum in Constancia de materia sanguinis (de communione calicis))

Inc. Prima conclusio: Christus post cenam. . . .

Expl. . . . minister meus erit.

MSS: 1. III G 9, f. 71–93
2. IV G 15, f. 166–192'
3. Mikulov, II. 123, f. 59–80
[etc.: neither Sedlák nor Bartoš lists the manuscripts.]

Subject: Defense of the necessity of communion in both kinds, against the condemnation of it by the Council of Constance.

Date: ca. July/August, 1415 (the Council's condemnation was issued on 15 June, 1415).

Authorship: Although sometimes ascribed to Jakoubek, it is claimed by Nicholas in several of his other works, and it contains references to works by him; the style is his and the canonistic citations are characteristic of him; some of the passages are the same as some in the *Tabule*.

Edition: by H. von der Hardt, *Magnum oecumenicum concilium Constantiense* (1698) **3**: 591–647 (ascribed to Jakoubek).

Literature: Sedlák, p. 29; Bartoš, p. 151; Sedlák, *ČKD* **54** (1913): pp. 404–408.

14. Super Pater Noster.

Inc. Pater noster etc. Prima peticio est. . . .

Expl. . . . ut nemo sine gracia spiritus sancti percipere possit, quam nobis concedat trinus et unus in secula seculorum deus benedictus. Amen.

MSS: 1. IV G 15, f. 44–81'
2. Bautzen, VIII 8, f. 193–262'

Subject: A discussion of the seven sins and of the vices of the clergy.

Date: Second half of 1415.

Authorship: It frequently cites other works by Nicholas.

Literature: Sedlák, p. 31 f.; Bartoš, pp. 145, 151.

15. Sermons on "Querite primum regnum dei."

Inc. Querite primum regnum dei et iusticiam eius. Et scribitur Mat. vi, Luc. xii. Ut adtestatur venerabilis Boecius. . . .

Expl. . . . cuncta conveniencia, que nobis prestare dignetur, qui vivit et regnat deus in secula seculorum benedictus. Amen.

MSS: 1. IV G 15, f. 100–141
2. O 73, f. 95–126
3. Mikulov, II 123, f. 110–144.

Subject: Various aspects of evangelical reform, including the perfectionist mandates of the Sermon on the Mount, etc.

Date: September/October, 1415

Authorship: The style and content are characteristic, and there are many references to Nicholas's other works.

Literature: Sedlák, pp. 31–39; Bartoš, pp. 137 f., 151.

16. Dialogus de purgatorio.

Inc. Circa peticionem pro peccatoribus. . . .

Expl. . . . in laudem, gloriam et honorem in revelacionem Jesu Christi.

MSS: 1. III G 8, f. 36–66
2. D 52, f. 21'–47'
3. Mikulov, II 123, f. 146–169

Subject: Arguments against the existence of Purgatory and refutation of arguments for it.

Date: ca. September/October, 1415. Sedlák supposes an earlier version, written by the end of 1411, but his reasons are inconsiderable.

Authorship: There are references to Nicholas's other works, and a contemporary writer, attacking this work, attributes it to Nicholas.

Literature: Sedlák, pp. 40–48; Bartoš, p. 151 f.

17. De imaginibus

Inc. Est secundum genus reliquiarum, scil. verbum dei, de veneracione cuius vide in Punctis. . . . Tercium genus reliquiarum est sacramentum eukaristie. . . .

Expl. . . . Hec ille. Et tantum de huiusmodi signis, sortilegiis et aliis supersticionibus.

MSS: 1. Mikulov, II 123, f. 169–181
    2. XXIII F 204

Subject: Attack on contemporary cult of holy images.

Date: ca. September/October, 1415 (see next §).

Authorship: Refers to other works by Nicholas, including the *De purgatorio,* and is referred to in the *Querite primum regnum dei.*

Literature: Sedlák, *Studie a texty* 3, i: pp. 89–92; Bartoš, p. 152; the text in MS. 2 is mentioned by Bartoš, "Nové spisy Petra a Mikuláše z Drážďan," *Reformační sborník* 8 (1946): 64 f. Also: Jana Nechutová, "Traktát Mikuláse z Drážďan 'De imaginibus' a jeho vztah k Matěji z Janova," *Sborník prací filosofické fakulty Brněnské University* E 9 (1964), pp. 149–161.

18. De proprio sacerdote et casibus

Inc. Dominus noster Jesus Christus, lapis angularis, assit huic nostro principio. . . .

Expl. . . . sanguinem dedit. Hec Augustinus.

MSS: 1. Mikulov, II 123, f. 83–88
    2. XXIII F 204

Subject: Defense of right of Hussite laymen in Catholic parishes to take communion from utraquist priests in other parishes.

Date: 1415.

Authorship: Style and content point to Nicholas, with whose other works it appears in both codices.

Literature: Bartoš, p. 152 f.; Bartoš, "Nové spisy," p. 64 f.

Part II: Works Possibly Attributable to Nicholas

1. De Christi victoria et Antichristi casu. *Inc.* Christus verus deus et verus homo. . . . *Expl.* . . . in pecunia divinabunt etc. Michee 3. There is no known manuscript; the text survives in Brunfels's edition (see next item). Bartoš, p. 148, attributes the work to Nicholas on the basis of its content, and dates it 1412/1414. For discussion see A. Kraus, *Husitství v literatuře* (Prague, 1917) 1: p. 172; K. Chytil, *Antikrist v naukách* . . ., pp. 182–184.

2. Processus consistorialis martyris Joannis Huss, cum correspondentia legis gratiae ad ius papisticum. *Inc.* Sancimus, ut nullis. . . . *Expl.* . . . ut dealbentur. Dan. xi. The text survives only in the printed edition by Otto Brunfels (Strassburg [?], 1524/25), based on a manuscript sent from Bohemia to Ulrich von Hutten and turned over by him to Brunfels. Bartoš, p. 153, attributes it to Nicholas because of its similarity to the *Tabule* and its sharp rejection of oaths; he dates it *ca.* 1415. For translations into German and Low German, see Bartoš, p. 153; for discussion see the works of Kraus and Chytil cited in the preceding paragraph.

3. Sermon on "Super cathedram Moysi sederunt scribe" (De heresi). *Inc.* Tunc Jesus locutus est ad turbas. . . . Super cathedram. . . . Hic Salvator ostendit. . . . *Expl.* . . . benedictus in secula seculorum *MS:* V E 28, f. 97'–102'. See Sedlák, p. 49 f.; Bartoš, p. 149.

4. De simonia. *Inc.* Ubi enim maius periculum. . . . *Expl.* . . . satis habetur ista materia. *MS:* V E 28, f. 104–129'. Sedlák, p. 49, conjectures that this is the "de simonia" referred to in several of Nicholas's works. *Cf.* Bartoš, p. 149 f.

5. Questiones circa quartam partem Sentenciarum. Nicholas refers to such a work in his *De purgatorio,* MS. D 52, f. 22; Bartoš, p. 148 f., conjectures that fragments of it *may* be found in MS. X D 10, f. 128'–163, 196'–201'.

6. De malicia cleri evitanda. *Inc.* Tu es sacerdos in eternum. . . . *Expl.* . . . rex pacificus Ihesus Christus. *MS:* V E 28, f. 142–149'. Sedlák, p. 49; Bartoš, p. 150.

7. De ecclesia. *Inc.* Ecce pro vera significacione ecclesie expresse. . . . *Expl.* (indeterminate). *MS:* Herrnhut, Unitätsarchiv, 220, f. 121–126'(?). Bartoš, p. 150, conjectures that this may be an early (*ca.* 1410?) work by Nicholas, even though not in his usual style; it is strongly Wyclifian.

8. Catechisms. Sedlák, p. 50 f., identifies two texts in MS. Kraków, Jagiellon Library, 2148, f. 2–11, f. 11–21, as probably by Nicholas: an *Exposicio decalogi* and a *De septem sacramentis*. A catechism, *Tractatus de fide catholica,* in MS. VII E 27, f. 81–90, is regarded by Bartoš, p. 150, as subsequent to these two, and also by Nicholas. This last has been published by E. Havelka, *Husitské katechismy* (Prague, 1938), pp. 192–205. *Cf. ibid.,* pp. 81–109, 160–171.

9. In his "Nové spisy Petra a Mikuláše z Drážďan," *Reformační sborník* 8 (1946): pp. 64–66, Bartoš lists a number of short compositions preserved, along with some of Nicholas's larger works, in MS. XXIII F 204 (formerly Lobkovic 322), f. 38–49'; he conjectures that they are by Nicholas. They are as follows: f. 38–40, De labore corporali; f. 40, a note on priests' fraudulent miracles with the consecrated host; f. 41–43', a critique of various occupations; f. 43'–46, an attack on luxury in women's clothing; f. 46', on the power of the sword; f. 46'–47, an attack on sinful priests; f. 47'–49', a defense of the chalice and the concomitant neglect of the use of the kiss-of-peace plaque in the liturgy.

TABULE VETERIS ET NOVI COLORIS

PREFACE

THE MANUSCRIPTS

B Basel University Library, A X 66, f. 296–304.

Catalogued by F. M. Bartoš, "Husitika a bohemika nekolika knihoven německých a švýcarských," *Věstník královské české společnosti nauk* (1931), No. V: pp. 55–57; the codex was part of the estate of John of Ragusa, a leading figure at the Council of Basel: Bartoš conjectures (p. 57) that he had bought it in Prague. The codex also contains several works of John Hus, Jakoubek of Stříbro, John Wyclif, and other works of Nicholas of Dresden. The *Tabule* ends with a scribal *explicit,* "Anno domini MCCCCXIIII, Dominico die post festum Sancti Bartholomei Apostoli," but this is crossed out and was presumably copied, absent-mindedly, from the scribe's model. The model, now unknown, can thus be dated 26 August, 1414; the copy, however, cannot be dated, except to some time after 1417, the date of composition of its latest item (Jan Čapek's "Otázka nynie taková běžie," f. 371′–373′).

K Kraków, Jagiellon Library, 2148, f. 111′–118.

The *Tabule* has the scribal *explicit,* "sub anno domini MCCCCXIIII, Sabbato ante Esto michi"—i.e., 18 February, 1414; this is the oldest known datable text. The codex contains several other works by Nicholas of Dresden.

L Karlsruhe, Badische Landesbibliothek, 346, f. 120–127′.

The codex dates from the sixteenth century, according to the catalogue, and contains, in addition to the *Tabule:* the Lollard commentary on Apocalypse, *Opus arduum valde;* a series of authorities "contra pluralitatem beneficiorum"; an anti-utraquist tractate and the answer thereto (the first is Gerson's tractate published by Von der Hardt, *Concilium Constantiense* 3: pp. 765–780; the second is by Jakoubek of Stříbro: *cf.* F. M. Bartoš, *Literární činnost M. Jakoubka ze Stříbra* (Prague, 1925), No. 47). A copy of this manuscript text was obtained only after the collation of all the others; it has been consulted for certain problematical passages but not collated—the text is very close to that of *S* and seems to offer nothing of value.

P Prague, University and National Library, IV G 15, f. 232–240.

Catalogued by Josef Truhlář, *Catalogus codicum manu scriptorum latinorum . . .* (Prague, 1905) **1**, No. 747. Two of the works in this codex have scribal *explicits* with the date 1417 (f. 99, f. 249), and since the hand seems uniform throughout, it may be supposed that the whole codex was copied in that year. Of 249 folios, 216 contain works by Nicholas of Dresden, the others works by John Hus and Jakoubek of Stříbro; the whole was evidently written by or at the order of a Hussite. Although the text of the *Tabule* here lacks all of the picture-titles and most of the references to the "old Color" and "new Color," it is otherwise very good, and has been taken as the basis of the present edition.

Q Prague, University and National Library, V G 15, f. 84–92.

Catalogued by Truhlář, *op. cit.,* **1**, No. 967. The codex is fifteenth-century and evidently Hussite; it contains works by Hus, Jakoubek, and others, through the early 1430's; the *Tabule* is the only work by Nicholas in the codex. The scribe made many errors, a good number of which were corrected in a contemporary hand, by comparison with the model.

R Prague, Cathedral Chapter Library, A 79/5, f. 256–261.

Catalogued by A. Podlaha, *Soupis rukopisů knihovny metropolitní kapitoly pražské* (Prague, 1910) **1**. The copy is the work of an anti-Hussite and seems relatively late.

S Prague, Cathedral Chapter Library, N 7, f. 30′–35.

Catalogued by Podlaha, *op. cit.* (Prague, 1922) **2**. The codex is dated in the catalogue as first half of the fifteenth century; it includes works by Hus and some of his immediate predecessors at the University of Prague, as well as some standard patristic and medieval texts; the *Tabule* is the latest work in the codex.

T Prague, Cathedral Chapter Library, O 50, f. 127–132′.

Catalogued by Podlaha, *op. cit.* **2**, and dated there in the first half of the fifteenth century. The codex includes many diverse items, including works by anti-Hussites; nothing seems later than the 1420's. The *Tabule* is followed, on f. 133–137′, by a treatise refuting it, and is preceded by letters of anti-Hussite exiles.

V Vienna, Nationalbibliothek, 4902, f. 181–186.

Catalogued in the *Tabulae codicum manu scriptorum . . .* (Vienna, 1869) **3**. The text of the *Tabule* is here incomplete, beginning with a short part of the third table (§§ 7 & 8) and then, with the fourth table, running through to the end. The hand looks like one of the first half of the fifteenth century.

W Vienna, Nationalbibliothek, 4488, f. 64–67′

Catalogued in the *Tabulae codd. mss. . . .* **3**, but in an unusually inadequate way; the codex contains a great variety of items, many on odd sheets tipped in during the binding, and seems to have been a repertory of "authorities" and tractates compiled by a Hussite. The antitheses of the *Tabule* are actually in facing columns, thus manifesting the sense of the work, but the arrangement seems to be derived from the writer's understanding of the material, rather than from an original model. There are no picture-titles or numberings of items, and some of the errors of quotation and reference common to *W*'s group have been corrected. Both before and after the *Tabule* there is more material, also arranged in the style of antitheses; on the preceding folio-side there is a reference to Pius II that sets the *terminus a quo* of the copy in ca. 1459, and this late date is confirmed by the handwriting. Almost the whole of the fifth table, which does not lend itself to the plan of facing columns, is lacking

Y Vienna, Nationalbibliothek, 4343, f. 181–188.

Catalogued in the *Tabb. codd. mss. . . . 3*; the text has been printed by Johann Loserth, "Ein kirchenpolitischer Dialog aus der Blütezeit des Taboritentums," *Mitteilungen des Vereins für Geschichte der Deutschen in Böhmen* **46** (1908): pp. 114–121, but not very accurately. It is in any case only a fragment of the whole, beginning with the tenth item of the first table and ending about one-quarter of the way through the fifth. The picture-titles are in part preserved, but as indications of the speakers in a dialogue, and where the titles were lacking, the scribe supplied speakers of his own, representing the "new color" by "Iurista" and the "old color" by "Theologus." It is evident that the scribe's model contained more of the picture-titles than any other of our texts, except *Z*. *Y* also contains one picture, truncated in the binding and trimming, of a horseman holding a balance (at the beginning of the fifth table, f. 187), but it cannot be said whether the source was the scribe's model or a suggestion drawn from the text.

Z Vienna, Nationalbibliothek, 4875*, f. 29–34.

Catalogued in the *Tabb. codd. mss. . . . 3*. The copy is well written in what seems to be a mid-fifteenth-century hand, but it is very erroneous. It preserves many more of the picture-titles (or instructions for drawing pictures, or descriptions of pictures) than any other known text.

H Codex 220 of the Unitätsarchiv, in Herrnhut, contains (f. 93'–f. 97) what seems to be an early sketch of what would become the *Tabule;* it is mentioned by J. Th. Müller, "Magister Nikolaus von Dresden," *Zeitschrift für Brüdergeschichte* **9** (1915): p. 85 n. 13, who calls it "ein Entwurf." It begins with a paragraph headed "Statera," and containing, in a variant form, the opening texts of the Fifth Table (up to "suo sensui coaptant"), together with some related material. The paragraph begins: "Fidelis cristianus racionis aperiens oculum debet legem Cristi et legem humanam ponere in pondere vel statera. . . ." It ends: "Pensare ergo debet ponderosius Cristi dicipulus legem Cristi quam legem humanam, ut ponitur in exemplo Cristus in sua conversacione cum discipulis et sua lege ex uno latere; et papa cum suis statum suum magnificantibus cum sua lege." There follow the two series of authorities, one headed "Pars Cristi," the other "Pars pape," and disposed on facing pages. In the second diptych (f. 94'–f. 95) the headings are amplified: "Pars Cristi que [*sic*] debet depingi baiulans crucem"; "Pars pape que [*sic*] debet depingi iuxta tenorem privilegii." A few of the authorities are not in the *Tabule;* others contain either more or less of the original passage than do their counterparts in the *Tabule;* still others, the greater number, are identical. But with one or two exceptions, the material in Tables Five through Eight does not appear in *H,* which, for the rest, groups its related texts differently and in a different sequence from that of the *Tabule.* It has therefore not been included in the collation.

THE EDITION

The problem of establishing a text for the *Tabule* has been resolved by a compromise between the two classical methods, of reconstructing an *Urtext* and of following the "best" manuscript copy; like all compromises this one has both virtues and defects, and the latter require some justification. First of all, it must be admitted that, after wasting many delightful hours in the attempt to determine a *stemma,* the editors have had to accept failure, and with it the inability to reconstruct the lost original. On the other hand, the dated manuscripts closest to the time of the composition (*ca.* 1412, as we shall see)—*B* and *K,* one copied from a 1414 text and the other itself copied in 1414—are not the best: they contain errors that are probably not those of the author, and they do not have the fullest number of picture-titles. Manuscript *P,* copied in 1417, has what seems to be the best text, but no picture-titles at all; manuscript *Z* has by far the most picture-titles, but is very inaccurate and, probably, late. Persuaded, for reasons that will be discussed below, of an original close association between the text and the now-lost pictures, the editors have decided to print the text of *P* with the addition of picture-titles from *Z* (and others), and with the correction of what seemed to be obvious errors. The result is a text including all the important elements that were associated in the tractate during its period of circulation and significance; the objectionable aspects of this artificial conflation are mitigated by the *apparatus criticus,* which allows the reconstruction of every manuscript copy collated, except for textually insignificant variants. The spelling of the edition is that of *P,* unimproved and unhomogenized. To facilitate use of the edition by scholars unfamiliar with English, the editorial material in the apparatus and notes is in Latin, spelled in the medieval manner in order to make formally clear the otherwise obvious fact, that the editors can lay no claim to classical elegance of Latin style.

The relation between the textual material and the pictures that embodied it is not precisely clear, but that the pictures existed is known from several sources. A treatise refuting the *Tabule* and written perhaps *ca.* 1417 refers to the pictures, not only by using the word "depingunt" but by describing the relationship of various figures in pictures that the author had, evidently, seen.[1] From his description it is obvious that these

---

[1] The text of the refutation has been printed incompletely and badly, from MS. Prague, Cathedral Chapter Library, O 50, f. 133–137', by K. Chytil, *Antikrist v naukách a umění středověku a husitské obrazné antithese* (Prague, 1918), pp. 237–247. The anonymous author complains about the Hussites who

pictures were in fact those of the *Tabule*.² A chronicle written as late as 1476 but embodying much circumstantial material,³ tells how the Germans of the Dresden School in Prague carried "written and painted tables" (*tabulas . . . scriptas et pictas*) attacking the papacy; the only example he gives, the antithesis between Christ riding on an ass, the apostles following barefoot, *vs.* the Pope and cardinals riding, sumptuously clothed, on mules, does not correspond to anything in the *Tabule*, which opposes Christ carrying his cross to the Pope on horseback, but the "many other tables" he mentions probably included those of the *Tabule*. The context seems to refer to events of 1415/1417, and we may thus be fairly sure that by this period the pictures were in existence.

But were they in existence from the first, from *ca.* 1412? Here we must begin by disqualifying one line of inference used by some scholars before: the words *tabula* and *color* did not necessarily refer to pictures, nor did the word *cortina*, with which Nicholas himself designated his work.⁴ *Tabula* can mean a picture but it can also mean a collection of authorities, a compendium or structured florilegium,⁵ and this is clearly the meaning of the word in our context, for the "Prima tabula," "Secunda tabula," etc. were not single pictures but rather groups of citations, each *tabula* including material for more than one picture. *Cortina* means tapestry or banner, but also, figuratively, a collection of authorities,⁶ and we may equate it here with *tabula*. Similarly the phrases, *de novo colore* and *de veteri colore*, refer not to actual colors but to the new and old systems, that of the modern church and Primitive Church respectively.⁷ These considerations, however, do not end the matter; the case for an original picture-text association rests on other foundations. If we suppose that Nicholas began by compiling "tables" of authorities for his own use—a practice attested by some of his other works⁸—and arranged them under topical headings to show the contrast between the two "colors," we can easily imagine him being struck with the idea of presenting the contrast in pictures that could get his point across to the illiterate laity. It would seem to be the first stage of this idea that is represented by manuscript *H*, which envisions the two pictures now at the beginning of the First Table, documented respectively by the left and right halves of a diptych extending through three sets of facing pages in the codex. At the beginning there may have been a picture of the Apocalyptic rider with his scales (now at the beginning of the Fifth Table), and at the end, perhaps, a picture of Antichrist (now at the beginning of the Ninth Table).

Having gone this far, Nicholas was in a position to bring his plan to the higher stage of development represented by the *Tabule* as it appears in the other manuscripts. More pictures were imagined; these allowed him to regroup his authorities in more telling antitheses, to add new authorities (and drop one or two), and, perhaps, in the process, to think up still other pictures. The result was a union of texts and pictures that can be inferentially reconstructed from the surviving textual part: the picture-titles tell their own story, and the sequence of authorities, which do not follow a simple

---

attack the Roman Church, "scrutantes in omnibus scripturis veteris et novi testamenti, in decreti canonibus et novis juribus, ubicunque contrarietates et repugnationes statui romanae ecclesiae potuerint invenire"—a clear reference to the *Tabule*—and goes on to say that all this "lucide apparet in tabulis et picturis ipsorum. Depingunt enim in una parte tabulae papam equitantem. . . . In alia vero parte depingunt Christum pauperem, crucem suam in humeris bajulantem . . ." (p. 237). He also describes other pictures.

² The following pictures of the *Tabule* are described: Christ carrying his cross, *vs.* the Pope riding a horse (Tab. I); Constantine and Louis the Pious making their donations to the pope, *vs.* Christ with a crown of thorns, saying "The foxes have holes . . ." etc., and *vs.* Peter on his cross (all from Tab. I); the Pope sitting on his throne and having his feet kissed, *vs.* Christ kneeling and washing the disciples' feet (Tab. VIII).

³ *Chronicon Procopii notarii Pragensis,* in K. Höfler, *Geschichtschreiber der husitischen Bewegung in Böhmen,* I, *Fontes rerum Austriacarum* (Vienna, 1856) I. Abt., **2**: p. 72.

⁴ None of the manuscript copies nor any contemporary source refers to the work as the *Tabule*, but the subdivisions of the work are called *tabule* in the manuscripts. The alternations between the old and new dispensations in the Church are often signalled in the manuscripts by the phrases "de novo colore" and "de antiquo (*or veteri*) colore"; both *B* and *K* end with the phrase, "Finitus est novus color et antiquus," while *P* ends with "Finis est novi et antiqui coloris." Thus the work as a whole was thought of as "The New and Old Color." As for Nicholas's own title, we know it from his citation of certain passages in the work in his later tractates, the "Puncta" and the "Super Pater Noster"—he calls it the "Cortina" or the "Cortina de Anticristo" (see J. Sedlák, *Mikuláš z Drážďan* (Brno, 1914), p. 8).

⁵ Chytil, *op. cit.*, p. 148, understands the word "tabule" as "painters' terminology," but in fact a *tabula* was merely a "table" in the sense of "the tables of the law," and any more specific meaning would be acquired according to the use to which the table was put. *Cf.* Master John Příbram's *Apologia,* written *ca.* 1427 (MS. Prague, Cathedral Chapter Library, D 49, f. 333'): "Magister Petrus [*scil.* Payne, or "Anglicus"] fecit plurima opuscula seu tabulas abreviatas ex sentenciis pociorum librorum Wikleph, quasi quedam comentariolla et explanaciones breves ipsorum librorum . . ."—here is a meaning of the word *tabula* that corresponds to the sort of thing represented by Nicholas's work. *Cf.* Sedlák, *op. cit.*, p. 13 n. 3, for a similar view: *tabule* means "tractate."

⁶ For the first meaning see Sedlák, *op. cit.*, p. 8, n. 4, and F. M. Bartoš, "Vznik a počátky táborství," *Husitství a cizina* (Prague, 1931), p. 131; for the second see Chytil, *op. cit.*, p. 150.

⁷ Thus MSS *R* and *T* have a note, at the end of the Fourth Table: "Lex divina antiquus color, lex humana novus color." A short discussion of the nature and divisions of the law—anonymous but probably by Nicholas of Dresden—has at its head the following: "Color duplex, novus et vetus. Novus qui noviter est inventus, vetus qui ab antiquo. Et secundum hoc eciam duplex lex" (MS. Prague, University and National Library, III G 16, f. 127'). Sedlák, *op. cit.*, p. 9 n. 6, rightly interprets the "old and new color" as "the old and new system," but Chytil, *op. cit.*, p. 148 refers it to painters' terminology.

⁸ Above all the *Puncta: cf.* Sedlák, *op. cit.*, p. 18 f.

one-for-one pattern of antithesis, bears witness to a principle of grouping that can best be understood in terms of the pictures. For example, §§ 7, 8, 9, and 10 of Table One all belong to the same "color," and must have been associated in a picture of Jesus. Similarly §§ 5, 6, 7 of Table Six must have been grouped in a single picture, a procession of prelates. Again, it will be noted that Table Five contains three noncontrasting pictures, and Table Nine documents a single picture.

These conclusions are confirmed by two codices, one in Göttingen, the other first found in Jena but now in Prague, which contain, along with much other material, a Czech redaction of the *Tabule,* in its pictorial form. Both manuscripts are very late, dating from the latter part of the fifteenth century or the first part of the sixteenth, but some at least of their pictures correspond precisely to the arrangement suggested by the Latin text and its titles, and it may be supposed that the pictures themselves derived from a tradition based originally on the illustrated Latin *Tabule,* either in the form of a book, or on placards used for agitation in the streets, or on wall-paintings in Bethlehem Chapel and the walls of the Dresdeners' house, "At the Black Rose." [9] Unfortunately, it has not been possible to work with these codices directly but only with summary or fragmentary discussions of them in the literature, where a few illustrations of them may be found; [10] the precise determination of the relationship between these Czech redactions and the Latin original must therefore be left to others.

Enough has been said, at any rate, to support some inferences regarding the origin of our text. Nicholas may well have prepared a final version containing instructions for the artist, but this would presumably have been much clearer in its dispositions than anything to be inferred from the surviving manuscripts. It must therefore be regarded as lost, along with the original pictures themselves. But soon after the pictures were completed, someone must have copied the textual material from them; in fact more than one such copy may have been made. The Czech redactions show that even in the pictures, the paragraphs of textual material carried their paragraph-numbers ("Primus," "Secundus," etc.), so that the order would not have been radically changed by different copyists. The original picture-text combination must therefore be considered the archetype. The stemma joining it to the surviving texts has not, as already noted, been determined by the editors, but a few general notes may be offered instead. *B, K, L, S,* and *V* agree in preserving a certain number of picture-titles, and also in some other respects; perhaps they go back to a single source, copied rather early (*K* was itself copied in 1414, and *B*'s exemplar dated from that year). *R* and *T* often agree against all the others; they have only a few titles, but they correspond in some points to the text used by the author of the refutation of the *Tabule,* who wrote *ca.* 1417 and who had seen the pictures.[11] *P,* copied in 1417, has virtually no trace of the titles, but offers an excellent text; it must go back to an early copy, from which *Q* and *W* were perhaps also descended. *Z* has the most titles; it sometimes varies with *R* and *T,* but it joins *B, L, S,* and *V* in omitting a good section from the end of the Fifth Table; it may be regarded as a late copy of a text that separated from the others at an early stage. In fact, the manuscript tradition must have been very highly ramified during the first five years of the work's existence; none of our texts is copied from another, and a great number must have been lost.

Finally, it may be observed that a work such as the *Tabule,* consisting almost entirely of quotations from more or less well-known authorities, was peculiarly susceptible to meliorative contamination. In many cases, for example, *B* and *W* differ from the other manuscripts but agree with the Bible, and must have been corrected by comparison with the latter. It is for this reason that we have included the reading of the original source (designated "*O*") along with the variants, where necessary (although major deviations from the original are noted in the explanatory notes). By the same token, the reconstruction of the *Urtext* is not as important as it would be in an edition of some literary composition.

AUTHORSHIP AND DATING

Although two of the manuscripts (*T* and *Z*) ascribe the *Tabule* to John Hus, and no manuscript identifies it as the work of Nicholas of Dresden, there can be no doubt that Nicholas was in fact its author. He refers to it in three of his known works and, as we have seen, calls it the *Cortina* or *Cortina de Antichristo.*[12] In manuscripts *B, K,* and *P* the *Tabule* appears together with other works by Nicholas, and its style is very much like that of some works indubitably by him.[13] *R* notes at the end of the work:[14]

---

[9] See Chytil's discussion, *op. cit.,* p. 142 ff. The first antithesis of the *Tabule,* Christ carrying his cross *vs.* the pope riding sumptuously on a horse, was seen in Bethlehem and described by fifteenth-century observers; the recent reconstruction of the Chapel on its original site in Prague's Old Town rightly reproduces these pictures on the walls, even though we do not know what the originals looked like.

[10] See Chytil, *op. cit.,* pp. 139–172, 235 f., 248–257; also Václav Husa, "O době vzniku jenského kodexu," *Sborník historický* 5 (1957): pp. 71–108; both reproduce some of the pictures. See also F. M. Bartoš, "Jenský kodex a jeho původce," *Ze zápasů české reformace* (Prague, 1959), pp. 64–74.

[11] See the text in Chytil, *op. cit.,* p. 237; it would seem to be the First Table that the subtitle referred to ("... huic tabulae asscribunt titulum 'Incipit conversatio Christi opposita conversationi antichristi'").

[12] See note 4 above.

[13] Sedlák, *op. cit.,* p. 8: a characteristic feature of Nicholas's style is that it is always full of citations from the canon law and its expositors.

[14] For the Latin text see the *Apparatus criticus;* for the history of the Dresdeners and their school see the Introduction.

These texts, collected in this heretical sense, were compiled in this form by the Dresdeners, who, having been expelled from Dresden, seduced many; they did not believe in the existence of Purgatory or in the suffrages of the saints, but taught the opposite.

Since, as we have seen, the pictures containing and illustrating the text were carried in the streets by the Dresdeners, it was natural for others to regard the *Tabule* as the work of the group as a whole; thus understood, *R*'s testimony reinforces the attribution to Nicholas, virtually the only member of the Dresden group who published work.

As for the date, all that can be said with certainty is that the *Tabule* must have preceded Nicholas's *De quadruplici missione,* which refers to it, and which was written in September or October of 1412.[15] The *terminus a quo,* however, cannot be fixed so clearly. Sedlák dated the work in 1410, but for reasons that have since been invalidated,[16] and it would be safest to suppose that Nicholas began to function as a literary figure in Hussite Prague only with the advent of the Dresden School, in late 1411 or early 1412.[17] Thus the work can be most reasonably dated in the first part or middle of 1412, a year filled with the turbulence and popular agitation that could have prompted Nicholas to produce so outspoken an instrument of mass propaganda. Since as we have seen, the structure of the work presupposes the association of text and pictures, it would seem probable that the latter also existed in 1412, and perhaps were used in street processions, even though no other source provides evidence of this. The alternative possibility, that the work Nicholas referred to in 1412 and again in 1413 was only a first draft of the *Tabule*—i.e., a collection of contrasting texts that had not yet been prepared for illustration, deserves mention; the version in manuscript *H* seems indeed to be such a collection. But this is only a possibility. By 1414, at any rate, the *Tabule* as we know it was in existence, and if the above speculations about the manuscript tradition are correct, manuscript *K,* copied on 18 February, 1414, must have been flanked or preceded by several lost copies of the pictorial archetype.

---

[15] The date is established by Bartoš, "Studie k Husovi a jeho době," *Časopis českého musea* **89** (1915): pp. 5 f.; he shows that Nicholas was refuting a sermon preached by Stephen of Páleč on 4 September, 1412—which for its part was an attack on John Hus's defense, earlier that summer, of Wyclif's position on freedom of preaching. See also the following note.

[16] Sedlák's argument ("Vlivy valdské," *Studie a texty* (Olomouc, 1914) **1**: pp. 82 ff.) was that the *De quadruplici missione* must have been composed before Hus's defense of Wyclif's article on free preaching, in July/August, 1412, because the two works have substantial portions in common and this circumstance can be best explained by supposing that Hus copied from Nicholas. The other possibility is less probable, he argues, because Hus habitually copied from others, while Nicholas was an independent, original spirit. On this line of reasoning, the *De quadruplici missione* must have been finished by mid-1412, and since Nicholas in that work refers to the *Tabule,* this work must have been written before then. Doubtless motivated by the momentum of this argument, Sedlák guessed that the *Tabule* was written in 1410, an early dating that he reinforced by the observation that the *Tabule* must have been among Nicholas's earliest works, for in it he does not refer to any of his others (*Mikuláš z Drážďan,* p. 14). But as Chytil noted (*op. cit.,* p. 150), the nature of the *Tabule* as a series of quotations made reference to other of Nicholas's works unlikely in any case, and as Bartoš argued (see note 15 above), the *De quadruplici missione* was written after Hus's defense of Wyclif, from which Nicholas drew substantial passages. Bartoš also rejected Sedlák's high opinion of Nicholas's originality—Nicholas, Bartoš argued, was not a Waldensian, as Sedlák believed, but a follower of Wyclif and the common Hussite tradition. Thus there is no reason to push the date of the *Tabule* back earlier than mid-1412.

[17] See the discussion in the Introduction; *cf.* Bartoš, "Vznik a počátky táborství," p. 129.

TABULE VETERIS ET NOVI COLORIS SEU CORTINA DE ANTICRISTO

[B 296, K111', P232', Q 84, R 256, S 30', T 127, W 64, Z 330]

1 *Incipit conversacio Cristi opposita conversacioni Anticristi.*
  Prima Tabula
  Primus: *Scilicet, Cristus portans crucem dicit:*
5 Novissimus virorum. *Isa. liii.*[1] Si quis vult post me venire, tollat crucem suam et sequatur me. *Mat. xvi.*[2]
  Secundus: *Scilicet, papa equitans in equo dicit:* Summus pontifex utens insigniis apostolice digni-
10 tatis. *Extra de privilegiis, Antiqua.*[3]
  Tercius: Lege vitam Cristi ab utero matris usque

THE TABLES OF THE OLD AND NEW COLOR
(English translation)

The Conversation of Christ contrasted with the Conversation of the Antichrist.

The First Table

1. *Christ carrying the cross says:* The last among men (*Isa. liii, 3*). If any man would come after me, let him take up his cross and follow me (*Mat. xvi, 24*).

2. *The Pope riding a horse says:* The Supreme Pontiff, employing the insignia of the apostolic office (*Decretals, V, xxxiii, 23*).

3. Read the life of Christ from the womb of his mother to his death on the cross, and you will find nothing but the marks of poverty. In regard to these things

---

Apparatus criticus

[1. A typical entry is constructed as follows: an Arabic numeral indicates the line of the text, and it is followed by the pertinent word or words of the text, after which there is a square bracket; then the variant reading is given, and finally the letters designating the manuscripts in which the variant appears. Different variants and their MSS are separated by semicolons.

2. These letters are ordinarily in alphabetical order, except when the variant differs slightly in certain MSS; then the letters for these are placed at the end of the series, set off from the others by commas, with the deviant words in parentheses. The letter "O", designating the original reading of quoted material (from the Vulgate, the *Decretum*, etc.), is always put at the end of the line; it is included only when the quotation varies significantly.

3. All editorial material is in italics.

4. Absence of a word or words is indicated by *"deest"*; presence by *"sic."* *"Ceteri"* stands for all MSS except those specified in the entry by letter. (But the reader is reminded that a few MSS are incomplete.)

5. Although the basis of the edited text is that of MS P, with the variants representing disagreements with P, the readings of other MSS have sometimes been followed instead; in such cases "P" will appear with the variants.

6. Certain classes of variants have not been noted:

  a. deviations in spelling.
  b. deviations in the mode of citing authorities.
  c. errors in citing chapter-numbers, etc.
  d. scribal errors that have resulted in ungrammatical or nonsensical readings, and which appear in only one MS.
  e. minor reversals of word-order in only one MS.

  f. the absence of paragraph-numbers (Primus, Secundus, etc.) in MSS W and Y; such numbers are invariably absent in these MSS.]

1 Incipit . . . Anticristi] *Titulus, ut speratur, primitivus seu ad minus propinquus origini, de codicibus RT desumptus; alii tituli aliis in codicibus habentur, in RT quoque:* Invecciones hereticorum contra papam et prelatos ecclesie *B;* Sequitur tractatus hereticorum reprehendencium et blasphemancium ecclesiam romanam, in hac forma. Incipit conversacio Cristi opposita conversacioni anticristi. Hic reprehendit papam propter insignia et temporalia recepta ab imperatore. *R;* Hic statuta legis Cristi contra statuta modernorum appostolicorum. Semper Cristus et eius exempla opponuntur modernis papis. *S;* Hic continetur husitarum heresis venenosa. Habetur ut cognoscatur et vitetur, quia malum non vitatur nisi congnitum, ut dicit Crisostomus. Incipit conversacio Cristi opposita conversacioni anticristi, ut patet ibi. Hic reprehendit Hus hereticus papam et ecclesiam propter insignia et temporalia ab imperatoribus accepta. *T;* De Cristo et anticristo pulcrum. (*in capite prime columne:*) Cristus. *W;* Sermo Johannis Hussi de Hussinecz, magister heretice pravitatis. *Z* // 3 Prima Tabula] *deest BRSTWZ;* Prima Tabula. Cristus portans crucem *K* // 4 Primus] *deest T;* Primus, de antiquo colore *S* // 4 Scilicet . . . crucem] *sic BKLSZ* (*scilicet deest BKZ*); *deest PQRTW* // 4 dicit] *sic K,Z* (dicit primo); *deest ceteri* // 5–6 post me venire] venire post me *QRSWZ* // 6 tollat] abneget semetipsum, tollat *BO* // 8 Scilicet . . . dicit] *sic BKL,S* (dicitur), *Z* (equitando); *deest PQRTW* // 9 Summus] supremus *B* // 11 Tercius] Tunc Tercius *B;* Tercius est Bernhardus ad Eugenium Papam *R, T* (est *deest*) // 11 Lege] unde lege

---

Explanatory Notes

[1. Abbreviations: "Friedberg" designates E. Friedberg's edition of the canon law, *Corpus iuris canonici* (Leipzig, 1879), 2 vols.

"Edit. Lugdun." designates the three-volume edition of the canon law: I. *Decretum Gratiani* (Lyons, 1613); II. *Decretales D. Gregorii Papae IX.* (Lyons, 1613); III. *Liber sextus . . . [etc.]* (Lyons, 1613). It contains the ordinary glosses.

"MPL": Migne, *Patrologia Latina*.
"MPG": Migne, *Patrologia Graeca*.

2. Minor and relatively insignificant discrepancies between Nicholas's quotations and the original text are not noted.

Where the fact of discrepancy seems noteworthy it is indicated by *"non verbatim"* or some other such phrase. Where Nicholas has radically compressed or distorted his source, the latter is quoted.]

Prima Tabula
[1] *Cf.* Isa. liii, 2–3: ". . . et vidimus eum . . . despectum, et novissimum virorum . . ." *etc.*
[2] Mat. xvi, 24.
[3] *Decretales,* V, xxxiii, 23 (Friedberg, II, 866): "Dominicae vero crucis vexillum ante se faciant ubique deferri, nisi in urbe Romana, et ubicumque summus Pontifex praesens exstiterit, aut eius legatus, utens insigniis apostolice dignitatis."

ad patibulum crucis et non invenies nisi stigmata paupertatis.[4] In hiis Constantino successisti et non Petro. *Bernhardus ad Eugenium Papam.*[5]

15 Quartus: *Scilicet, fides ceca dicit:* Cristus verus deus et verus homo.

Quintus: Papa, id est admirabilis, nec deus nec homo. *Johannes Andree in Prohemio Clementinarum.*[6]

20 Sextus: *Scilicet, Constantinus:* [K 112] Beato Silvestro et successoribus eius tradimus pallacium imperii nostri. Decernimus ut mappulis et lintheaminibus, id est candidissimo colore decoratos equos equitent, conferentes eciam diversa orna-
25 menta imperialia et omnem gloriam potestatis nostre, et possessionum predia contulimus et rebus diversis ditamus. *XCVI. di., Constantinus.*[7]

Septimus: *Ihesus:* Vulpes foveas habent et volucres celi nidos; filius autem hominis non habet
30 ubi caput suum reclinet. *Mat. viii.*[8]

Octavus: Ihesus autem cum cognovisset quod venturi essent ut caperent eum et facerent eum regem, fugit in montem ipse solus. *Joh. vi.*[9]

Nonus: *De veteri colore:* Homo, quis me consti-
35 tuit [R 256'] iudicem aut divisorem super vos? Videte et cavete ab omni avaricia. *Luc. xii.*[10]

Decimus: [hic incipit Y181] Induunt eum purpura et imponunt ei plectentes spineam coronam. *Mat. xxv.*[11] [Z 330']

40 Undecimus: *De novo colore:* Ego Lodovicus Imperator concedo tibi beato Petro et successoribus imperpetuum sicut a predecessoribus nostris usque nunc in vestra potestate et dicione tenuistis et disposuistis, civitatem romanam cum ducatu suo

you are the successor of Constantine, not of Peter (*Bernard to Pope Eugene III*).

4. *Blind Faith says:* Christ, true God and true man.

5. The Pope—a wondrous being, neither God nor man (*John Andree, Gloss on the Preface to the Clementines*).

6. *Constantine:* We give to Blessed Silvester and his successors the palace of our Empire. We decree that they may ride horses decked out in caparisons and coverings of purest white, and we also confer upon them the various imperial ornaments and all the glory of our power, as well as giving them the estates that we possess and enriching them with various properties (*XCVI. dist., c. 14*).

7. *Jesus:* The foxes have holes and the birds of the sky have nests; but the Son of Man does not have where to lay his head (*Mat. viii, 20*).

8. When Jesus therefore perceived that they would come and take him, to make him a king, he fled to a mountain himself alone (*Joh. vi, 15*).

9. (*The Old Color.*) Man, who made me a judge or a divider over you? Take heed and beware of all covetousness (*Luk. xii, 14, 15*).

10. They clothe him in purple and weave a crown of thorns and put it on him (*Mar. xv, 17*).

11. (*The New Color.*) I, the Emperor Lewis, grant to you, Blessed Peter, and to your successors, the city of Rome with its duchy and suburbs and territories, in perpetuity, just as you have held them in your power and sway from our predecessors to the present, and have disposed over them (*LXIII. dist., c. 30*).

Z // 11 usque] *deest Z* // 12 et] *deest W* // 13 hiis] *deest Z* // 13 Constantino successisti] successisti Constantino *QW* // 14 Bernhardus] hec Bernhardus *QW* // 14 Bernhardus ad Eugenium Papam] *deest in loco RT* // 14 Papam] *deest Z; Post hoc in L habetur longus paragraphus de opere Bernardi, De consideracione, sumptus; Post hoc:* Sequitur *P* // 15 Scilicet . . . dicit] *sic Z; deest Ceteri* // 16 et verus homo] *deest Z* // 16 homo] homo. Hec est fides nostra *Q;* homo. Hec Bernhardus *RT* // 17 admirabilis] mirabilis *S* // 17 deus] deus est *BQRW;* deus es *TZ* // 20 Scilicet, Constantinus] *sic Z;* de novo colore *BKS;* Cesar Constantinus *RT; deest Ceteri* // 21 Silvestro] Petro *W* // 22 Decernimus] decrevimus *RST* // 22 ut] ut et *QW;* et *Z* // 22 mappulis] manipulis *T* // 23 id est] et *Z* // 24 equitent] equitaret *S;* equitant *Z;* equitent. Insuper coronam quam ex capite nostro illi con-

cessimus, ex auro purissimo et gemmis preciosis, uti debeant pro honore beati Petri. *Q* // 27 ditamus] ditavimus *BKTW* // 28 Ihesus] *sic T;* Johannes *R; deest Ceteri* // 30 ubi . . . reclinet] etc. *W* // 31 quod] quia *WO* // 32 caperent] raperent *BTO* // 33 in montem ipse solus] *deest W* // 34 de veteri colore] *sic B; deest Ceteri* // 37 Induunt] Induerunt *Y* // 38 imponunt] imposuerunt *Y* // 40 de novo colore] *sic BKS;* Ludwicus Imperator *Y; deest Ceteri* // 40 Imperator] *deest Q* // 41 tibi] *deest RT* // 41 beato Petro] *sic Ceteri et O;* Petro beato *P* // 41 successoribus] successoribus tuis *W* // 44 disposuistis] disposicionem tenuistis *B* // 44 civitatem romanam] Romam *Z* // 45 et suburbanis] eciam suburbanis *S* // 47–48 Scilicet . . . dicit] *sic BKLS,Z* (dicit *deest*); Petrus contradicit Ludwico pendens in cruce *Y; deest Ceteri* // 47–48

---

[4] *Non inventum.*

[5] Bernardus Clarevallensis, *De consideracione*, IV, iii (MPL, 182, col. 776).

[6] *Glosa in verbum "Papa", in Proemio Clementinarum (Friedberg, II, 1130):* "Admirabilis. Et dicitur a Papae [*sic*], quod est interiectio admirantis, et vere admirabilis: quia vices Dei in terris gerit. Inde dixit ille Anglicus in poëtria nova: *Papa stupor mundi,* et circa finem: *Qui maxima rerum. Nec Deus es,* nec homo, quasi neuter es inter utrunque . . ." (*Editio Lugdun., Clem., col. 4*).

[7] XCVI. dist., c. 14 (Friedberg, I, 342–345); *citacio e fragmentis confecta.*

[8] Mat. viii, 20.

[9] Joh. vi, 15.

[10] Luc. xii, 14, 15.

[11] *Recte* Mar. xv, 17.

45 et suburbanis et territoriis eius. *LXIII. di., Ego Lodovicus.*[12]
Duodecimus: *Scilicet, Petrus pendens in cruce dicit:* Scientes quod non corruptibilibus [Q 84'] auro et argento redempti estis de vana vestra
50 conversacione, sed precioso saguine quasi agni inmaculati Ihesu Cristi. *I. Pet. i.*[13] [B 296']
Tredecimus: *Scilicet, Cristus:* Quid ad te, tu me sequere. Extendes manus tuas et alius te cinget et ducet quo tu non vis. *Joh. ultimo.*[14]

1 Secunda Tabula [Y 181']
Primus: *Scilicet, papa dicit:* Decernimus ut sine titulo facta ordinacio irrita habeatur. *LXX. di., Sanctorum.*[1]
5 Secundus: Nolite possidere aurum nec argentum. *Mat. x.*[2] In quamcumque civitatem aut domum intraveritis, in ea manete edentes et bibentes que apud illos sunt [P 233] *Luc. x.*[3]
Tercius: *Scilicet, idem papa:* Non habens titulum
10 beneficii vel patrimonii unde possit congrue sustentari non debet ad ordines promoveri. *Extra de prebendis, Episcopus.*[4]
Quartus: *Scilicet Petrus:* Aurum et argentum non est michi. *Act. iii.*[5]
15 Quintus: *Scilicet, idem pre ore, papa:* Non licet ulli episcopo ordinare clericos et nullas eis prestare alimonias, sed vel non faciat clericos, vel si fecerit det [Y 182] illis unde vivere possint. *Extra de prebendis, Non liceat.*[6]
20 Sextus: *Idem Petrus:* Ecce nos reliquimus omnia et secuti sumus te; quid ergo erit nobis? *Mat. xix.*[7] [T 127']

12. *Peter hanging on the cross says:* Knowing that you were not redeemed with corruptible things, gold and silver, from your futile way of living, but with precious blood, like that of a spotless lamb, the blood of Jesus Christ (*I Pet. i, 18–19*).

13. *Christ:* As for you, follow me. You will stretch out your hands and another will gird you and lead you where you do not wish to go (*Cf. Joh. xxi, 22, 18*).

The Second Table

1. *The Pope says:* We decree that an ordination made without title of assignment to a church should be considered void (*LXX. dist., c. 2*).

2. Do not possess gold or silver (*Mat. x, 9*). Into whatsoever city or house you enter, in the same remain, eating and drinking such things as they have (*Luk. x, 5, 7*).

3. *The same Pope:* He who has no title to a church benefice, or a patrimony sufficient for his proper support, should not be promoted to holy orders (*Decretals, III, v, 4*).

4. *Peter:* Gold and silver I have none (*Act. iii, 6*).

5. *The same Pope (the words are in front of his mouth):* No bishop may ordain clerics without providing them with subsistence. Let him either not create clerics, or, if he does, let him provide them with enough to live on (*Decretals, III, v, 2*).

6. *The same Peter:* Behold we have forsaken all and followed you; what shall we have therefore? (*Mat. xix, 27*).

Duodecimus . . . Scientes] Duodecimus: Argentum et aurum non est michi. *Act. iii.* Scientes *RT* // 48 quod] quia *BW* // 48 non] non in *Y* // 50 conversacione] conversacione paterne tradicionis *WO* // 50–51 quasi . . . inmaculati] Cristi quasi agni incontaminati et inmaculati *W* // 52–54 Tredecimus . . . ultimo] *deest Q* // 52 Scilicet Cristus] *sic BKLSZ;* Cristus ad Petrum dicit *Y; deest Ceteri* // 52 tu] *deest Y* // 52–53 me sequere] sequere me *KY* // 53 Extendes] extendens *WZ* // 54 ducet] ducet te *BKRTYZ (Sed non O)* // 54 tu] *deest BW*

Secunda Tabula

1 Secunda Tabula] *deest BWYZ;* Hic obicit contra beneficia, dignitates. Beneficia denunciat et propria ecclesiasticorum *R;* Sequitur tabula secunda *S;* Materia secunda. Hic obicit contra beneficia et dignitates personarum ecclesie et contra divicias et propria ecclesiasticarum personarum *T* // 2 Primus] *deest RT;* Primus in secunda tabula *BSZ* // 2 Scilicet papa dicit] *sic BKZ; deest PQW;* Scilicet papa *S;* Papa. Primus *RT;* Papa *Y* // 2 Decernimus] Decrevimus *QR* // 3 ordinacio] ordine *R;* ordinacione *S* // 3 habeatur] habeatur ut patet *T* // 4 sanctorum] *deest RT* // 5 Secundus] Theologus contradicit pape dicens *Y* // 5 nec] neque *BQR;* et *WY* // 6 civitatem aut domum] domum aut civitatem *BR;* domum vel civitatem *QW* // 7 in ea] *deest Y;* in eadem *Ceteri* // 7–8 edentes . . . sunt] *deest W* // 8 illos] istos *Z* // 9 Scilicet idem papa] *sic BKS; deest Ceteri;* Papa *Y;* Idem primus papa *Z* // 10 possit] posset *BRZ* // 8 debet] non hoc debet *S* // 11 ad ordines promoveri] ordinari neque promoveri *Q* // 12 Episcopus] Episcopus et c. Tuis *WZ* // 13 Scilicet Petrus] *sic Ceteri; deest PQRTW;* Pater contra *Y* // 15 Quintus] *deest RT* // 15 Scilicet . . . papa] *sic Z;* scilicet idem papa *B;* scilicet papa *K;* idem papa *S;* contra papam *Y; deest Ceteri* // 18 illis] eis *BW* // 18 possint] possunt *R;* possent *S* // 20 Sextus] *deest S;* Quintus *R* // 20 Idem Petrus] *sic B;* Scilicet papa *K;* Scilicet Petrus *S;*

---

[12] LXIII. dist., c. 30 (Friedberg, I, 244 f.); *lacunose citatum.*
[13] I. Pet. i, 18–19.
[14] Cf. Joh. xxi, 22, 18.

Secunda Tabula
[1] LXX. dist., c. 2 (Friedberg, I, 257).
[2] Mat. x, 9.
[3] Luc. x, 5, 7.
[4] *Decretales,* III, v, 4 (Friedberg, II, 465); *summarium capituli.*
[5] Act. iii, 6.
[6] *Decretales,* III, v, 2 (Friedberg, II, 465).
[7] Mat. xix, 27.

Septimus: *Scilicet papa:* Episcopi non debent constitui ad modicam civitatem, ne vilescat nomen episcopi, sed ad honorabilem tytulum preficiendus est et honorandus. *LXXX. di., Episcopi.*[8]

Octavus: Pastores invenerunt Mariam et Yoseph et infantem positum in presepio. *Luc. ii.*[9] Non habemus hic manentem civitatem sed futuram inquiramus. *Heb. ultimo.*[10]

Nonus: *Scilicet, idem papa:* [Y 182'] Tamen qui altari servit et vivere debet de altari [K 112'] et qui ad onus eligitur repelli non debeat a mercede. *Extra de prebendis, Cum secundum.*[11]

Decimus: De altari et evangelio vivunt qui nichil habere proprium volunt, nec habent, nec habere concupiscunt. Quid est aliud de evangelio vivere, nisi laborantem ubi laborat necessaria vite percipere? *Prosper. I. q. ii, Sacerdos.*[12]

Undecimus: Nonne deus pauperes elegit in hoc mundo? *Jac. ii.*[13] Non multos sapientes secundum [S 31] carnem, non multos potentes, non multos nobiles, sed que stulta sunt mundi elegit deus ut confundat sapientes. *Prima Cor. i.*[14]

Duodecimus: *De novo colore:* [Y 183] [W 64'] Ymmo expedit ecclesie plures habere [B 297] divites clericos ut eam possint melius defensare. Et imperium et fiscus habundabit utens subiectis locupletibus. *In Autentica. Ut iudices sine quoquo suffragio. Par. I. Collatio II.*[15]

Tredecimus: *Idem doctor:* Circa sublimes personas et literatas [Q 85] cum maioribus beneficiis sunt honorande; cum sic racio postulaverit, per sedem apostolicam poterit dispensari circa plures dignitates aut personatus. *Extra de prebendis, De multa.*[16]

Decimus quartus: Ille cum quo fuerit dispensa-

7. *The Pope:* Bishops should not be established in small cities, in order that the name of bishop not be cheapened. A bishop should be set over a worthy benefice, and he should be honored (*LXXX. dist., c. 3*).

8. The shepherds found Mary and Joseph, and the infant lying in a manger (*Luk. ii, 15, 16*). Here have we no continuing city, but let us seek one to come (*Heb. xiii, 14*).

9. *The same Pope:* But he who serves the altar should live from the altar, and he who has been chosen for a burden should not be excluded from a reward (*Decretals, III, v, 16*).

10. They live from the altar and the gospel who wish to have nothing of their own, who neither possess nor desire to possess. What else is it to live from the gospel, but that the worker draws the necessities of life from the place where he works? *Prosper (I. q. ii, c. 9).*

11. Did not God choose the poor in this world? (*Jas. ii, 5*). Not the many who are wise according to the flesh, not the many mighty, not the many noble, but the foolish things of the world did God choose, that he might confound the wise (*I Cor. i, 26, 27*).

12. (*The new color.*) It is to the advantage of the church to have many rich clerics, who can defend her better. Both the empire and the treasury will flourish if they can employ wealthy subjects (*Authentica, II, ii, Pref., Par. i*).

13. *The same Doctor:* As for high-born and learned persons, they are to be honored with larger benefices. When reason may require it, the Apostolic See can grant dispensations in the matter of multiple dignities or offices (*Decretals, III, v, c. 28*).

14. He who has received a dispensation shall have the exemption as far as the Church Militant is con-

---

Theologus *Y; deest Ceteri //* 23 Septimus] sextus *R //* 23 Scilicet papa] *sic Z;* Unus de novo colore *B;* Papa *RST;* Episcopus *Y //* 25 preficiendus] *deest BKQW //* 26 est] *deest Z //* 27 Octavus] Septimus *R;* Contra episcopum *Y //* 27 Pastores] Tamen pastores *Y //* 28 et infantem] *et deest Z //* 28–29 non habemus] Octavus. Non habemus *R;* Eciam non habemus *Y //* 28–30 Non habemus . . . Heb. Ultimo] *deest W //* 29–30 sed futuram inquiramus] *deest BRSTY //* 31 Scilicet idem papa] *sic SZ;* Dicit papa *B;* Scilicet papa *K;* Episcopus respondet theologo *Y; deest Ceteri //* et] *deest QRSZ //* 38 debeat] debet *KRS //* 40 Decimus] Theologus contra episcopum dicit *Y //* 40 altari] *sic Ceteri;* altario *P //* 40 et evangelio] *sic Ceteri; deest P;* et de evangelio *W //* 40–41 nichil habere proprium] nichil proprii habere *B;* nichil proprium habere *W //* 41 volunt] *deest Z //* 43 nisi] nec *T;* non *Z //* 43 percipere] potest percipere *K //* 45 Undecimus] Theologus *Y* (*Nota: In RT materia paragraphi xi in xii datur et vice-versa*) // 45 Nonne] Nam *Z //* 45 deus pauperes elegit] pauperes deus elegit *BW //* 46 Non] Iam non *Y //* 46 Non multos] Non multa *S //* 47 potentes] nobiles *R //* 48 nobiles] potentes *R,* volentes *Z //* 48–49 que stulta sunt mundi elegit deus] que sunt stulta mundi deus elegit *QW //* 49 ut] non *Y //* 49 confundat] confundit *Z //* 49 Prima] *sic Ceteri; deest P //* 50 De novo colore] *sic BKSZ; deest Ceteri;* Iurista contradicit theologo *Y //* 52 divites] *deest W //* 52 possint melius] melius possint *QWZ //* 56 Idem doctor] *sic Z;* Ibidem iurista *Y; deest Ceteri //* 57 literatas] literatas personas *Q //* 58 sunt] sint *S //* 58 sic] *deest R //* 59 dispensari] defensari *Y //* 62 Decimus quartus] Theologus contradicit

---

[8] LXXX. dist., c. 3 (Friedberg, I, 280); *summarium capituli.*
[9] Luc. ii, 15, 16.
[10] Heb. xiii, 14.
[11] *Decretales,* III, v, 16 (Friedberg, II, 469).
[12] I. q. ii, c. 9 (Friedberg, I, 410).
[13] Jac. ii, 5.
[14] I Cor. i, 26, 27.
[15] *Authentica,* II, ii, Praefacio, Par. i (*Edicio Lipsiensis,* 509); *citacio tamen desumpta videtur e glosa ordinaria in verbum "necessitatem", Decretum, XXI, i, 1* (*Edit. Lugdun., col. 1231*).
[16] *Decretales,* III, v, 28 (Friedberg, II, 477–8).

tum habebit excepcionem quoad eclesiam militantem, sed quoad deum, ubi iudicabitur [Z 331]
65 eo teste quo iudice, hec allegacio non valebit.[17] Nec papa eius conscienciam potest immutare quia vis animo fieri non potest. *XXXII. q. v, Par. I. et c. I et II.*[18] [R 257]

1 Tercia Tabula [Y 183']
Primus: *Scilicet papa de novo colore:* Falsarius litterarum pape [P 233'] in perpetuum carcerem includi debet; pane doloris et aqua angustie sus-
5 tentandus est. *Extra de verborum significacione, Novimus.*[1] Qui in ecclesia vel ministris aliquid iniurie importaverit, capitali sentencia ferietur. *XVII. q. iiii, Si quis suadente, Qui Autem.*[2]
Secundus: *Scilicet, Cristus cum flagellatur:* Cor-
10 pus meum dedi percucientibus. Ego autem non contradico. *Isa. l.*[3] Nescitis cuius spiritus estis. Filius hominis non venit animas perdere, sed salvare. *Luc. ix.*[4] Orate pro persequentibus et calumpniantibus vos et benefacite hiis qui oderunt
15 vos. *Mat. v.*[5] *Augustinus:* (*Infra Cristum et papam. Sed nulla est imago.*) Religionem nostram quam dominus noster Ihesus Cristus in paucissimis sacramentorum celebracionibus voluit esse liberam, quidam servilibus premunt oneribus;

cerned, but this has no force with respect to God in Whose tribunal judge and witness are one. Nor can his conscience be changed by the Pope, since the mind is not subject to coercion (*Decretals, III, xxxiv, 5, gloss; XXXII. q. v, part 1, gloss*).

The Third Table

1. *The Pope (the new color):* A forger of papal letters is to be locked in prison for life, to live on the bread of pain and the water of sorrow (*Decretals, V, xl, 27*). Whoever does injury to the church or priesthood will be sentenced to death (*XVII. q. iv, c. 29*).

2. *Christ, as he is being whipped:* I gave my body to the smiters and have not been rebellious (*Isa. l, 5–6*). You know not what manner of spirit you are. The Son of Man has come not to destroy lives but to save them (*Luk. ix, 55–56*). Pray for those who persecute you and slander you, and bless those who hate you (*Mat. v. 44*). *Augustine* (*Below Christ and the Pope. But this is not a picture*): Our religion which our Lord Jesus Christ wished to be free, with only the fewest of sacramental rites, is so oppressed by some with servile burdens that more bearable is the condition of the Jews, who are subjected not to human presump-

---

iuriste Y // 62 quo] *sic Ceteri; deest PQ* // 64 sed quoad deum] sed non quoad deum *Q;* sed aput deum *W* // 64 iudicabitur] iudicabit *RT* // 65 eo] *deest RT* // 65 quo iudice] qui iudicat *Z* // 65–67 Hec allegacio . . . non potest] *deest Q* // 67 vis animo] ius a minimo *B* // 68 et II.] *Post hoc in R sequitur paragrafus iste, qui in T eciam habetur, sed in folio particulari:* Augustinus ad Jeronimum, de hoc quod scriptum est, "Si totam legem observaverit, offendat autem in uno, factus est omni reus," Epistola xviii, sic dicit: Si quid ergo in eis est quid erudicionem offendat tuam, queso ut rescribendo [*sic T; R:* ut refert Beda] ammoneas et me corrigere non graveris. Infelix est enim qui non tantos eciam sanctos tuorum studiorum labores, et digne honorat et de hiis domino nostro Ihesu Cristo, cuius munere talis es, gracias agit. Unde cum libencius debeam a quolibet discere quod utiliter [*sic!*] ignoro quam prompcius docere quod scio, quantocius hoc abs te caritatis debitum flagito, cuius doctrina es in nomine et adiutorio domini tantum in latina lingwa ecclesiastice littere adiute sunt, quantum numquam ante ea patuerunt; maxime tamen istam sentenciam, "quicumque totam legem servaverit" etc., si quo alio modo exponi posse novit dileccio

tua, per dominum obsecro ut id nobiscum communicare digneris. [*T:* Hec Augustinus ubi supra.]

Tercia Tabula

1 Tercia Tabula] *deest WYZ;* Tercia Tabula: Hic vult quod papa non debeat iudicare sed pocius iudicari *T, R* (*deest* Tercia Tabula); Sequitur Tabula Tercia *S* // 2 Primus] Primus in Tercia Tabula *B;* Primus: Dicit *K;* Papa Primus *R* // 2 Scilicet . . . colore] *sic Z;* Papa *Y; deest Ceteri* // 2 Falsarius] *Ante verbum "falsarius" habetur in RT paragraphus "Augustinus . . . de Religione cristiana", qui in ceteris codicibus habetur post secundum paragraphum.* // 5 est] *deest BQRSTWYZ* // 6 ministris] misteriis *K;* in ministris *Z* // 6 aliquid] *deest K* // 7 ferietur] punietur *Y* // 8 quis] quid *WK* // 9 Scilicet . . . flagellatur] *sic Z;* Scilicet Cristus *K;* Cristus flagellatus dicit *Y; deest Ceteri* // 10 dedi] dedit *B* // 10–11 Ego . . . contradico] *deest W* // 11 nescitis] nescitur *Z* // 14–15 oderunt vos] vos oderunt *QW* // 15–16 Augustinus . . . imago] *sic Z;* Infra ista duo Augustinus *BS;* Infra ista duo *K;* Augustinus *Ceteri; deest R* // 19 quidam] quam

---

[17] *Glosa in verbum "adimplere," Decretales, III, xxxiv, 5* (*Friedberg, II, 590*): "Si iusta causa subest . . . alias non est securus, quoad deum, cum quo papa dispensat, nisi subsit causa dispensandi . . . Habebit tamen exceptionem quoad ecclesiam ille, cum quo sine causa dispensatum est . . . Quoad deum sibi allegatio non valebit, ubi iudicabitur eo teste, quo iudice . . ." (*Edicio Lugdun., Decretales, col. 1280; cf. Innocencium III, MPL, 217, 988*C).

[18] *Glosa in verbum "vis," XXXII. q. v, 1 pars* (*Friedberg, I, 1132*): "non potest inferri animo vis." (*Edicio Lugdun., Decretum, col. 1621.*)

Tercia Tabula
[1] *Decretales,* V, xl, 27 (*Friedberg, II, 924*); *citacio composita.*
[2] XVII. q. iv, c. 29 (*Friedberg, I, 822*); *est compressum: cf.* "Qui autem de ecclesia vi aliquem exemerit vel in ipsa ecclesia vel loco vel cultui sacerdotibus et ministris aliquid iniuriae inportaverit ad instar publici criminis et laesae majestatis accusabitur, et convictus sive confessus capitali sententia a rectoribus provinciae ferietur."
[3] Isa. l, 5–6.
[4] Luc. ix, 55–56.
[5] Mat. v, 44.

20 adeo ut tollerabilior sit condicio iudeorum, qui non humanis presumpcionibus sed divinis subiciuntur institutis. *Hec ille, De religione cristiana. XII. di., Omnia.*[6] **[Y 184]**

Tercius: *Scilicet, doctor de novo colore:* Papa in
25 hiis que vult est ei pro racione voluntas. *Institutiones, de Iure Naturali, Sed quod principi.*[7] Nec est qui ei dicat, cur ita facis. *De penitencia, di. III, Ex persona.*[8] Secundum plenitudinem potestatis de iure possumus supra ius dispensare.
30 *Extra de concessione prebende, Proposuit.*[9]

Quartus: Alligant onera gravia et importabilia et imponunt **[B 297']** in humeros hominum: digito autem suo nolunt ea movere. *Mat. xxiii.*[10] **[K 113]**

35 Quintus: Non addetis ad verbum quod loquor vobis neque auferetis ex eo. Maledictus qui non permanet in sermonibus legis huius nec eos opere perficiunt. *Deut. iv et xxvii.*[11] **[Y 184']**

Sextus: Non veni solvere legem sed adimplere.
40 *Mat. v.*[12] A meipso facio nichil sed sicut docuit me pater, hoc loquor. *Joh. viii.*[13] **[hic incipit V 181]**

Septimus: Reges humiliabit et sermones contra excelsum loquetur et sanctos altissimi conteret et
45 putabit quod possit mutare tempora et leges. *Dan. vii.*[14]

Octavus: *Unus et est doctor de novo colore:* Sacro[**Q 85'**] sancta romana ecclesia ius et auctoritatem sacris canonibus impertitur sed non eis
50 alligatur. *XXV, q. i, § Hiis ita.*[15]

Nonus: Licet ille qui constituit legem non sit subditus legi adhoc quod puniatur ab homine si faciat contrarium, tamen obligatus est ad legem implendam, et gravius punietur a Deo si faciat

tions but to divine institutions. (*On the Christian Religion; cf. XII. dist., c. 12.*)

3. *A Doctor (the new color):* In those things which the Pope desires, his will is sufficient reason. (*Institutiones, Liber I, de Iure Naturali et Gentium et Civili, Par. 3*). Nor is there anyone who may say to him, why do you do thus? (*De penitencia, dist. III, c. 11*). According to our plenitude of power we are able to dispense, by law, from the requirements of the law (*Decretals, III, viii, 4*).

4. They bind heavy burdens and grievous to be borne, and lay them on men's shoulders; but they themselves will not move them with one of their fingers (*Mat. xxiii, 4*).

5. You shall not add to the word that I command you, nor shall you diminish from it. Cursed be he who does not persist in the words of this law and who does not work to carry them out (*Deut. iv, 2 and xxvii, 26*).

6. I have come not to destroy the law but to fulfill it (*Mat. v, 17*). I do nothing of myself, but, as my father has taught me, I speak this (*Joh. viii, 28*).

7. He shall subdue kings and he shall speak words against the exalted and shall wear out the saints of the most High, and he shall think that he is able to change times and laws (*Dan. vii, 24–25*).

8. *One man, a Doctor (the new color):* The holy Roman Church imparts justice and authority to the sacred canons, but it is not bound by them (*XXV. q. i, c. 16*).

9. Although he who has established the law is not subject to the law in such a way that he would be punished by men if he should act against it; nevertheless, he is obligated to carry out the law and he will be the more severely punished by God if he should act against it, because his transgression is more serious, on

---

quidam *S* // 20 condicio] *deest W* // 21 presumpcionibus] *deest P* // 22 ille] Augustinus *RY* // 22 Religione] vita *RT* // 23 XII. di., Omnia] *sic W*; *deest Ceteri* // 24 Scilicet . . . colore] *sic Z*; Scilicet *K*; Iurista *Y*; *deest Ceteri* // 26 quod] *deest RT* // 27–28 Nec est . . . Persona] *deest W* // 27–30 Nec . . . proposuit] *in Y ista particula sequitur quartum paragraphum et habet titulum: iurista ex parte Episcopi* // 27 qui] quis *BKQSTYZ* // 27 ei] *deest Z* // 27 penitencia] optime *Y* // 28 Secundum] Sed *KZ*; Nam secundum *Q* // 29 supra] super *BKSTY* // 30 proposuit] proposui *Q* // 31 Quartus] Theologus opponit *Y* // 31 Alligant] Alligant enim *O* // 32 imponunt] imponunt ea *Q* // 32 humeros] humeris *QZ*

// 33 ea movere] *deest W* // 35 Quintus] Theologus *Y* // 35 quod] quid *R* // 36 ex] ab *R* // 36 qui] homo qui *Z* // 37 in] *deest Y* // 37 huius nec] ut *B*; huius ut *R* // 37 eos] vos *Y* // 38 perficiunt] perficiat *B*; perficit *YZO* // 39 Sextus] Theologus *Y* // 40 A meipso . . . sicut] *sic Ceteri*; A meipso sed nichil sicut *P* // 41 pater] pater meus *R* // 41 hoc] *sic RT* // 41 loquor] loquitur *Z* // 43–61 Septimus . . . Presule] *deest W* // 43 Septimus] Unde Daniel dixit *Y*; *hic incipit V* // 43 sermones] *sic Ceteri*; sermonem *P* // 47 unus . . . colore] *sic Z*; Iurista *Y*; *deest Ceteri* // 49 canonibus] *deest RT* // 51 Nonus] Theologus *Y* // 51–61 Nonus . . . Presule] *deest*

---

[6] Augustinus, *de Religione Cristiana. Recte:* Epistola quam Augustinus scripsit ad Inquisitiones Ianuarii (MPL, 33, col. 221). *Cf. XII. dist., c. 12 (Friedberg, I, 30); citacio composita. Et cf. Lyra, super Mat. xxiii, ubi est verbatim.*

[7] *Institutiones*, I, ii, 6 (*Editio Lips.*, 3); *Hec citacio, que in Institutionibus refert ad Imperatorem, sumpta est forsan de Glosa ordinaria in Decretales, I, vii, 3, in verbum, "Veri Dei vicem," ubi refert ad papam.*

[8] XXXIII. q. iii (de Penitencia) III. dist., c. 21 (Friedberg, I, 1215); *non recte laudatum. Cf. Job ix, 12: "Cur ita facis . . ."*

[9] *Decretales*, III, viii, 4 (Friedberg, II, 489).

[10] Mat. xxiii, 4.

[11] Deut. iv, 2, et xxvii, 26.

[12] Mat. v, 17.

[13] Joh. viii, 28.

[14] Dan. vii, 24–25.

[15] XXV. q. i, c. 16, §1 (Gracianus) (Friedberg, I, 1011).

55 contrarium, quia transgressio eius gravior est propter scandalum. **[Y 185]** Hec Lira, Mat. xxiii.[16] Et Bartholomeus Brixiensis loquens de presule romane sedis dicit: Imo sine venia puniri **[T 128]** debet sicut dyabolus; et sine spe venie condemp-
60 nandus est ut dyabolus. *IX. q. iii, Aliorum; II. q. iiii, Presule.*[17]

account of scandal (*Lyra, on Mat. xxiii, 4*). And Bartholomew of Brescia speaking about the ruler of the Roman See says: Nay, he should be punished as a devil without indulgence and he should be condemned as a devil without the hope of forgiveness (*Glosses on IX. q. iii, c. 14, and II. q. iv, c. 2*).

1 Quarta Tabula
Primus: *Episcopus dicit:* Non est a plebe arguendus **[P 234]** vel accusandus episcopus, licet sit inordinatus. *II. q. vii, Non est.*[1] Nullus laicus
5 crimen audeat clerico inferre. *Ibidem, Nullus.*[2] Romana ecclesia phas habet de omnibus iudicare, nec cuiquam de eius liceat iudicare iudicio. *IX. q. iii, Cuncta, i.*[3]
Secundus: *Scilicet Cristus, de antiquo:* **[Z 331′]**
10 Quis ex vobis arguet me de peccato? *Ioh. viii.*[4] **[S 31′]** Sic si peccaverit in te frater tuus, corripe eum. *Mat. xviii.*[5] Vos estis sal terre. Quod si sal evanuerit? Ad nichilum valet ultra, nisi ut mittatur foras, et conculcetur **[R 257′]** ab homini-
15 bus. *Mat. v.*[6] **[Y 185′]**
Tercius: *De veteri colore:* Vos, qui reliquistis omnia et secuti estis me, sedebitis et vos iudicantes xii tribus Israhel. *Mat. xix.*[7]
Quartus: *Andree Johannes, de novo colore:* Epis-
20 copi et magni clerici non debent cogi in obprobrium proprium coram iudicibus pannosis litigare, et eciam in favorem apostolice sedis, ne vilipenda-

The Fourth Table

1. *A Bishop says:* A bishop is not to be accused or charged by a layman even if his conduct is irregular (*II. q. vii, c. 1*). Let no layman dare to bring a charge against a cleric (*II. q. vii, c. 2*). The Roman Church has the right to judge concerning all things, nor may it be permitted to anyone to pass judgment on its decision (*IX. q. iii, c. 17*).

2. *Christ (the old color):* Which one of you accuses me of sin? (*Joh. viii, 46*). If your brother has sinned against you, tell him his fault (*Mat. xviii, 15*). You are the salt of the earth, but if the salt has lost its savor, it is thenceforth good for nothing but to be cast out and to be trampled under foot by men (*Mat. v, 13*).

3. (*The old color:*) You, who have abandoned all and followed me, you will sit judging the twelve tribes of Israel (*Mat. xix, 28*).

4. *John Andree (the new color):* Bishops and high-ranking clerics should not be forced, to their own ignominy, to litigate before mean judges; and this provision is also in favor of the Apostolic See, lest it be

---

V // 52 quod] ut *BQRSZ //* 52 si] *deest B //* 53–55 tamen . . . contrarium] *deest Z //* 54 gravius] magis *R //* 56 Hec Lira] *deest P //* 58 dicit] *deest RTZ //* 60 ut] sicut *R*

Quarta Tabula

Quarta Tabula incipit: Hic vult quod persone ecclesiastice debent iudicari seculariter et conculcari ut sal infatuatum. *R;* Hic dicit quod episcopi et persone ecclesie debent accusari, iudicari seculariter et conculcari ut sal infatuatum. *T //* 1 Quarta Tabula] *deest BWYZ;* Sequitur Tabula Quarta *S //* 2 Primus] Primus in Quarta Tabula est *Z,B* (est *deest*); Primus: De novo colore *V //* 2 Episcopus dicit] sic *Z;* Episcopus (*ante inicium tabule*) *T;* Iurista *Y; deest Ceteri //* 2 Non est a plebe . . . episcopus] Episcopus a plebe non est . . . *R //* 3 vel accusandus] *deest WO //* 4 Non est] Non est et cetera *Y //* 5 crimen audeat clerico] audeat clerico crimen *KVO;* audeat crimen clerico *RW //* 5 audeat] debeat *Y //* 5 clerico] *deest B //* 6 Romana] Nam Romana *Q //* 7 eius] eis *B //* 9 Scilicet Cristus] sic *Z;* Theologus *Y; deest Ceteri //* 9 de antiquo] sic *Z;* de veteri *V; deest Ceteri //* 10 ex vobis] *deest Q //* 11 Sic] *deest BRSTVWYZ;* Sic quod *K;* et *Q //* 11 in te] *deest R //* 11–12 corripe eum] corripe eum inter te et ipsum *WO //* 13 evanuerit] evanuerit in quo salietur *BO //* 13 ad nichilum] nichil *RS //* 16–24 *Paragraphus tercius est paragraphus quartus et vice versa in T //* 16 Tercius] *deest Z //* 16 de veteri colore] sic *V;* Theologus *Y; deest Ceteri //* 16 qui] *deest BZ //* 17 et vos] *deest W //* 18 Israhel] *deest W //* 19 Quartus] *deest B //* 19 Andree Johannes] sic *Z;* Iurista *Y; deest Ceteri //* 19 de novo colore] sic *VZ; deest Ceteri //* 19 Episcopi] Episcopus *R //* 20 et] *deest QS //* 20 cogi] *deest S //* 20 in] ad *S //* 21 proprium] *deest BV //* 21 iudicibus pannosis] pannosis iudicibus *RZ //* 22 sedis] *deest Z //* 23

---

[16] Lyra, super Mat. xxiii, 4.
[17] *Glosa ordinaria in verbum "aliorum," IX. q. iii, c. 14 (Friedberg, I, 610); et Glosa in verbum "Presule," II, q. iiii, c. 2 (Friedberg, I, 466). Cf. De pen., dist. II, §"Quia ergo" (in principio); hoc citatum in codice H.*

Quarta Tabula
[1] II. q. vii, c. 1 (Friedberg, I, 483).
[2] II. q. vii, c. 2 (Friedberg, I, 483).
[3] IX. q. iii, c. 17 (Friedberg, I, 611).
[4] Joh. viii, 46.
[5] Mat. xviii, 15.
[6] Mat. v, 13.
[7] Mat. xix, 28; *citacio composita.*

tur in tali ministerio. *Johannes Andree super capitulo Statutum de rescriptis, libro sexto.*[8]

25 Quintus: *Doctor, de novo colore:* Executor **[B 298]** si sciat sentenciam iniustam esse nichilominus exequi tenetur eandem. *Extra, de officio delegati, Pastoralis.*[9] Iudex pronuncciet in nomine domini, secundum allegata et deponat con-
30 scienciam. *Huguccio.*[10]

Sextus: *De antiquo colore:* Ex verbis tuis iustificaberis et condempnaberis. *Mat. xii.*[11] Omne quod contra conscienciam sit edificat in iehennam. *Augustinus.*[12] Qualis hinc quisque egreditur talis
35 **[Y 186]** in iudicio apparebit vel presentabitur. *Gregorius.*[13]

Septimus: *Magnus Monachus elevans manus, de novo colore:* Conditor canonis vel legis **[Q 86]** potest michi dare rem alienam et tutus ero.
40 *Digestum, de eviccionibus, lege Lucius.*[14] **[W 65]** Qui iuravit cum aliqua contrahere, et vult religionem ingredi, contrahere debet, **[K 113']** et demum ante carnalem copulam religionem ingredi. *Extra de sponsalibus, Commisum.*[15]

45 Octavus: *De antiquo colore:* Non exies inde, donec reddes novissimum quadrantem. *Mat. v.*[16] Non concupiscas domum proximi tui. *Exo. xx.*[17] Quod deus coniunxit, homo non separet. Non licet viro uxorem suam dimittere, excepta forni-
50 cacionis causa. *Mat. v et xix.*[18]

Nonus: *De colore antiquo:* Si religionis causa coniugia de se dissolvi dicantur, sciendum est, quia etsi lex humana hoc concessit, lex divina tamen prohibuit. Ecce qualiter, quod lex humana
55 concessit, lex divina prohibuit. *Gregorius, X. di.*

held in low esteem on account of such an official (*John Andree, Gloss on Liber Sextus, I, iii, c. 11*).

5. *A Doctor (the new color):* Even if the executor knows the sentence to be unjust, he is bound, nevertheless, to execute it (*Decretals, I, xxix, 28*). Let the judge pronounce sentence in the name of the Lord, according to the facts of the case, and let him put aside his conscience (*Huguccio*).

6. (*The old color:*) By your words you will be justified, and by your words condemned (*Mat. xii, 37*). Whatever is against conscience builds for Gehenna (*Augustine*). Such as he is when he leaves this world, so will each appear, or be brought to appear, on Judgment Day (*Gregory*).

7. *A big monk, his arms raised (the new color):* The author of canons and law can give me another's property, and I will be safe (*Digest, de eviccione, lex Lucius*). He who has sworn to contract marriage with another and wishes to enter a religious life should contract the marriage, and then, before the carnal union, enter the monastery (*Decretals, IV, i, 16*).

8. (*The old color:*) You shall not come out thence till you have paid the last farthing (*Mat. 5: 26*). Covet not the house of your neighbor (*Exo. 20: 17*). What God has joined together let no man separate (*Mat. xix, 6*). A man may not put his wife aside except for adultery (*Mat. v, 36*).

9. (*The old color:*) If marriages may be said to be dissolved for the sake of the religious life, let it be known that even if human law has granted this, divine law, nevertheless, has prohibited it. Behold how what human law has granted, divine law has prohibited (*Gregory: XXVII. q. ii, c. 19; X. dist., c. 4*).

---

tali ministerio] tali officio ministro (*sic*) *S* // 23 super] in *Z* // 25 Doctor] *sic Z*; Iurista *Y*; *deest Ceteri* // 25 de novo colore] *sic VZ*; *deest Ceteri* // 26 sciat] scit *RV* // 26 nichilominus] *deest R*; non *TZ* // 27 eandem] *deest B* // 29 allegata et deponat] allegata et probata et deponat *QR* // 30 Huguccio] Huguccio in glosa *W* // 31 de antiquo colore] *sic Z*; de veteri *V*; Theologus *Y*; *deest Ceteri* // 33 in] ad *BKQRSTVYZ* // 35 in iudicio] ante iudicem *S* // 35 vel] et *R* // 35 presentabitur] presentatur *BSYZ* // 36 Gregorius] *sic Ceteri*; *deest P* // 37 *Paragraphus septimus octavum sequitur Y; eadem transposicio incepta sed tunc correcta T* // 37–38 Magnus . . . colore] *sic Z*; de novo *V*; Iurista *Y*; *deest Ceteri* // 39 michi dare] iudicare *B* // 40 Digestum] super Digestum *Q* // 40 Lucius] bullas *S* // 41 iuravit] iuraverit *VTQ* // 41 religionem] postea religionem *Q* // 42 ingredi] ingredi potest *Q* // 45 de antiquo colore] *sic Z*; de veteri colore *V*; Theologus *Y*; *deest Ceteri* // 47 concupiscas] concupisces *BRTVWO* // 48 Quod] Quos *BKRTVWYZ* // 48–50 "Quod . . . separat" *sequitur* "Non . . . causa" *QW* // 50 causa] *deest V* // 51 de colore antiquo] *sic Z*; de veteri *V*; Theologus *Y*; *deest Ceteri* // 52 de se dissolvi] de lege dissolvi *B*; debere dicantur dissolvi *WO* // 52 sciendum] tamen sciendum *Q* // 53 quia] *sic BKSTVWYZO*; quod *PR*; *deest Q* // 53 etsi] *sic BKQRSTVYZO*; si *PW* // 53 lex divina] lex *deest R* // 53 etsi lex humana hoc concessit] si licet humana lex est concessit *W* // 54 tamen] *deest B* // 55 lex divina] lex *deest R* // 54–55 Ecce . . . prohibuit] *deest QWZ* // 55–56 Gregorius . . . dicunt] Hec Gregorius, *X. di., Lege*. Ecce, quomodo lex Cristi et lex pape sibi inficem (*sic pro* invicem) repugnant in isto et in multis aliis ut patet in precedentibus

---

[8] *Glosa ordinaria in verbum "committantur," Liber Sextus, I, iii, 11 (Friedberg, II, 941–942):* "Dicebat Bernardus et omnes post eum . . . poterat pars huic iuri renunciare. Introductum est enim in ipsorum favorem, ne scilicet in opprobrium proprium cogantur episcopi et magni clerici coram rudibus et pannosis clericis litigare . . . Sed hodie per finem istius decretalis, credo contrarium . . . quia hoc videbitur non solum in favorem partium inductum, sed eciam in favorem ipsius Apostolicae sedis, ne vilipendatur in tali ministro." (*Edit. Lugdun., III, col. 38.*)

[9] *Decretales, I, xxix, 28 (Friedberg, II, 172–173).*

[10] *Glosa ordinaria in verba "tenetur ea[n]dem," Decretales, I, xxix, 28 (Friedberg, II, 173–175; Edicio Lugdun., Decretales, col. 365). Huguccio nominatur in glosa.*

[11] Mat. xii, 37.

[12] *Cf. XXVIII. q. i, §"Ex his," post c. 14, ubi dictum reperitur, sed non Augustino adscriptum.*

[13] *Non inventum.*

[14] *Non inventum; citacio non recte laudata est.*

[15] *Decretales, IV, i, 16 (Friedberg, II, 667.)*

[16] Mat. v, 26.

[17] Exo. xx, 17.

[18] Mat. v, 32; xix, 6.

*Lege; et XXVII. q. ii, Sunt qui dicunt.*¹⁹ **[Y 186']**
Decimus: *Idem monachus magnus previus nominatus:* Propter religionem multa contra racionem sunt statuta. *Digestum de religiosis, Sunt per-*
60 *sone.*²⁰ **[T 128']**
Undecimus: *Papa, de novo colore:* Non sufficit cuiquam nude asserere, quod ipse sit missus a Deo, cum hoc quilibet hereticus assereret: sed opportet, **[P 234']** quod astruat illam invisibilem
65 missionem per operacionem miraculi, vel scripture testimonium speciale. *Extra de hereticis, Cum ex iniuncto.*²¹

Duodecimus: *De antiquo colore:* Adventus filii perdicionis, id est anticristi, est secundum opera-
70 cionem sathane in omni virtute, signis, et prodigiis mendacibus, et in omni seduccione **[V 181']** iniquitatis. *II. Thes. ii.*²²

Tredecimus: *De veteri:* Generacio mala et adultera signum querit. *Mat. xvi.*²³ A fructibus
75 eorum cognoscetis eos. *Mat. vii.*²⁴ Nolite prohibere: qui enim non est adversum nos, pro nobis est. *Mat. ix.*²⁵ Quis tribuat, ut omnis populus prophetet. *Num. xi.*²⁶

Decimus Quartus: *De antiquo colore:* **[Y 187]**
80 Ve vobis, legisperitis, qui tulistis clavem sapiencie, ipsi non introistis, et eos qui introibant, prohibuistis. *Luc. xi.*²⁷

Decimus Quintus: *Et sunt tres Iudei, unus in iacca, secundus in toga, tercius in pileo accuto:*
85 Hec dicens nobis, contumeliam facis, **[B 298']** et ceperunt legisperiti et pharisei graviter insistere,

10. *The same big monk:* Because of religion many things contrary to reason have been decreed (*Digest, de religione, Sunt personae*).

11. *The Pope (the new color):* It is not enough for someone to assert simply that he is sent by God, since any heretic might assert this, but it is necessary that he demonstrate that invisible mission by the working of a miracle or by some special testimony of scripture (*Decretals, V, vii, 12*).

12. (*The old color:*) The coming of the son of perdition, that is, Antichrist, is according to the working of Satan with all power and signs and lying wonders and with all the seduction of unrighteousness (*II Thes. ii, 9–10*).

13. (*The old color:*) A wicked and adulterous generation seeks a sign (*Mat. xvi, 4*). You shall know them by their fruits (*Mat. vii, 16*). Do not forbid him, for he who is not against you is for you (*Mar. ix, 39*). Would that he would grant that every people were prophets (*Num. xi, 29*).

14. (*The old color:*) Woe unto you, lawyers, who have taken away the key of knowledge: Yourselves, you have not entered, and you have forbidden those who were entering (*Luk. xi, 52*).

15. *Here there are three Jews, one in a jacket, the second in a toga, the third in a pointed skull-cap:* Saying these things, you reproach us. And the scribes and Pharisees began to urge him vehemently and to provoke him to speak of many things, trapping him (*Luk. xi, 45, 53–54*).

---

et sequentibus Q // 57 Idem . . . Nominatus] *sic* Z; de novo V; Iurista Y; *deest Ceteri* // 58 Propter] Per Z // 59 religiosis] religiosis et super ipsum Z // 60 *Post decimum paragraphum:* Hic dicit quod predicare debent non missi nec prohiberi, licet non faciant miracula aut signa T; Predicare debent non missi licet non faciant miracula aut signa R // 61 Undecimus] *deest* BR // 61 Papa, de novo colore] *sic* Z; de novo V; *deest Ceteri* // 62 nude] *deest* R; nude tamen V // 63 assereret] asseverit K; asservat R; asseveret QWYO; asserveret T // 63 sed] et B // 64 quod] ut W; nec Z // 64 astruat] construat B // 65 per] et B // 66 speciale] *deest* RT // 68 Duodecimus] Secundus R; Paulus, Duodecimus T // 68 De antiquo colore] *sic* Z; de veteri V; Theologus propheta Y; *deest Ceteri* // 70 virtute] virtute et B // 71 in] *deest* B // 73 Tredecimus] *deest* Q; Tercius R // 73 de veteri] *sic* V; Theologus Y; *deest Ceteri* // 73 mala] prava QVW // 75 Nolite] Noli Z // 75 prohibere] eum prohibere BT; prohibere eum RV // 76 enim] *deest* W // 76 adversum] *deest* V // 76–77 nobis est] est *deest* W // 77 tribuat] tribuerit V // 77 omnis] *deest* RT // 78 prophetet] prophetiset et deus det ei spiritum R; prophetet et deus det eis spiritum suum TZ // 79–82 Decimus Quartus . . . Luc. xi] *deest* R // 79 Decimus Quartus] Tredecimus Q // 79 De antiquo colore] *sic* Z; de veteri V; Theologus Y; *deest Ceteri* // 80 sapiencie] sciencie WO // 81 ipsi] et ipsi BKTVYZ // 81 introibant] intrabant KQ // 83 Decimus Quintus] Quintusdecimus BKST; Quartusdecimus Q; Quintus R // 83–84 Et . . . accuto] *sic* Z; De veteri V; Advocati Y (Iurista *et* Legati et cardinales pape *deleta sunt in loco*);*deest Ceteri* // 85 Hec dicens] *deest* RT // 86 et pharisei] *deest* QW // 86 insistere] resistere K //

---

¹⁹ XXVII. q. ii, c. 19 (Friedberg, I, 1067); X. dist., c. 4 (Friedberg, I, 19).

²⁰ *Cf. Digestum*, XI, vii, 43 (Edicio Lipsiensis, 273), *citacio tamen prevaricata:* "Sunt personae, quae quanquam religiosum locum facere non possunt, interdicto tamen *de mortuo inferendo* utiliter agunt: ut puta dominus proprietatis, si in fundum, cujus fructus alienus est, mortuum inferat, aut inferre velit: nam, si intulerit, non faciet justum sepulchrum: sed, si prohibeatur, utiliter interdicto, qui de jure dominii queritur, aget. Eademque sunt in Socio, qui in fundum communem invito socio mortuum inferre vult: nam *propter publicam utilitatem, ne insepulta cadavera jacerent, strictam rationem insuper habemus: quae non nunquam in ambiguis religionum quaestionibus omitti solet: nam summam esse rationem, quae pro religione facit.*"

²¹ *Decretales,* V, vii, 12 (Friedberg, II, 784).
²² II Thes. ii, 9–10.
²³ Mat. xvi, 4.
²⁴ Mat. vii, 16.
²⁵ Mar. ix, 39–40 (*q.v.*).
²⁶ Num. xi, 29; "Ac ille (*Moyses*): Quid, inquit, aemularis pro me? Quis tribuat ut omnis populus prophetet, et det eis Dominus spiritum suum?"
²⁷ Luc. xi, 52.

et os eius opprimere de multis, insidiantes ei. Luc. xi.[28]

Sedecimus: [Z 332] *De antiquo colore:* Dura cervice, et incircumcisis cordibus, vos semper spiritui sancto restitistis; sicut patres vestri: qui occidebant eos qui annunciabant de adventu Cristi, cuius vos nunc proditores et homicide fuistis. Act. vii.[29]

95 Decimus Septimus: *De antiquo colore:* Audientes [Q 86'] hec dissecabantur cordibus suis, et stridebant dentibus in eum. Act. vii.[30]

1 Quinta Tabula

In medio ponitur equus niger et unus habens stateram in manu et ibi ponitur ista scriptura. [Y 187'] Ecce equus niger et qui sedebat super eum habebat stateram in manu sua. Apok. vi.[1] *Glosa:* Statera est scriptura quia sicut per stateram cognoscitur quanti ponderis sit corpus, sic per sacram scripturam cognoscitur quanti ponderis sit spiritus. Sancti enim doctores habent scienciam a scriptura, quia humiliter se subiciunt scripture, sensum suum illi coaptantes. Sed heretici habent scienciam in manu sua, quia quasi doctores illam suo sensui coaptant. Quicumque igitur aliter scripturam [R 258] intelligit quam sensus spiritus sancti flagitat, a quo scripta est, hereticus appellari potest. Et in hanc insipienciam cadunt qui cum ad cognoscendum veritatem [S 32] aliquo impediuntur obscuro, non ad propheticas voces, non ad apostolicas litteras, nec ad evangelicas auctoritates, sed ad semetipsos recurrunt, et ideo magistri erroris existunt, quia veritatis discipuli non fuerunt.[1a] *Jeronimus:* Veteres scrutans hystorias [P 235] invenire non possum [K 114] scidisse ecclesiam,

16. (*The old color:*) You stiffnecked and uncircumcised in heart, you have always resisted the Holy Spirit, just as your fathers, who slew those who told of the coming of Christ, of whom you have been now the betrayers and the murderers (*Act. vii, 51*).

17. (*The old color:*) When they heard these things they were cut to the heart and they gnashed their teeth at him (*Act. vii, 54*).

The Fifth Table

In the middle there is a picture of a black horse and a man with a balance in his hand, and this text is written there: Lo a black horse, and he that sat on him had a balance in his hand (*Apok. vi, 5*). *Gloss:* The balance is the scripture, because just as the weight of a body is known by a balance so by the holy scripture is known the weight of a spirit. For the holy doctors have their knowledge from the scriptures because they humbly subject themselves to scripture, adapting their understanding to it. But heretics have knowledge from their own hands, for, pretending to be doctors, they adapt it to their understanding. Whoever, then, interprets the scripture other than as the sense of the Holy Spirit, by whom it is written, demands, can be called a heretic. And they fall into this folly who, when hindered by some difficulty in learning the truth, turn not to the words of the prophets, not to the letters of the apostles, not to the authority of the gospels, but to themselves. Therefore they are masters of error, because they have not been disciples of truth. *Jerome:* Scrutinizing ancient histories, I cannot find anyone to have divided the church and to have seduced the people

---

87 eius] *deest SY //* 87 ei] *deest S //* 89 Sedecimus] Decimus quintus *Q;* Sextus *R //* 89 De antiquo colore] *sic Z;* de veteri *V;* Theologus *Y; deest Ceteri //* 90 incircumcisis] incircumcisi *BRT //* 90 cordibus] corde *B //* 90 semper] *deest R //* 91 restitistis] resistitis *QRS //* 91 qui] ita et eos qui *Q //* 91–92 qui occidebant ... Cristi] ita et vos etc. *W //* 92 occidebant] occiderunt *Q //* 92 eos] vos *Q //* 92 annunciabant] pronunciabant *Q //* 92 de] *deest Q //* 92 Cristi] Anticristi *B //* 93 proditores] proditores estis *V //* 95 Decimus Septimus] Decimus Sextus *Q;* Septimus *R //* 95 de antiquo colore] *sic Z;* de veteri *V;* Advocati curie pape *Y; deest Ceteri //* 96 cordibus] incordibus *BVW;* dentibus *T*

Quinta Tabula

Tabula Quinta deest in W, uno paragrapho dempto, qui in fine tractatus invenitur; cf. infra // Ante inicium Tabule Quinte: Hic confundit doctores et sacerdotes ecclesie. Lex divina antiquus color, lex humana novus color. *RT; figura equi et equitantis stateram tenentis delineatur in superiori margine Y, sed caput equitantis detonsum est. In statera duo libri, lex divina et lex humana, ponderantur, ille gravior hoc. //* 1 Quinta Tabula] *deest BRY;* Sequitur Quinta Tabula *S;* Tabula quinta alteram partem continens libri precedentis *V //* 2–3 In medio ... scriptura] *sic Z; deest Ceteri //* 4 Ecce] Primus in Quinta Tabula: Ecce *B;* Primus: Ecce *Q //* 6 scriptura] scriptura sacra *QY //* 6 quia sicut] *deest Y //* 6 stateram] scripturam *B //* 7 sit] est *B //* 9 scienciam a scriptura] sacram scripturam *B //* 9 scriptura] scriptura sacra *Q //* 10 suum] *deest R //* 11 coaptantes] coaptant *Q //* 14 sensus] *deest RST //* 14 sancti] sanctus *RST //* 15 scripta] scriptura *BSVZ //* 15 est] *deest R //* 15 potest] non potest *Q //* 16 insipienciam] scienciam *Q //* 16 cadunt] cadunt illi *S //* 18 non] nec *S //* 19 sed] et *Z //* 22 scrutans] scrutantes *K //* 23 possum] possunt *K;* possumus *S //* 23 scidisse] cecidisse

---

[28] Luc. xi, 45: "hec dicens nobis, contumeliam facis"; Luc. xi, 53–54: "et ... ei."
[29] Act. vii, 51.
[30] Act. vii, 54.

Quinta Tabula
[1] Apok. vi, 5.
[1a] *Non inventum.*

et de domo domini populos seduxisse, preter eos, qui sacerdotes a deo **[Y 188]** positi fuerant et prophete. Isti ergo vertuntur in laqueum tortuosum, in omnibus locis ponentes scandalum. *Idem:* Transferunt principes Iude terminos, quos posuerunt patres eorum, quando inmutant mendacio veritatem, et aliud predicant quam ab apostolicis acceperunt. *Hec XXIIII. q. iii, Transferunt; et c. Quid autem; et c. Heresis.*[2] *Gregorius VII:* Pervenit ad nos fama sinistra, **[T 129]** quod quidam episcoporum non sacerdotibus proprie dyocesis cristianorum oblaciones conferrant, **[B 299]** sed pocius laicalibus, personis militum sive servitorum, vel, quod gravius est, consaguineis. Unde si quis amodo episcopus inventus fuerit huius divini precepti transgressor, inter maximos hereticos et anticristos non minimus habeatur, et qui dat episcopus, et qui recipiunt ad eo laici, sive precio, sive beneficio, eterni incendii ignibus deputentur. *I. q. iii, Pervenit.*[3] Sed quis aliquando vidit clericum cito penitenciam agentem; etsi deprehensus humiliaverit se, non ideo dolet quia peccavit, sed confunditur quia perdidit gloriam **[Q 87]** suam. *Hec Crisostomus, de penitencia, I. di., Quis aliquando.*[4] Sed symoniacos, velut primos et precipuos hereticos, patet ab omnibus fidelibus respuendos esse, omnia **[V 182]** enim crimina ad comparacionem symoniace heresis quasi pro nichilo computantur. *I. q. ultima, Patet.*[5] Tolerabilior est enim Macedonii et eorum, qui circa ipsum sunt, sancti spiritus impugnatorum, impia heresis. Illi enim creaturam et servum dei patris et filii sanctum spiritum delirando fatentur, isti vero eundem spiritum sanctum **[Z 332']** efficiunt suum servum. *I. q. i, Eos.*[6] Et cum primo contra sanctam ecclesiam symoniaca heresis sit exorta, cur non perpenditur, cur non cavetur. *I. q. i, Quibusdam.*[7] Ideo non est aliquid requirendum sive exigendum pro sepulturis et exequiis mortuorum, et benediccionibus nubencium, seu aliis sacramentis conferendis sive

from the house of the Lord except those who had been instituted as priests or prophets by God. They are thus turned into tortuous snares and everywhere give scandal. *The same:* The princes of Juda move the boundaries that their fathers established, when they change truth to falsehood and preach other than they have received from the apostles (*XXIV. q. iii, c. 33, 30, 27*). *Gregory VII:* A nasty rumor has reached us, that certain bishops are conferring the gifts of the Christian people not on priests of their own diocese, but rather upon laymen—knights, servitors, or, what is worse, relatives. Because of this, if any bishop, henceforth, shall be found a transgressor of this divine precept, let him be held not least among the greatest heretics and antichrists, and the bishop who gives, and laymen who receive from him, either as a payment or as a benefice, are to be consigned to the flames of eternal fire (*I. q. iii, c. 13*). But who ever sees a cleric readily performing penance? Even if when caught he humbles himself, he does not grieve because he has sinned, but he is confounded because he has lost his reputation (*XXXIII. q. iii (de Penitencia) I. dist., c. 87*). But it is clear that symoniacs, as the first and foremost heretics, are to be rejected by all the faithful. For all crimes are reckoned as nought in comparison with the symoniac heresy (*I. q. vii, c. 27*). More tolerable indeed is the impious heresy of Macedonius and those who follow him, assailants of the Holy Spirit. These profess, in their madness that the Holy Spirit is the creature and slave of God the Father and of the Son; the symoniacs, however, enslave the Holy Spirit to themselves (*I. q. i, c. 21, par. 1*). And why was the symoniac heresy not studied and avoided when it first appeared (*I. q.i., c. 117, par. 1*)? Therefore, nothing is to be required or exacted for burials and rites for the dead, blessings for those being married, or other sacraments conferred or to be conferred, nor for ordinations of clerics, for investiture, or for reception into a monastery. And likewise with other cases: *Decretals, V, iii, 9; V, iii, 39, and others, like V, iii, 7,* where it is said that neither minister nor notary, in his ordination, ought to sell voice or pen. Thus no

---

RTVZO // 25 fuerant] erant *R* // 27 locis] *deest V* // 27 ponentes] ponent *Z* // 27 scandalum] scandala *V* // 27 Idem] Ibidem *RTZ* // 28 principes] *deest V* // 29 inmutant] inmutat *K* // 30 predicant] *sic Ceteri et O; deest P* // 32 Gregorius VII] *deest Y;* VII *deest Z* // 36 militum] militibus *Y* // 37 vel] sed *V* // 37 est] *deest B* // 38 amodo] omnino *B* // 38 fuerit] fuit *Q* // 40 et qui] et *deest R* // 41 recipiunt] *sic Ceteri et O; deest P* // 43 Sed] Si *W* // 46 sed] sed quia *B* // 48 *Hic titulus:* Hic condempnat ecclesiam quia (ex eo quod *T*) symoniaci sunt in ea. Nota: Quod id (illud *T*)

quod sequitur pertinet ad illos quos Cristus eiecit de templo. *RT* // 48 I.di.] Hic desinit *Y.* // 48 Quis] Si quis *RT* // 49 ab] in *R* // 52 nichilo] nullo *V* // 53 est enim] enim est *KQSTV* // 53 est] *deest Z* // 54 qui] que *S* // 55–56 et servum] et *deest V* // 56 sanctum spiritum] spiritum sanctum *BKQRSVO;* et spiritum sanctum *T;* et spiritum sancti *Z* // 56 spiritum sanctum] sanctum *deest RT* //58 efficiunt] appellant *V* // 58 suum servum] servum suum *BTV* // 60 sit] est *QR* // 62 aliquid] *deest R;* aliud *V* // 62 requirendum] relinquendum *Q* // 63 exequiis] obsequiis *R* // 64–65 seu . . . pro investitura] nec pro

---

[2] XXIV. q. iii, c. 33 (Friedberg, I, 999).
  Ibidem. c. 30 (Friedberg, I, 998).
  Ibidem. c. 27 (Friedberg, I, 997).
[3] I. q. iii, c. 13 (Friedberg, I, 417).

[4] XXXIII. q. iii (de Penitencia), I. dist., c. 87 (Friedberg, I, 1184).
[5] *Cf.* I. q. vii, c. 27 (Friedberg, I, 437–38).
[6] I. q. i, c. 21, par. 1 (Friedberg, I, 365).
[7] I. q. i, c. 117, par. 1 (Friedberg, I, 403–04).

65 collatis, nec pro ordinibus clericorum, pro investitura, pro recepcione in monasterium. Et sic de aliis. *Extra de symonia, Cum in ecclesia; Sicut pro certo;* [8] *et cetera in c. i,* ubi dicitur, quod nec minister nec notarius in ordinacione eius vocem
70 vel calamum vendere debet.[8a] Sic nullus clericus pro beneficio vel servicio ecclesie aliquid conferre audeat, aut fabricis ecclesie vel in donariis ecclesiarum sive eciam quod pauperibus sit erogandum [P 235′] quia qui aliquid male accipit ut bene
75 dispenset gravatur pocius quam iuvetur. *I. q. iii, Calcedonense.*[9] Nec excusat consuetudo quia non valet contra legem dei. *Ut XI. di. In hiis;* [10] dicitur: In hiis rebus, de quibus nil certi statuit divina scriptura, mos populi dei et instituta maiorum pro
80 lege tenenda sunt. Sed lex dei est; gratis accepistis, gratis date. *Mat. x.*[11] Ergo et cetera. Et si Cristus potuit [B 299′] pape legem ponere, potest papa symoniam comittere? Tancretus dicit papa potest incurrere vicium symonie sicut quilibet alius
85 homo, peccatum enim de tanto in aliqua persona est gravius, quanto maiorem obtinet locum. *XL. di. Homo cristianus.*[12] [K 114′] Unde quisquis per pecuniam ordinatur, ad hoc, ut fiat hereticus promovetur. *I. q. i, Quisquis.*[13] Et dicit *Am-*
90 *brosius, I. q. i:* [14] Cum ordinaretur episcopus, quid dedit aurum fuit, quid perdidit anima fuit; cum alium ordinaret, [Q 87′] quid accepit aurum fuit, quid [T 129′] dedit lepra fuit. *Hic Cristus expellit vendentes et ementes dicens:* Ihesus in-
95 venit in templo vendentes et ementes oves, [R 258′] et boves, et columbas, et nummilarios sedentes. Et cum fecisset quasi flagellum de funi-

cleric may dare to grant anything in exchange for a benefit or service for the church, for the fabric of the church, or for a contribution to the treasures of the churches, or even for funds to be given to the poor, because whoever accepts wrongly that he might give rightly is burdened rather than helped (*I. q. iii, c. 8*). Nor does custom excuse, because it does not avail against the law of God, as it is said in *XI. dist., c. 7*: In those matters about which nothing certain is decreed in the divine scripture, the custom of the people of God and the institutions of the elders are to be held for law. But the law of God is: Freely you have received, freely give (*Mat. x, 8*). And if Christ could set the law for the pope, may the pope commit simony? Tancred says that the pope can incur the vice of simony just as any other man. Indeed, sin is all the heavier in any person according to the greatness of the place he occupies (*XL. dist., c. 5*). Whence, whoever is ordained through money is promoted to this, that he be a heretic (*I. q. i, c. 5*). And Ambrose (*I. q. i, c. 14*) *says*: When he was ordained bishop, what he gave was gold, what he lost was his soul. When he ordained another, what he took was gold, what he gave was leprosy.

Here there is a picture of Christ driving out the buyers and sellers, and saying: Jesus found in the temple those that sold and bought sheep and oxen and doves, and the changers of money sitting. And when he had made a scourge of small cords, he drove them all out of the temple, and the sheep and the oxen, and poured out the changers' money (*Joh. ii, 13–15*). Thy money perish with thee! (*Act. 8: 20*).

1. (*Two old men:*) Behold, the gates of the orchard

---

ordinibus clericorum, nec pro aliis sacramentis consecrandis nec pro investitura *V* // 66 in] *deest Z* // 67 aliis] singulis *BKQS* // 67–68 Sicut pro certo et cetera] et *R* // 68 et ... ubi] et iii° capitulo In ordinando *Q* // 68 quod] *deest R;* quod sicut *B* // 69 in ordinacione] *deest R* // 70 sic] sicut *V* // 72 audeat] *sic V;* audet *Ceteri* // 72 donariis] donariis muneribus *RT* // 73 quod] *deest Z* // 74 aliquid] *deest B* // 77 contra] extra *B* // 78 de] *deest S* // 78 certi] *deest R;* certe *BZ* // 82 Cristus potuit] potuit Cristus *RT* // 82 pape legem] legem pape *RT* // 83 symoniam] symoniaca *RVZ* // 83 committere] dimittere *B* // 83 dicit] dicit quod *V* // 85 enim] est *Q* // 85 de] *deest V* // 85 de tanto] in tantum *B;* de quanto *RT* // 85 in] *deest RT* // 86 gravius] gravior *R* // 86 quanto] tanto *RT* // 86 locum] in ecclesia locum *Q* // 88 fiat hereticus] hereticus sit *B* // 89 promovetur] promoveatur *RTZ* // 89–90 I. q. i] I. q. i, Cum ordinaretur *V* // 91 dedit] *deest K* // 91–92 quid dedit ... ordinaret] *deest R* // 93 fuit] fuit. Hec Sanctus Ambrosius *RT* // 93–94 Hic ... dicens]

sic *Z; deest Ceteri* // 94 Hic insercio ante verbum "Ihesus": Ibidem: Et tu graciam, cum, ordinareris, non suscepisti, quia gratuito eam non meruisti. *Hec ibi per Ambrosium* [*I. q. i., c. 15; Friedberg, I, 361*]; *et Gregorium, I. q. prima, pars, Quia ergo* [*I. q. i., c. 16, II pars; Friedberg, I, 362*] dicit: Aput symoniacos sacerdocium non subsistit, benediccio eorum in maledictionem vertetur, aput eos manet anathema dandi et accipiendi, cum sancti non sint nec in Cristi constituti corpore, cum sint maledicti; nec sanctificare alios possunt, nec corpus Cristi tradere, vel accipere, nec benedicere aliis valent. *Ibidem*. Qui honorem non habuerit honorem dare non potuit, nec aliquid ille accepit, quia nichil erat in dante, sed dampnacionem quam habuit per pravam manus inposicionem dedit. *Ibidem in capitulo, Qui perfeccionum*. [*I. q. i., c. 17; Friedberg, I, 363*]. *V* // 95 vendentes et ementes] ementes et vendentes *RV* // 96 et columbas] et *deest R* // 96 et nummilarios] et *deest RT* // 97 quasi flagellum] *sic Ceteri et O;* flagellum

---

[8] *Decretales,* V, iii, 9 (Friedberg, II, 751); *Hic est fons, sed non verbatim.*
  Decretales, V, iii, 39 (Friedberg, II, 765).
[8a] *Decretales,* V, iii, 1 (Friedberg, II, 749).
[9] Sic ... iuvetur; I. q. iii, c. 8 (Friedberg, I, 413–415); *paraphrasis.*
[10] XI. dist., c. 7 (Friedberg, I, 25).

[11] Mat. x, 8.
[12] XL. dist., c. 5 (Friedberg, I, 146): Homo Christianus fortiter cadit in peccatum propter duas causas: aut propter magnitudinem peccati, aut propter altitudinem dignitatis. *Glosa, aut commentarius, Tancreti non inventa est.*
[13] I. q. i, c. 5 (Friedberg, I, 358).
[14] I. q. i, c. 14 (Friedberg, I, 361).

culis, omnes eiecit de templo, oves quoque et boves et nummilariorum effudit es. *Joh. ii.*[15]

100 Pecunia tua tecum sit in perdicionem. *Act. viii.*[16]

[S 32']

Primus: *Scilicet, duo senes:* Ecce hostia pomerii clausa sunt, et nemo nos videt, et in concupiscenciam tui sumus; consentire nobis et commiscere
105 nobiscum quod si nolueris, dicemus testimonium contra te quod fuit tecum iuvenis. *Dan. xiii.*[17]

Secundus: *Scilicet, Zuzanna:* Angustie sunt michi undique; si enim hec egero mors michi est. Si autem non egero non effugiam manus vestras.
110 Sed melius [V 182'] est michi absque opere incidere in manus vestras, quam peccare in conspectu domini. Et exclamavit voce magna Zuzanna; et exclamaverunt senes et duo presbiteri pleni iniqua cogitacione adversus eam. *Ibidem.*[18]

115 Tercius: *Scilicet Daniel:* Inveterate dierum malorum, nunc venerunt peccata tua, que operabaris prius, iudicans iudicia iniusta, innocentes opprimens, et dimittens noxios. *Ibidem.*[19]

Quartus: *Idem Daniel:* Semen Chanaan, et non
120 Iuda, species decepit te, et concupiscencia subvertit cor tuum. Sic faciebatis filiabus Israhel, et ille timentes loquebantur vobiscum, sed non filia Iuda hec sustinuit iniquitatem vestram. *Ibidem.*[20]

125 *Bartholomeus Brixiensis, XXXII. di., Nullus,*[21] *dicit:* Fornicator notorius per sentenciam vel per propriam confessionem, vel per rei evidenciam, quia mulierem suspectam [P 236] tenet in domo publice, vel forte sunt argumenta gradiencia super
130 [Z 333] terram, scilicet pueri, vitari debet. Eciam occultus symoniacus in ordine. Unde et ab occulto symoniaco quem scis esse symoniacum [B 300] non debes percipere sacramenta: *I. q. i, Si qui a symoniacis.*[22] Et illos symoniacos et

are closed and nobody sees us and we are desirous of you. Consent and have intercourse with us, because if you will not we shall give witness against you that a young man was with you (*Dan. xiii, 20–21*).

2. (*Susanna:*) I am completely distressed. If I submit I will surely die. If, however, I do not submit, I cannot escape your hands. But it is better for me to fall into your hands without complicity than to sin in the sight of God. And Susanna cried out in a loud voice, and the elders, the two priests with evil thoughts against her, cried out (*Dan. xiii, 22–24, 28*).

3. (*Daniel:*) Old men of evil days! Now your sins, which you committed earlier, come out; handing down unjust decisions, oppressing the innocent, and freeing the guilty (*Dan. xiii, 52–53*).

4. (*Daniel again:*) Seed of Chanaan and not Juda, beauty deceives you and lust subverts your heart. Thus you did things to the daughters of Israel, and they, fearing, talked with you, but not one daughter of Juda abided your iniquity (*Dan. xiii, 56–57*).

Bartholomew of Brescia (*XXXIII. dist., c. 5*) *says:* A known fornicator, whether he is known because of a sentence, or by his own confession, or by evidence —because he keeps a suspected woman in his house publicly, or perchance because there are arguments walking around on earth, namely children—should be shunned; and likewise a secret symoniac in orders. Thus, you ought not to receive the sacrament from a secret symoniac whom you know to be a symoniac (*I. q. i, c. 108*). And we can avoid those symoniacs and fornicators by simple right (*Decretals, II, xxvi, 12*). Do not wait for the sentence of a superior, who perhaps himself is such, upholding a symoniac for receipt of money, contrary to Chapter 13, *Decretals*, III, i. And the avoidance of such persons is enjoined, under pain of excommunication and the sin of idolatry (*XXXII.*

---

quasi *P;* flagellum *Z* // 99 es] *deest Z* // 100 pecunia ... perdicionem] *deest RT* // 102 *Ante "Primus":* Hic condempnat ecclesiam quod fornicatorii et concubinarii sunt in ea. *RT;* Sexta Tabula *VQ* // 102 *In margine:* Zuzanna *ST* // 102 Primus] Sequitur Primus *S* // 102 Scilicet, duo senes] *sic Z; deest Ceteri* // 104 commisceri] commisceri *STZ* // 106 te] *deest K* // 106 fuit] fuerit *SZ* // 107 Scilicet, Zuzanna] *sic Z; deest Ceteri* // 107 sunt] *deest S* // 107 michi] *deest K* // 108–109 mors ... egero] *deest Z* // 112 domini] dei *V* // 113 et exclamaverunt] et *deest R* // 113 senes] duo senes *Z* // 113 et duo] et *deest Q* // 115 Scilicet Daniel] *sic Z; deest Ceteri* // 119 Idem Daniel] *sic Z;* Daniel *B; deest Ceteri* // 121 faciebatis] faciebas *R* // 121 filiabus] *deest Z* // 122 ille] *deest S;* iste *Z* // 123 filia] filie *Z* // 123 hec] non ita *Q;* que *Z* // 125 *Hic insercio ante verbum "Bartholomeus":* Nota: ad idem infrascriptum immediate *RT* // 125 Bartholomeus] Et Bartholomeus *V* // 125 *Hic insercio post verbum "Brixiensis":* Nota: Quod iste auctoritates correspondunt ad quartam auctoritatem, scilicet Danielis *RT* // 125–126 Nullus dicit] dicit: Nullus *R* // 126 dicit] dicit se *S* // 126 Fornicator] Omnis fornicator *Q* // 126–127 per propriam] per *deest KQRTV* // 128 tenet] licet *R* // 129 publice] *deest Z* // 130 scilicet pueri] *deest Z;* ut sunt pueri eius, missa *Q* // 131 et] *deest R* // 134 Si qui] Quoniam *V* // 134 qui] quis *B;* autem *RT* //134 illos] *sic BKQRSTV;* istos *Z; deest P* // 134 et] *deest R;*

---

[15] Joh. ii, 13–15.
[16] Act. viii, 21.
[17] Dan. xiii, 20–21.
[18] *Ibidem,* 22–24; Angustie ... senes.
Ibidem, 28; et ... cogitacione.
Ibidem, 24; Adversus eam.
[19] *Ibidem.,* 52–53.
[20] *Ibidem.,* 56–57.
[21] *Glosa in verbum "Audiat," XXXII. dist., c. 5* (*Friedberg, I, 117*). (vel forte ... pueri, *non in glosa.*) (*Edicio Lugdun., Decretum, col. 156.*)
[22] I. q. i, c. 108 (*Friedberg,* I, 400–401); *non verbatim.*

135 fornicarios vitare possumus iure mero. *Extra de prescripcionibus, Cum non liceat:*²³ Non expecta sentenciam superioris²³ᵃ qui forte per se est talis illum sustinens obtentu pecunie, contra c. "Ut clericorum," **[Q 88]** *Extra de vita et*
140 *honestate clericorum*.²⁴ Et abstinencia a talibus sub pena excommunicacionis et peccati ydolatre precipitur: *XXXII. di., Nullus, et capitulo sequenti*.²⁵ Eciam in necessitate ab illis divisis ab unitate ecclesie, non debent recipi sacramenta: *Ut*
145 *XXXII. di., c. Verum*,²⁶ dicitur: Officium symoniacorum et in fornicacione iacencium nullomodo recipiatis, et quantum potestis, tales a sanctis misteriis ut opportuerit prohibeatis. *Unde XXVII. di., Quod autem*,²⁷ *dicitur:* Si quis frater nomi-
150 natur fornicator, aut avarus, aut ydolis serviens, cum huiusmodi nec cibum sumere nec ave ei dicere, nec in domum recipere, sed esse debet **[K 115]** sicut ethnicus et publicanus. Neque in sterquilinium utilis est, sed foris mittatur. Qui
155 habet aures audiendi audiat: *Luc. xiiii.*²⁸ Hec lex dei; etsi angelus de celo descenderet et aliud evangelizaret non esset credendum: *Gal. i.*²⁹ Quamvis multi contrarium senciunt, sicut *Augustinus super Johannem* ait contra **[T 130]** Donatistas, ubi
160 dicit: Quod talia sacramenta proprias habent virtutes et agentibus vel suscipientibus obsunt, nisi sola morte interveniente, ut puta ne sine baptismate vel communione decedant, in tantum eis obsunt, ut veri ydolatre sunt, cum talibus, scilicet
165 sacerdotibus. Ordinacionum et sacramentorum confeccio, et aliter quam permissum est scienter suscepcio vehementer a sanctis canonibus prohibeantur. Ait enim Samuel propheta: Quoniam peccatum ariolandi est repugnare, et quasi scelus
170 ydolatre nolle acquiescere.³⁰ Et ponitur *XXXII.*

dist., c. 5). Even in exigency the sacraments ought not to be received from those cut off from the unity of the church, *as XXXII. dist., c. 6, Part III, says:* In no case may you receive the ministration of symoniacs and those lying in fornication, and insofar as you are able, you must keep them from the holy mysteries, as is right. *Thus it says in XXVII. dist., Part I:* Even if a brother is called fornicator, or covetous, or idolator, with such a one do not eat, or greet him, or receive him into your home, but he ought to be treated just as a heathen or publican. He is not fit for the dungpit, but let him be cast out. He who has ears, let him hear (*Luc. xiv, 35*). This is the law of God: Even if an angel should descend from heaven and preach something else, this is not to be believed (*Gal. i, 8–9*). However, many have different opinions; *as Augustine writing on the Gospel of John (XXXII. dist., c. 6, Part III) says, against the Donatists:* that such sacraments have their own powers, and they are hurtful to those giving and receiving them, except only if death be imminent, lest, for example, people die without baptism or communion. They are so hurtful to them that they are true idolators, along with such priests. The ministration of ordinations and sacraments, and the receiving of them, knowingly, other than as permitted, are strictly forbidden by the holy canons. For the Prophet Samuel says: For to rebel is the sin of witchcraft and not to wish to obey is like the sin of idolatry. (*I Sam. xv, 23*). And it is to be found in *XXXII. dist., c. 6, Part III. And in the same place it is said:* Let not the dove fear the ministrations of the wicked, let it be mindful of the power of the Lord. But nevertheless Pope Nicholas and Pope Gregory ordered the faithful to abstain from masses of priests who are established clearly to be such, so that they

---

symoniacos vel K // 135 possumus] posset Z // 135 possumus iure mero] debemus Q // 135 iure] mere Z // 135 mero] merito T // 136 expecta] sic BSZ; expectata KPRTV, Q (*in hoc correctum*) // 137 sentenciam] sentencia KPQRTV // 137 per se] deest S // 138 illum] istum Z // 138 pecunie] deest Z // 138 Contra] deest R V // 141 excommunicacionis] deest R // 142 Nullus] deest K // 143 Eciam] Eciam nullus K // 144 recipi] sic BKRSTVZ; percipi PQ // 146 iacencium] iacencium scienter QO // 147 tales] sic Ceteri et O; deest P // 147 sanctis] sacris Q // 147 misteriis] ministeriis BVZ // 151 huiusmodi] hiis Z // 152 domum] domo RT // 152 esse debet] debet esse RT // 155 Hec] Hec est B // 156 de celo] deest B // 157 esset] sic Ceteri; est P // 157 credendum] ei credendum Q // 158 senciunt] *Hic Explicit Tabula Quinta BSVZ* // 160 dicit] sic dicit Q; ait R // 162 ut puta] utpote QO // 163 in tantum] interim RT // 164 sunt] sint KRTO // 164 scilicet] scilicet cum K // 167 suscepcio] suscipere R // 167 sanctis] sacris Q // 168 Ait enim] deest K (*spacium reservatum est*) // 168 Quoniam] Quod R // 170 Et poni-

---

²³ *Decretales*, II, xxvi, 12 (Friedberg, II, 385–86); *cf. glosam ordinariam in verbum* "*Recedere*" (*Edicio Lugdun., col. 861*): ". . . istas symoniacos, et fornicarios vitare possumus iure mero. . . ."

²³ᵃ *Cf. glosam citatam:* ("Cum non liceat a capite membra recedere . . .") *glosa:* "Recedere": Nisi ubi incidit in haeresim. . . . Vel in schisma . . . et in crimine notorio fornicationis, et in simoniaco in ordine, si possit probari. . . . In aliis autem criminibus etiamsi sint notoria, expectanda est sentencia. . . .

²⁴ *Cf. Decretales*, III, i, 13 (Friedberg, II, 452).

²⁵ XXXII. dist., c. 5 (Friedberg, I, 117); *non verbatim. Fons dicit de ydolatra nichil.*

²⁶ XXXII. dist., c. 6, III pars (Friedberg, I, 118–119).

²⁷ XXVII. dist., I pars (Friedberg, I, 98); *sed nescimus quo modo pertineret, citacio est forsan erronea.*

²⁸ I Cor. v, 11; Si . . . sumere; *non verbatim.*
II Joh. 10; nec . . . debet; *non verbatim.*
Mat. xviii, 17; sicut . . . publicanus; *non verbatim.*
Luc. xiv, 35; neque . . . audiat; *non verbatim.*

²⁹ Gal. i, 8–9; *non verbatim.*

³⁰ I Sam. xv, 23.

di. c. *Verum*; c. *Porro*.³¹ Et ibidem dicitur: Non horreat columba ministerium malorum, respiciat domini potestatem. Ac tamen Nicolaus Papa et Gregorius a missis sacerdotum, quos tales revera esse constiterit, **[R 259]** fideles abstinere decreverunt, [ut] et peccandi licenciam ceteris auferrent, et huiusmodi ad digne penitencie lamenta revocarent.

1 Tabula Sexta
Primus: *Scilicet, Cristus habens pellicium in manu et vestit Adam et Ewam:* Fecit quoque deus Ade et **[P 236′]** uxori eius tunicas pelliceas et induit eos. *Gen. iii.*¹ Id est, de pellibus animalium mortuorum, **[Q 88′]** in signum sue mortalitatis, eo quod tunc indigebant tegumento contra intemperiem aeris. *Lira ibidem.*²
Secundus, *de antiquo colore:* Cumque cognovissent se esse nudos, consuerunt ficus **[V 183]** folia et fecerunt sibi perizomata. *Gen. iii.*³ Quia senserunt rebellionem carnis et motum inordinatum membrorum, ideo studuerunt cooperire suam turpitudinem. *Lira.*⁴
Tercius: *Scilicet, Constantinus qualiter coronat papam, et ibidem incipit novus color, dicit:* Constantinus Imperator pontifici romane ecclesie imposuit coronam capitis sui ex auro purissimo et gemmis preciosis, et clamidem purpuream, atque omnia imperialia indumenta, exhibens illi stratoris officium. *XCVI. di., Constantinus.*⁵
Quartus: *Scilicet, Maria circa Cristum positum in presepio dicit:* Maria peperit filium suum primogenitum et pannis eum involvit et reclinavit eum in presepio. *Luc. ii.*⁶ Nascitur dei filius in cuius arbitrio erat quodcumque vellet eligere tem-

might take away the freedom of sinning from the others and recall such ones to the lamentations of worthy penance.

The Sixth Table

1. *Christ, with a garment of skins in his hand, and clothing Adam and Eve:* Also God made Adam and his wife tunics of skins and he clothed them (*Gen. iii, 21*). That is, from the pelts of dead animals, as a sign of their mortality, because then they needed a covering against the intemperance of the air (*Lira*).

2. (*The old color:*) And as they knew themselves to be naked, they sewed fig leaves together and made themselves aprons (*Gen. iii, 7*). Because they sensed a rebellion of the flesh and an uncontrolled movement of their members, they therefore were anxious to cover over their foulness (*Lira*).

3. *Constantine crowning the pope says (and here the New color begins):* The Emperor Constantine put the crown, made from purest gold and precious gems, from his own head on the pontiff of the Roman Church; and he put the purple cape and all the imperial garments on him, performing for him the office of strator (*XCVI. dist., c. 14*).

4. *Mary, next to Christ lying in the manger, says:* Mary bore her firstborn son and wrapped him in swaddling clothes and laid him in a manger (*Luk. ii, 7*). The son of God is born, in whose power it was to choose whatever time he wished. He chose the season most troublesome to the flesh, especially to an infant

---

tur] deest *QR* // 171 Non] deest *T* // 172 ministerium] sic *QRTO*; ministeriorum *K*; misterium *P* // 172 respiciat] sed respiciat *Q* // 173 Ac tamen] Attamen *RO* // 174 a] deest *K* // 175 fideles abstinere] sic *RO*; fideles esse abstinere *Ceteri* // 176 ceteris] cecorum *K* // 178 revocarent] revocarent. Hec ibidem *Q*

Tabula Sexta

1 Tabula Sexta] deest *BRTW*; Sexta Tabula *K*; Tabula Septima *V*; Septima Tabula *Q*; *Loco istius, titulus:* Hic reprehenduntur pape et clerici et preciosa vestimenta. *R*; Hic reprehendit pape et ecclesie personarum preciosa et honesta vestimenta. *T* // 2–3 Scilicet . . . Ewam] sic *Z*; deest *Ceteri* // 4 Ade] deest *W* // 5 id est] deest *B*; Glosa: id est *RT* // 6 in] et in *R* // 7 tegumento] vestimento *W* // 8 Lira ibidem] deest in loco *RT* // 9 de antiquo colore] sic *Z*; Lyra ibidem dicit *RT*; deest *Ceteri* // 9 Cumque] Quandocumque *V* // 11 sibi] deest *W* // 11 Quia] detur *Z* (*sic pro* ibidem?) // 13 suam] sic *BKRSTVZO*; deest *PQW* // 14 Lira] deest *Z*; Hec Lira ibidem *Q*; Lira ibidem *VW*; Hec ille *RT* // 15–16 Scilicet . . . dicit] sic *Z*; Scilicet *B*; Scilicet Constantinus *S*; Constantinus dicit pontifici *T*; deest *Ceteri* // 16 Constantinus] Constantinus dicit *R* // 17 Imperator] Imperator dupliciter *Q*; deest *R* // 17 imposuit] et imposuit *R* // 18 capitis sui] capiti suo *B*; capiti *R*; capitis *TZ* // 19 et] deest *VZ* // 20 exhibens illi stratoris] exhibent dicit strator *Z* // 21 Constantinus] Constantinus beato Silvestro *Q* // 22–23 Scilicet . . . dicit] sic *Z*; deest *Ceteri* // 23–36 Maria . . . Bernhardus] deest in loco *RT* (*inclusum est autem, infra, sub octavo*) // 23 suum] deest *RT* // 24 involvit et] et deest *TZ* // 25–30 Nascitur . . . reclinandum] deest *Q* // 25 dei] deus *W* // 25–26 in cuius] deest *Z*; in deest

---

³¹ XXXII. dist., c. 6, III pars (Friedberg, I, 118–119); *citacio composita.*

Sexta Tabula
¹ Gen. iii, 21 (. . . quoque dominus deus . . .).
² Lyra *super* Gen. iii.

³ Gen. iii, 7.
⁴ Lyra *super* Gen. iii; *citacio compressa.*
⁵ XCVI. dist., c. 14 (Friedberg, I, 342 ff.); *imperfecte laudatum.*
⁶ Luc. ii, 7.

pus. Elegit quod carni mo [B 300′] lestius est, presertim parvulo et pauperis matris filio, que vix pannos habebat ad [T 130′] involvendum,
30 presepe ad reclinandum. Primus Adam pelliciis vestitur tunicis; secundus pannis obvolvitur. Cristus utique qui non fallitur elegit quod carni est molestius, id ergo utilius, [S 33] id pocius eligendum, et quisquis aliud docet vel swadet, ab
35 eo tamquam [K 115′] a seductore cavendum est. *Hec Bernhardus*.[7]
Quintus: Scilicet patriarcha equitans in equo, et unus precedit cum cruce, dicit: Solus romanus pontifex in missarum solemniis palio semper utitur et
40 ubique, quoniam assumptus est in plenitudine ecclesiastice potestatis, que per palium figuratur. *Extra de auctoritate et usu palii, Ad honorem.*[8] Patriarche dominice crucis vexillum ante se ubique deferri faciant. *Extra de privilegiis, Antiqua.*[9]
45 *Sextus: Cardinalis:* Inferiores prelati quibus per privilegium conceditur usus mitre, [Z 333′] si sunt exempti, uti possunt mitris aurificatis non habentibus laminas aut gemmas; si non sunt exempti, albis et planis utantur. *Johannes Andree,*
50 *Libro sexto, de excessibus prelatorum, Ut apostolice.*[10]
Septimus: Iterum Cardinalis, equitans: Per palium confertur plenitudo pontificalis officii, et nomen archiepiscopale, sic quod ante tradicionem
55 palii non sit archiepiscopus appellandus. Et palium suum alteri commodare non debet, sed debet sepeliri cum eo. *Extra de auctoritate et usu palii, Nisi, Ad hoc.*[11]
Octavus: Qualiter Martinus tenet ruffam [clamidem?]: Martinus [Q 89] clamidem cum paupere
60 dimidiavit, [P 237] qui cum veste brevi atque hyspida, quinque argenteis comparata, oblaturus

and the son of a poor mother, who hardly had rags to wrap him in and only a manger to lay him in. The first Adam is dressed in hides, the second wrapped in rags. Christ, who does not err, chose what was more burdensome to the flesh, therefore more beneficial and rather to be chosen; and whoever teaches or persuades otherwise, beware of him as of a seducer (*Bernard*).

5. *A Patriarch riding a horse, and preceded by a man with a cross, says:* Only the Roman pontiff uses the pallium at all times and in all places in the celebration of the mass. This is because he has been elevated to the fullness of ecclesiastical power, which it represents (*Decretals, I, viii, 4*). Patriarchs are to have the banner of the Lord's cross borne before them wherever they go (*Decretals, V, xxxiii, 23*).

6. *A Cardinal:* Lesser prelates, to whom, by privilege, the use of the mitre is conceded, can use a gilt mitre without lamination or gems, if they are exempt. If they are not exempt, let them use white and unadorned mitres (*John Andree, gloss on Liber Sextus, V, vii, 6*).

7. *Another Cardinal, riding a horse:* The fullness of the pontifical office and the archiepiscopal dignity are conferred by the pallium: before the granting of the pallium no one may be called an archbishop. And he should not let his pallium be used by another, but it should be buried with him (*Decretals, I, viii, 3, 2*).

8. *Martin holding a red [cloak]:* Martin divided his cloak with the pauper and even though having but scant and coarse clothing, bought with only five pieces of silver, he proceeded to offer a sacrifice to God (*from the life of St. Martin*).

9. The soul would not choose to be clothed in sumptuous raiment unless it had previously been stripped of its virtues; and the cult of the body would not claim so much care unless the mind, barren of virtues, had not first been neglected (*Bernard*). They wandered around

---

R // 26 vellet] *deest* RV // 27 est] *deest* B // 28 parvulo] parvulus RT // 28 filio] filius RT // 30 ad reclinandum] reclinandi RT // 31 tunicis] et tunicis B // 31 secundus] is RT // 31 obvolvitur] convolvitur Z // 32 utique] *deest* W // 32-33 elegit ... pocius] *deest* Z // 33 est] esset K // 33 id pocius] illud pocius K // 34 eligendum] est eligendum B // 34 et] est R // 34 aliud] aliquid Z // 34 docet vel] *deest* Z // 34 vel] aut QW; aliud V // 34-35 ab eo] *deest* Z // 35 a] *deest* S // 36 Hec] *deest* BKSWZ // 36 Bernhardus] Sanctus Bernhardus T // 37 Quintus] *deest* RT // 37-38 Scilicet ... dicit] *sic* Z; *deest Ceteri* // 40 est] *deest* T // 40 in] ad R // 40 plenitudine] plenitudinem QRTZO // 41 ecclesiastice] *deest* QR // 42 Ad honorem] *deest* RT // 43 Patriarche] Quintus: Patriarche RT // 43-44 Patriarche ... faciant]

Patriarche dominice crucis vexillum ubique ante se deferri faciant B; Ante se ubique deferri faciant patriarche dominice crucis vexillum K; Patriarche dominice crucis ante se vexillum ubique deferri faciant W, Q (deferre) //45 Cardinalis] *sic* Z; *deest Ceteri* // 45 Inferiores prelati] Inferioribus prelatis R // 45 quibus *deest* RTZ // 45 per] *deest* BQW // 46 usus] et usus Q // 47 uti] *deest* RTZ // 47 uti possunt mitris] *deest* B // 48 sunt] sitis S // 50 de excessibus prelatorum] de privilegiis W // 52 Iterum Cardinalis, equitans] *sic* Z; *deest Ceteri* // 53 confertur] conceditur R // 55 sit] est *ceteri* // 56 commodare] accomodare BZ; commendare SV; comodari T // 59 Qualiter ... ruffam] *sic* Z; *deest Ceteri* // 59 clamidem] palium R // 61 brevi] *deest* V // 61 atque] *sic Ceteri*;

---

[7] *Bernardi Clarevallensis Sermo III. In nativitate domini, MPL, 183, 123; locus citatus a Wyclifo quoque, in tractatu De civili dominio, III, ed. J. Loserth (London, 1903), 59—sed amplius.*
[8] *Decretales, I, viii, 4 (Friedberg, II, 101).*
[9] *Decretales, V, xxxiii, 23 (Friedberg, II, 866).*
[10] *Recte, de privilegiis; cf. Liber Sextus, V, vii, 6 (Friedberg,* II, 1086). *Glosa recte laudata est (Editio Lugdun., Liber Sextus, col. 676), hoc dempto, quod post "si sunt exempti" sequitur: "in provincialibus et Episcopalibus conciliis."*
[11] *Decretales, I, viii, 3, 2 (Friedberg, II, 100 ff.). Cf. glosam ordinariam in verbum "nominis" (I, viii, 3; Edit. Lugdun., col. 221):* "Et ita licet consecratus sit in episcopum, non est appellandus archiepiscopus, ante palii receptionem."

deo sacrificium procedit. *Ut patet in Passionali.*[12]
[**W 65'**]

65 Nonus: Non optaret anima indui vestibus preciosis nisi prius virtutibus esset spoliata, et non curaretur tantum corporis cultus nisi prius neglecta fuisset mens inculta virtutibus. *Bernhardus.*[13] Circuierunt in melotis, in pellibus caprinis, egentes,
70 quibus dignus non erat mundus. *Heb. xi.*[14] Melota est vestis facta de pelle taxi illius animalis, que [**V 183'**] hirsuta est, pendens usque ad lumbos. *Huguccio.*[15]

Decimus: Non est pompositate respuendum,
75 ymmo est defendendum quod doctores togati, variati, et ornati incedant, ut per eos dignitas doctoratus appareat. Sed sunt scolastici reprehendendi qui sibi vestes solum doctoribus congruentes assumunt. *De excessibus prelatorum,*
80 *Ut apostolice, Libro sexto, Johannes Andree in glosa.*[16] [**B 301**]

Undecimus: Incrassatus, inpigwatus, dilatatus, dereliquit deum factorem suum et recessit a deo salutari suo et recalcitravit. *Deut. xxxii.*[17]

85 Duodecimus: Possunt clerici secundum conswetudinem regionis preciosis vestibus [**R 259'**] uti, ut conforment se moribus eorum inter quos vivunt, et ne vilescat dignitas clericalis. Purpuram et cyndatum ferre possunt, nam vestis Domini pur-
90 pura fuit. *XXI. q. iiii, Omnis, Bartholomeus Brixiensis in glosa.*[18]

Tredecimus: Milites plectentes coronam de spinis et imposuerunt capiti eius, et veste purpurea circumdederunt. *Joh. xix.*[19] Hoc totum factum est
95 illusorie. *Lira.*[20] Ideo sequitur, "et dabant ei alapas." *Ibidem.*[21] Ut ei illuderent factis sicut illuserant signis et verbis, cum dicebant, "Ave rex

in sheepskins [*in melotis*] and goatskins, destitute; of whom the world was not worthy (*Heb. xi, 37–38*). A *melota* is a garment made from the tanned hide of a hairy animal, and it hangs down to the loins (*Huguccio*).

10. It is not to be rejected as pomp, but rather defended, that doctors should go about elaborately and ornately gowned, that in them the dignity of the doctorate may be apparent. But schoolmasters who wear the clothing fitting only for doctors are to be censured. (*John Andree, gloss on Liber Sextus, V, vii, 6.*)

11. He waxed fat, grew gross, swelled up; he forsook God his maker; he turned away from God his saviour; he lashed out (*Deut., xxxii, 15*).

12. Clerics may wear costly clothing, according to local custom, in order to conform to the practice of those among whom they live, and so that the clerical estate not be cheapened. They may wear purple and silk, for the robe of the Lord was purple. (*Bartholomew of Brescia, gloss on XXI. q. iv, c. 1.*)

13. The soldiers wove a crown of thorns and put it on his head, and they put a purple robe on him (*Joh. xix, 2*). This was all done in mockery (*Lira*), hence it continues: "and they smote him with their hands" (*ibidem*), so that they might mock him in deed, as they had mocked him in gesture and word, when they said, "Hail, King of the Jews" (*Lira*). As it is said in Luke *xxiii, 11:* And Herod set him at naught and mocked him and arrayed him in a gorgeous robe. For in this way fools were mocked in those times (*Lira, ibidem*).

14. And having food and raiment, let us be therewith content (*I Tim. vi, 8*). Anything more is of evil. Therefore a garment that covers is enough for the servants of Christ, nor would one be suitable that

---

et *P; deest V* // 63 procedit] *deest B;* procidit *S;* precedit *Z* // 63 Ut patet] *deest Ceteri* // 63 Passionali] *post hoc, in RT, habetur paragrafus, quartus, "Maria . . . Bernhardus" (supra, ll. 16–25)* // 66 virtutibus esset] esset virtutibus *RW* // 66 et] *deest VZ* // 67 corporis] corporum *R* // 67 nisi] ubi *Z* // 68 fuisset] fuit *S* // 69 in pellibus] et in pellibus *RTV;* in *deest Q* // 69 egentes] egentibus *Q;* egentes, angustiati, afflicti *RTO* // 70 erat] esset *Z* // 70 Melota] Melotus *V;* Melior *Z* // 71 pelle taxi] pellis taxis *Z* // 72 usque] *deest V* // 74 pompositate] *sic BKQRSTVZO;* pompositati *PW* // 74 respuendum] *sic BQRSTWZO;* respiciendum *K;* resistendum *P;* respondendum *V* // 75 ymmo est defendenum] *deest RTZ;* ymmo non est defendendum *S* // 75–76 togati, variati] variati, togati *RTZ* // 76 et ornati] paliati et ornati *S* // 76 incedant] incedunt *K* // 76 per eos] *deest K* // 77 doctoratus] *deest V* // 77 scolastici] *sic BQRSTZO;* scolastice *KPVW* // 77 reprehendendi] respuendi *B* // 78 doctoribus . . . De] *deest Z* // 84 salutari] *sic KQRSTVWZO;* salvatore *BP* // 88 clericalis] clericorum *QW;* clericalis. XXI. q. iiii, Omnis talis *S* // 88 purpuram et] *deest K; hic in margine, alia manu:* Si optatis purpuram, optate eciam alapas etc. Sed wana *S* // 89 cyndatum] syndonem *R; deest W (spacium tamen in codice reservatum est)* // 90 xxi. q. iiii] *deest in loco S* // 91 Brixiensis] *deest RT* // 92 coronam de spinis] *sic Ceteri et O;* de spinis coronam *P* // 93 et] *deest BQRST* // 93 et veste] et *deest Q* // 93 circumdederunt] circumdederunt eum *QRWO* // 94 Hoc] Lira ibidem dicit: Hoc *RT;* Hoc autem *QW* // 95 Lira] *deest in loco RT* // 96 ei] eum *W* // 97 illuserant]

---

[12] *Non inventum.*
[13] "Non curaretur . . . virtutibus," *Bernardi Clarevallensis Apologia ad Guillelmum*, x, §26, *MPL, 182, 913.*
[14] Heb. xi, 37, 38.
[15] *Non ad manum.*
[16] *Recte, de privilegiis; cf. Liber Sextus, V, vii, 6 (Friedberg, II, 1086). Glosa recte laudata est (Editio Lugdun., Liber Sextus, col. 676), demptis paucis, et sane:* "ymmo *ratione* defendendum," "ut per *illa*"; "rogati" *loco* "togati" *est in edicione, sed sine dubio est error.*
[17] Deut. xxxii, 15.
[18] *Glosa ordinaria in verba "quod vero," XXI. q. iv, c. 1 (Friedberg, I, 857–858). (Editio Lugdun., col. 1238.)*
[19] Joh. xix, 2.
[20] Lyra, *super* Joh. xix.
[21] *Ibidem.*

iudeorum." *Lira.*[22] Sicut dicitur *Luc. xxiii.*[22a]
Sprevit autem illum Herodes, et illusit indutum
100 veste alba. Sic enim illudebatur tunc fatuus.
Lira, ibidem.[23]

Decimus Quartus: Habentes alimenta et quibus
tegamur, hiis contenti simus. *I. Tim. ultimo.*[24]
Quod amplius est a malo est. Itaque servis Cristi
105 **[Q 89′]** talis habitus sufficit qui tegat, nec expedit qui vestit vel ornat. *Glosa, ibidem.*[25] Omnis
iactancia et ornatura a sacro ordine aliena est.
Priscis enim temporibus omnis sacratus vir cum
mediocri aut vili veste conversabatur. Omne
110 quippe quod non propter necessitatem sed propter
venustatem accipitur elacionis habet calumpniam.
[K 116] Sed neque ex sericis texturis vestem quis
variatam induebat, nec apponebat variorum colorum ornamenta. Audierant **[P 237′]** enim quia
115 qui mollibus vestiuntur in domibus regum sunt.
XXI. q. iiii, Omnis.[26] Confusio vero et ignominia est Ihesum Cristum pauperem et esurientem
farsitis sive farsis predicare **[S 33′]** corporibus,
et ieiuniorum doctrinam rubentes buccas tumen-
120 ciaque ora proferre; si in apostolorum loco sumus,
non solum sermonem eorum imitemur sed conversacionem **[Z 334]** et abstinenciam. *XXXV. di.,
Ecclesia.*[27] **[V 184]**

1 Septima Tabula
Primus: *Et est dives epulo:* Homo quidam erat
dives, et induebatur purpura et bisso, etc. Et
mortuus est et sepultus est in inferno. Et erat
5 quidam mendicus, nomine Lazarus, qui iacebat ad
ianuam eius, ulceribus plenus, etc. Hic in sinum

clothed them in style or adorned them (*Gloss, ibidem*).
All ostentation and adornment are alien to holy orders;
for in early times every holy man went about in simple
or cheap garments. Indeed everything taken not on
account of necessity, but for the sake of elegance, is
open to the accusation of pridefulness. Nor did anyone
use to wear a variegated garment of silk fabrics, or
attach ornaments of various colors. For they had heard
that "they that wear soft clothing are in kings' houses"
([*Mat. xi, 8*] *XXI. q. iv, c. 1*). It is a confusion
indeed and a disgrace to preach Jesus Christ, the poor
and hungry, with stuffed bodies, and to proclaim the
doctrine of fasts with flushed cheeks and bulging
mouths. If we occupy the place of the Apostles, let us
imitate not only their words but their way of life and
their abstinence (*XXXV. dist., c. 4*).

The Seventh Table

1. *A rich banqueter:* There was a certain rich man
and he was clothed in purple and fine linen, etc. And
he died and he was buried in hell. And there was a
certain beggar, named Lazarus, who lay at his gate,

---

illuserunt *KRTVW* // 98 Lira] *deest RTZ* // 98 sicut]
sic *KS* // 98 Sicut ... xxiii] *deest QW* // 99 illum]
istum *Z* // 99 et] *deest V* // 100 Sic] Sicut *B* // 100
illudebatur tunc] illudebantur tunc *R*; tunc illudebant *V* //
100 fatuus] fatuis *BT*; fatui *R*; fatuos *V* // 102 et] et
hiis *R*; *deest T* // 104 Quod] Quid *RS* // 104 servis
Cristi] sic *BKQSVW*; Cristi *deest P*; servo Cristi *RT*
// 106 qui vestit] ut vestiat *R* // 106 ornat] armat *B*;
ornet *R* // 107 iactancia] iactancia corporalis *W* // 108
Priscis] Pristinis *K* // 108 omnis sacratus] sanctus *K*;
execratus *R*; ex sacratus *T* // 109 mediocri aut vili veste]
sic *BKRSVZO, T* (mediocriter), *P* (veloci); mediocri
veste aut vili *Q*; vili et mediocri veste *W* // 109–115 Omne
... regum sunt] *deest W* // 110 quod] quid *R* 110–111
sed propter venustatem] *deest Q* // 111 accipitur] accipit
B // 112 ex] *deest Z*; a *B* // 113 apponebat] apparebant
R; apparebat *T*; opponebat *Z* // 114 enim] sic *Ceteri*;
deest P // 116 vero] enim *Z* // 117 est] *deest R* // 117
et esurientem ... abstinenciam] *deest W* // 117 esurien-
tem] esurienti *B* // 120 loco] locis *RT* // 121–122 conversacionem et] conversacionis *V*

Septima Tabula

1 Septima Tabula] *deest BRTWZ*; Octava Tabula *QV* //
2–8 Primus ... Luc. xvi] *deest W* // 2 Primus] Primus
in alia tabula *Z* // 2 Et ... epulo] sic *Z; deest Ceteri* //
4 est in] est *deest BSTZ* // 4 et erat] Erat autem *RTZ*
// 5 quidam] sic *BKQRSTZO; deest PV* // 5 nomine
Lazarus] Lazarus nomine *RT* // 6 ulceribus plenus] plenus
ulceribus *BR* // 6 etc] et desiderabat saturari de micis que
cadebant de mensa divitis, sed nemo illi dabat, sed et canes
venientes lingebant ulcera eius *B*; cupiens saturari de micis
que cadebant de mensa divitis et nemo illi dabat, sed et canes
veniebant et lingebant ulcera eius *K*; sed nemo illi dabat sed
canes veniebant et lingebant ulcera eius *QST*; sed nemo
illi dabat rem sed canes veniebant et lingebant ulcera eius
R; et nemo illi dabat sed canes veniebant et lingebant ulcera
eius *V*; et non illi dabat *Z* // 6 Hic in sinum] Qui insanum
V // 6–8 Hic ... portatur] *deest RT* // 6 Hic] Autem

---

[22] *Ibidem.*
[22a] Luc. xxiii, 11.
[23] Lyra, *super* Joh. xix.
[24] I Tim. vi, 8.
[25] *Non ad manum.*
[26] XXI. q. iv, c. 1 (Friedberg, I, 857–858).
[27] XXXV. dist., c. 4 (Friedberg, I, 132).

[B 301'] Abrahe dum moritur ab angelis portatur. *Luc. xvi.*[1]

Secundus: Iohannes habebat vestimentum de pilis camelorum, zonam pelliceam circa lumbos eius. Esca autem eius erant locuste et mel silvestre. *Mat. iii.*[2] Non surrexit maior [T 131] inter natos mulierum Iohanne Baptista. *Mat. xi.*[3]

Tercius: Si cultus preciosarum vestium non esset in culpa servis Dei, non tam manifeste exprimeret quod dives indutus purpura et bisso descendit ad inferos. *Gregorius.*[4] Si abieccio vilis vestimenti virtus non esset, evangelista de Iohanne tam vigilanter non diceret: Erat indutus pilis camelorum. *Gregorius in Omelia.*[5]

Quartus: Fili, recordare quia recepisti bona in vita tua, et Lazarus similiter mala; nunc autem hic consolatur, tu vero cruciaris. *Luc. xvi.*[6] Nec obtinuit guttam aque. *Ibidem.*[7]

Primus impugnans indumentum humile et commendans statum, dicit: Cristus [Q 90] iubet nos attendere a falsis prophetis qui veniunt in vestimentis ovium nam interius sunt lupi rapaces. *Mat. vii.*[8] *Hec ille de novo colore.*

Sequitur solucio: Linis parietem, sed absque palea et temperamento, cum non dicit a vestibus sed a fructibus eorum, id est ab operibus cognoscetis eos. Et sic multum pro abiectis et humilibus indumentis. *Unde Thomas:*[9] Numquid lupi et ypochrite putarent suam maliciam sub humilibus vestibus posse paleare nisi proprium esset ovibus solere abiectis vestibus indui. *Augustinus:*[10] Non ideo debent oves odisse vestimentum suum quod plerumque illo se occultant lupi.

[V 184'] *Secundus impugnans:* [W 66] Alii

full of sores, etc. When he died, he was carried by angels into Abraham's bosom (*Luke, xvi, 19, 20, 22*).

2. John had his garment of camel's hair and a leather girdle about his loins. His meat was locusts and wild honey (*Mat. iii, 4*). Among them that are born of women there has not risen a greater than John the Baptist (*Mat. xi, 11*).

3. If the cult of expensive clothing were not a fault in the servants of God, he would not have pointed out so clearly that the rich man, dressed in purple and fine linen, descended to hell (*Gregory*). If the lowliness of humble clothing were not a virtue, the Evangelist would not so carefully have said of John that he was dressed in camel's hair (*Gregory, in a Homily*).

4. Son, remember that you did receive good things in your lifetime, and likewise Lazarus bad things; but now he is comforted and you are tormented (*Luke, xvi, 25*). And he did not receive even a drop of water (*ibid.*).

The first assailant of humble attire and supporter of pomp says: Christ commands us to beware of false prophets, who come in the clothing of sheep, for underneath they are ravening wolves (*Mat. vii, 15*). (*Thus far the New Color.*)

The solution is as follows: You plaster the wall, but without chaff and without a proper mixture; for he does not say "by their clothing" but "by their fruits," that is by their works, "will you recognize them." And thus this weighs heavily on the side of lowly and humble clothing. Thus Thomas says: Would wolves and hypocrites reckon that they might be able to cover their malice under humble attire if it were not proper to sheep to be customarily covered with lowly clothing? And Augustine says: Nor should sheep hate their

---

hic *Z* // 6 sinum] *sic KQSO*; sinu *Ceteri* // 7–8 ab angelis portatur] deportatur *B*; portatur *K* // 9 pilis] pellibus *W* // 10 zonam et zonam *QRSTWZ* // 11 eius] vestros *B*; suos *W* // 11 erant] erat *RZ* // 12–13 inter natos … Baptista] Iohanne Baptista inter natos mulierum. *RT* // 16 et bisso] *Sic BKQRSTVWZ*; *deest P* // 16 descendit] descenderit *R* // 17 vilis] et utilitas *Z* // 18 non esset] non *deest R* // 19–20 erat indutus pilis camelorum] *deest Q* // 19 pilis] vestibus *K* // 20 camelorum] *deest W* // 21–24 Quartus … Ibidem] *deest RTW* // 21 quia] quod *B* // 23 vero] autem *BQSV* // 25 Primus impugnans] *deest W*; *ante hoc in S*: De novo colore // 25–26 indumentum … dicit] *deest RT* // 28 interius] intrinsecus *QRT*; intus *S*; intricus autem *W* // 28 sunt lupi rapaces] lupi rapaces sunt *RT* // 29 Hec ille de novo colore] *sic Z*; *deest Ceteri* // 30 Sequitur solucio] *deest W*; sequitur *deest BKQRS*; Solucio primi *TVZ* // 31–32 a vestibus … operibus] a fructibus id est operibus *B*; a vestibus sed a fructibus idem est operibus eorum *V* // 32 ab] *deest KQRSTWZ* // 32 cognoscetis] eorum cognoscetis *Z* // 33 sic] *deest B*; sic facit *QW* // 34 indumentis] vestibus *R*; vestimentis *SVWZ* // 34–35 indumentis … humilibus] *deest Q* // 34 Unde Thomas] *deest W* // 34 Numquid] Numquam *V* // 36 paleare] palliari *BKQRSTVW*; salvari *Z* // 37 solere] humilis solere *Q*; solum *R*; humilibus solere *W* // 37 abiectis] *deest QW* // 37 Augustinus] Nunquam se lupi sub illis occultant. Augustinus *Q* // 38 ideo] *deest Z* // 38–39 vestimentum suum quod] vestimenta sua que *V* // 39 illo] illi *RT* // 40 Secundus impugnans] *deest W* // 40 impugnans] repugnans *BRST*;

Septima Tabula

[1] *Cf.* Luc. xvi, 19, 20, 22.
[2] Mat. iii, 4.
[3] Mat. xi, 11.
[4] *Cf.* Gregorii Magni, *XL Homiliarum in Evangelia* (MPL, 76, 1305).
[5] Gregorii Magni, *XL Homiliarum in Evangelia* (MPL, 76, 1305). Mat. iii, 4.
[6] Luc. xvi, 25.
[7] *Cf.* Luc. xvi, 24–6.
[8] *Cf.* Mat. vii, 15.
[9] *Non inventum.*
[10] Augustini, *De Sermone Domini in Monte*, II, xxiv (MPL, 24, 1306).

scandalizantur in huiusmodi habitus abieccione et humilitate cum non sit ceteris similis. Ideo quilibet debet se cum aliis conformare. *Hec ille* [P 238] *de novo colore.*

45 *Solucio secundi:* [W 65'] Scandalizat quemquam vestis fuscior, scandalizet Iohannes quo inter natos mulierum maior nullus fuit, qui angelus dictus Dominum quoque baptizavit, qui camelorum [R 260] vestitus tegumine zona pellicea cingebatur.
50 [W 66] Cibi displicent viliores. Nichil vilius est locustis. Illi Cristianos oculos scandalizant pocius, qui purpura et bisso [vestiuntur] et quibusdam [K 116'] fucis ora oculosque depingunt. *Ieronymus*.[11] *Et Ambrosius dicit*, quod qui sic ornatur,
55 vel cuius cervix auro premitur, domus est omnium demonum infernalium. *Hec ille in libro de virginitate.*[12]

Tercius impugnans: In corde latet virtus non in vestibus, quare eque bene potest quis deo servire
60 in tunica preciosa dummodo corde bono et intencione recta, sicut in tunica vilissima. *Hec ille de novo colore.*

[V 184] *Solucio tercii:* Stultum est dicere, "Que cura de exteriori vestitu cum virtus in corde
65 [B 302] consistat?" Nam eodem modo diceretur, "Que cura de elemosina, cum virtus in corde consistat?" Et sic de omnibus aliis actibus virtutum, quorum habitus et virtutes sunt in anima. Certe de corde venit quod preciosum pannum
70 emistis et vilem sprevistis, de corde venit quod sic ornate fecistis vestimenta consui, quia sine corde et sine premeditacione non fecistis. Ex cordis thezauro sine dubio procedit quidquid foris apparet viciosum. *Bernhardus.*[13] Non potest
75 fieri ut habeat mala facta, qui bonas [Q 90'] habet cogitaciones. Facta enim de cogitacione procedunt nec quisquam potest facere aliquid aut ad aliquid agendum [V 184'] membra movere, nisi

clothing merely because wolves often hide themselves under it.

The second assailant: Some feel offended by the lowliness and humbleness of such clothing, since it is different from that of others. Therefore everyone should conform with the rest. (*Thus far the New Color.*)

The solution of the second: Let anyone who likes take offense at rough clothing! Let anyone who likes take offense at John, than whom there has been no one greater among them that are born of women, who has been called an angel, and who baptized the Lord! He, dressed in the hide of camels, was girded by a leather belt! Does inferior food displease? There is no food lower than locusts. They offend Christian eyes, rather, who dress in purple and fine linen, and paint their lips and eyes with red colors (*Jerome*). And Ambrose says that he who is decked out in this manner, and whose neck is weighed down with gold, is the dwelling-place of all the demons of hell (*On Virginity*).

The third assailant: Virtue lies in the heart, not in garments. Therefore someone can equally well serve God in an expensive tunic, provided only that he do so with good heart and proper intention, as in the cheapest tunic. (*Thus far the New Color.*)

Solution of the third: It is stupid to say, "Why worry about external garments, when virtue resides in the heart?" For in the same way it might be said: "Why worry about alms, when virtue resides in the heart?" And so with all the other acts of the virtues, of which acts the habits and virtues are in the soul. And certainly it came from the heart that you have bought expensive cloth and scorned the cheap, it came from the heart that you had garments sewn so ornately, for you did not do it without heart and without premeditation. Whatever seems vicious externally undoubtedly proceeds from the chambers of the heart (*Bernard*). It cannot happen that one who has good intentions would

---

impugnans dicit *V* // 41 habitus] *deest B;* habitu *W* // 42 sit] *deest RST* // 43–44 Hec ille de novo colore] *deest R;* Hec ille de novo *Z* // 45 Solucio secundi] *deest RW;* solucio *Q* // 45 Scandalizat] Scandalizet *KRSTZ* // 45 quemquam] *sic QRSTVWZ;* quamquam *BKP* // 46 fuscior] iustior *B* // 46–47 scandalizet . . . maior] *deest Z* // 47 maior nullus fuit] non fuit maior *R;* maior fuit *W* // 47 dictus] dignus *R* // 48 quoque] *deest R;* que *B* // 48 baptizavit] baptizat *VZ* // 49 vestitus] vestibus *KSW* // 49 tegumine] pilis et *Q* // 49 zona] *deest V* // 50 cibi] tunc *V* // 50 vilius est] *deest Z* // 50 est] *deest W;* sunt *K;* nisi *Q* // 51 Cristianos] Cristiani *Z* // 51 scandalizant] scandalizent *BRTVZ;* scandalizat *K* // 52 et bisso] *deest et R* // 52 et quibusdam] et *deest V* // 53 oculosque] oculos *W* // 54 ornatur] ornantur *BQRS* // 55 premitur] pretingitur *W* // 56 libro] libro tercio *W* // 58 Tercius impugnans] *deest W* // 58 impugnans] *deest B;* repugnans *RT;* impugnans. De novo colore *S;* impugnans dicit *V* //

59 eque bene potest quis] potest quis eque *B* // 59 bene] *deest KQSW* // 60 bono] *deest W* // 60 bono et] recto et bona *R* // 61 recta] *deest R* // 61 in] *deest W;* ut in *Z* // 61 Hec ille] *deest RZ* // 61–62 de novo colore] *sic QTV;* deest Ceteri* // 63 Solucio tercii] *deest W;* Solucio *QR* // 63–64 Que cura de] De cura *K* // 64 exteriori vestitu] vestitu exteriore *Q;* exteriori vestimento *RT;* exteriori parte vestitu *Z* // 64–65 cum virtus in corde consistat] *deest QW* // 65–67 Nam eodem . . . consistat] *deest Z* // 65 diceretur] et diceretur *Q* // 66 cura de] cura est de *W* // 67 omnibus] *sic ceteri; deest P* // 67 aliis actibus] actibus aliis *S* // 69 Certe] Et enim *KS;* et *Z* // 69 de] *deest S* // 69 venit] exivit *B;* veniunt *V* // 70 emistis] emisti *Q* // 70 et] *deest R* // 70 sprevistis] sprevisti *Q* // 70 venit] exivit *B* // 71 fecistis] fecisti *Q* // 72 fecistis] fecisti *Q* // 73 cordis] corde *Z* // 73 procedit] processit *B* // 73 quidquid] quicquid *RSV* // 75

---

[11] *Non inventum.*
[12] *Non inventum.*

[13] "Ex cordis . . . viciosum," *Bernardi Clarev., Apologia ad Guillelmum,* x, § 26, *MPL, 182,* 913; *q.v.*

precesserit primo iussio [Z 334'] cogitacionis.
80 *Hec Augustinus.*[14] [S 34] Si ergo humilitas est in corde certe iubet fieri habitum humilem, econtra si superbia. Sic si castitas fuerit in corde, amat [*sic*] habitum castum, econtra si luxuria. Ita ut vix casti possunt dici qui habitum deferunt im-
85 pudicum. Quid aliud pollicemur et aliud ostendimus? Ligwa personat castitatem et totum corpus prefert impudiciciam. *Ieronymus.*[15]
Quartus impugnans dicit: Tamen Augustinus in libro iii, De doctrina cristiana et ponitur XLI. di.,
90 *Quisquis,*[16] [T 131'] *dicit:* Quisquis rebus transeuntibus striccius utitur quam se habet consuetudo eorum, cum quibus vivit, aut intemperans, aut supersticiosus est. Ergo quilibet in habitu exteriori debet se aliis conformare et non abieccius
95 ceteris vestiri. *Hec ille de novo colore.*
Solucio quarti: Exemplaria habent sic: "aut temperans, aut supersticiosus est." Sic doctores, [P 238'] scilicet sanctus Thomas et alii, allegant. Ex quo patet quod in decreto XLI. di. *Quis-*
100 *quis,*[16a] textus vicio scriptorum sit corruptus; vel Gracianus ibi defecit, sicut in multis aliis locis.
Quintus impugnans: Immo Cristus, cuius omnis accio nostra est instruccio, preciosas et competentes vestes habuit, quia tunica eius inconsutilis
105 erat desuper contexta per totum. *Joh. xix.*[17] Si enim indumenta eius vilia fuissent, tunc milites ea non tam sollicite divisissent, ut quis quid acciperet sortirentur. Igitur et nos debemus eum imitari. *Hec ille de novo colore.*[18]
110 *Solucio quinti:* Superius indumentum Cristi sicut dicitur et legitur, procuravit sibi mater gloriosa eius, que utique preciosum indumentum procurare non potuit. Nam ipsamet urgente paupertate unam tunicam habuit, non ad ornamentum sed ad

do evil deeds, because deeds follow intentions. No one can do anything, or move his limbs to do anything, unless first his mind has ordered it (*Augustine*). Therefore if humility be in the heart, it will certainly order a humble habit; and contrariwise with pride. So, if chastity be in the heart, it will love a chaste habit; and contrariwise with lust. Those, therefore, can hardly be called chaste who wear immodest attire. Why then do we promise one thing and manifest another? The tongue voices chastity and the whole body betrays immodesty. (*Jerome.*)

The fourth assailant says: But Augustine says in the third book of *On Christian Doctrine* (*cited in dist. XLI, c. 1*): "whoever uses transitory objects less freely than is the custom of those among whom he lives is either intemperate or superstitious." Therefore, everyone should conform to others in his external attire and should not dress in a manner more lowly than that of others. (*Thus far the New Color.*)

The solution of the fourth: There are copies [of this text] where it reads "is either temperate or superstitious." The doctors, for instance Saint Thomas and others, cite it so. From this it is evident that in the *Decretum XLI. dist., "Quisquis,"* the text has been corrupted by fault of the scribes; or Gratian made a mistake, as he did in many other places.

The fifth assailant: But Christ, whose every action is our instruction, had valuable and appropriate clothing, for his tunic was without seam, woven from the top throughout (*Joh. xix, 23*). And if his garments were cheap, the soldiers would not have been so solicitous to divide them and cast lots to see what each should receive. Therefore, it is for us to imitate him. (*Thus far the New Color.*)

Solution of the fifth: It is said and written that the outer clothing of Christ was provided for him by his

---

habet] habent Q // 79 iussio] visio B // 79 cogitacionis] cogitacionis et voluntatis Q; cogitacionum Z // 80 Si] Sic Q // 80 humilitas] humilis STV // 81 iubet] ipsa iubet RT // 81 iubet fieri] ipsa membra fiunt Z // 81 fieri] deest K // 81–82 si superbia] si deest Z; si superbia est in corde iubet fieri habitum superbum Q // 82 castitas] castus RT // 82 amat] amavit B; iubet si Q // 84 casti possunt dici] casti dici possunt BQ; casti esse possunt W // 85 ostendimus] ostendamus KW // 88–101 Quartus . . . aliis locis] deest W // 88 Quartus] deest Z // 88 impugnans] repugnans R // 88 in] deest KQTVZ // 90 dicit: Quisquis] deest Z; Quisquis RT; De K; dicit: Quod quisquis V // 92 quibus] quilibet S // 92 intemperans] intemperatus B // 93 exteriori] exterius T // 94–95 et non . . . novo colore] deest S // 95 ceteris] aliis K // 95 vestiri] deest RT // 95 Hec ille de novo colore] deest RZ; Hec ille V; Hec ibi de novo colore T // 96 quarti] deest QR // 96 sic] se K // 99 quod] deest BK // 100 scriptorum] scriptoris Q // 101 ibi] ubi S // 101 sicut] et sicut V // 102 Quintus impugnans] deest W // 102 impugnans] repugnans R // 102 omnis] deest RVW // 103 nostra est] est nostra RTW // 103 instruccio] informacio V // 104 inconsutilis] sic Ceteri; deest P // 106–107 tunc milites ea non tam sollicite divisissent] sic B; milites non tam sollicite eam divisissent KPQRSTV (eam deest RT); non tam sollicite divisissent ea W; milites cur tam sollicite dividissent Z // 108 Igitur] Tunc igitur T; Ergo VW // 109 de novo colore] sic QTVWZ; deest Ceteri // 110 Solucio quinti] deest W; Solucio QR // 110 Superius] deest W // 110 Superius indumentum Cristi sicut] Indumentum Cristi sicut superius Q // 111 dicitur] deest Z // 111 mater gloriosa] gloriosa mater Ceteri // 114 unam] unicam R // 114–115 unam tunicam habuit . . . nuditatis] non ad ornamentum sed ad tegumentum nuditatis unam tunicam habuit K // 114 ornamentum] ornatum

---

[14] *Non inventum.*
[15] Hieronymi, *Epistola* (MPL, 22, 553).
[16] XLI. dist., c. 1 (Friedberg, I, 148); *cf.* Augustini, *De Doctrina Christiana* III, c. xii (MPL, 34, 73).

[17] Joh. xix, 23; *cf. infra*, n. 2a ad Tabulam octavam.
[18] *Cf.* Joh. xix, 23–24.

115 tegumentum nuditatis. *Chrysostomus dicit:* [19] Et qualem tunicam habere potuit carpentarii [V 185] pauperis [Q 91] uxor? Quomodo ergo Cristo [K 117] emere potuit preciosum vestimentum qui ad hoc [B 302'] de celo venerat ut pauper-
120 tatem assumeret et sua assumpcione eam nobis preciosam faceret? *Idem dicit:* [20] Et dividunt vestimenta quod in valde vilibus et abiectis et nichil habentibus fit. Illa ergo divisio non ostendit vestimentorum Cristi preciositatem, sed mili-
125 tum dividencium vilitatem et paupertatem. Erant enim tortores viles et pauperes, qui eciam pauperrimorum [R 260'] indumenta occissorum dividere consueverunt. Et in Palestina pauperes utuntur vestimentis reticulato opere factis ad mo-
130 dum Ciliciorum, sic tunica Cristi erat contexta, *secundum Iohannem Chrysostomum.*[21]

glorious mother, who certainly could not provide valuable clothing. For she herself, under the stress of poverty, had only one tunic, not for adornment but as a covering for nakedness. *Chrysostom says:* And what kind of tunic could the wife of a poor carpenter have? When therefore could she buy valuable clothing for Christ, who came from heaven in order to assume poverty and by assuming it make it precious to us? *The same author says:* And they divide the clothing—this is something that would be done by lowly, mean men, who possessed nothing. That division, therefore, does not show the costliness of Christ's clothing but the meanness and poverty of the soldiers who divided it up. For the executioners were mean and poor; they used to divide up the clothing even of the poorest ones who were executed. And in Palestine the poor use knitted clothing, like that of the Cilicians; and the tunic of Christ was woven thus, according to John Chrysostom.

1 Octava Tabula
Sextus impugnans dicit: Sanctus Bartholomeus vestitur purpura, induitur palio albo quod per singulos angulos singulas gemmas habet pur-
5 pureas; sicut et testatur Berith dyabolus, *in Passionali.*[1]
Solucio Sexti: Ille homicida erat ab inicio et in veritate non stetit, quia non est veritas in eo; quia mendax est et pater eius. *Joh. viii.*[2] Non
10 enim est nobis dictum, omnis accio Bartholomei, sed Cristi nostra est instruccio.[2a]
Septimus impugnans dicit, de novo colore: Sebas-

The Eighth Table

The sixth assailant says: St. Bartholomew is clothed in purple, and wears a white pallium that has purple gems in each corner, as Berith the devil says, in the Life of St. Bartholomew.
The solution of the sixth: He was a murderer from the beginning and abode not in the truth, because there is no truth in him. For he is a liar and the father of the lie (*Joh. viii, 44*). Nor has it been said to us that every action of Bartholomew, but rather of Christ, is our instruction.

RTZ // 115 tegumentum] tegumen *V* // 115 Chrysostomus dicit] Hec Chrysostomus *RT* // 117 Cristo] Cristus *Z* // 120 eam nobis] nobis eam *QV* // 121 dividunt] diviserunt *Q;* dividuntur *R* // 123 fit] fuit *RT;* sicut *Z* // 125 dividencium] dividenciam *S* (*sic pro* diffidenciam) // 126 pauperrimorum] pauperiorum *KRTZ* // 127 indumenta] vestimenta *K* // 128 consueverunt] consueverant *SVZ* // 129 vestimentis] vestibus *R* // 129 reticulato] reticulatis *R* // 130 sic] sicut *KRTZ* // 130 Cristi] deest *S*

Octava Tabula
1 Octava Tabula] deest *BQRSTWZ;* Tabula Nona *V* // 2 Sextus ... dicit] deest *W* // 2 dicit] deest *RTV;* humilia vestimenta seu humilem habitum dicit *Q* // 2 Sanctus] Beatus *K* // 2-3 Bartholomeus vestitur] Bartholomeus ut in Passionali legitur vestitus *R*; Bartholomeus in Passionali vestitur *T* // 3 induitur] indutus *R* // 3 quod] et *Q* // 3 per] deest *S* // 4 angulos] annos *R* // 4 singulas] deest *S* // 4 habet] habebat *W* // 5 sicut] sicut dicit *BQSTVWZ* // 5 et testatur] testatur et dicit *R* // 5 dyabolus] deest *Z* // 7 Solucio] deest *W* // 7 Sexti] deest *QRWZ* // 9 quia] sed *Q* // 9-10 Non enim] Eciam non *Q*; Et non enim *R* // 10 est nobis dictum] dictum est nobis *B*; nobis est dictum *TW* // 11 sed Cristi] deest *B;* deest in loco *QS* // 11 nostra est] est nostra *BRSTW* // 11 instruccio] informacio *V*; *post hoc:* Sed Cristi *QS* // 12-45 Septimus ... Mat. xxiii] deest *W* // 12 dicit, de novo colore] sic

---

[19] *Non inventum.*
[20] *Non inventum.*
[21] *Cf.* Johannis Chrysostomi, *In Joannem Homilia* (MPG, 59, 461).

Octava Tabula
[1] *Acta Sanctorum Bollandiana,* XXXIX, 34 (Acta fabulosa S. Bartholomaei, *c. i,* § 4): "Dixerunt autem cultores ad Berith idolum [*cf.* § 2: . . . daemonium . . . cui nomen erat Berith]: Dic nobis signa Bartholomaei, ut possimus invenire eum. . . . Respondit daemon: Capillo nigro capitis est. . . . Vestitur colobio albo clavato purpura; indutus est pallio albo, habente per singulos angulos gemmas purpureas."

[2] Joh. viii, 44.
[2a] *Versum hexametrum,* "Omnis Cristi accio nostra est instruccio," *laudabant Hussite frequencius; reperitur autem alibi, apud scriptores illius etatis renovacionem evangelicam promoventes—cf.* F. M. Bartoš, "Hus, Lollardism and Devotio moderna in the Fight for a National Bible," Communio viatorum, *III* (1960), 251 f. *Origo versus nescitur; nonnumquam ascribitur Alberto Magno,* Super canone misse, *ut in tractatu M. Jacobelli,* De cerimoniis, *ed.* J. Sedlák, Studie a texty, *II, 151, 158; cf. Von der Hardt, III, 759 f. Sed invenitur eciam apud Wyclif (e.g.,* De civili dominio, *I, 199), et forsan exhinc Hussite eum habebant.*

tianus, vir cristianissimus, militarem clamidem ferebat. *In Passionali.*³

15 *Solucio Septimi:* Sed ad hoc tantum ut cristianorum animas quas in tormentis videbat confortaret. *Ibi.*⁴ Nec in habitu tali Cristum sequebatur per martyrium, sed ipso deposito et fide Cristi ab eo confessa spoliatus **[P 239]** est habitu tali et pro
20 Cristo trucidatus.

Conclusio: Si omnia que de vilitate habitus sanctorum, scilicet Martini, Petri et Pauli, Jacobi et aliorum apostolorum et sanctorum, **[Z 335]** leguntur scriberentur, prolixum opus fieret et adhuc
25 prolixius si omnia eorum dicta que innumera sunt super hoc allegarentur. *Hec Ieronimus.*⁵ Narraverunt michi iniqui fabulaciones, sed non ut lex tua. *Psalmista.*⁶ **[T 132]**

Post hoc ponitur Cristus lavans pedes discipu-
30 *lorum [et] dicit:* Scitis quid fecerim vobis? Vos vocatis me magister **[Q 91′]** et domine et bene dicitis, sum etenim. Si ergo ego lavi pedes vestros, magister et **[S 34′]** dominus, et vos debetis alter alterius lavare pedes. Non est servus maior
35 domino suo; neque apostolus maior est illo qui misit illum. Si hec scitis, beati eritis si feceritis ea. Non de omnibus vobis dico; ego scio quos elegerim. *Joh. xiii.*⁷ Vos autem nolite vocari rabi, unus enim est magister vester Cristus, omnis
40 autem vos fratres estis. Patrem nolite vocare super terram, **[B 303]** unus est enim pater qui in celis est. Qui maior est **[K 117′]** vestrum erit minister vester. Quia omnis qui se exaltat humiliabitur; et qui se humiliaverit exaltabitur. *Mat.*
45 *xxiii.*⁸

Tunc post hoc lavit et ponitur ibi: Ihesus surgit a cena et cepit lavare pedes apostolorum.⁹

The seventh assailant says (the New Color): Sebastian, a most Christian man, wore a soldier's cape. (*In the Life of St. Sebastian.*)

The solution of the seventh: But for this purpose only, that he might comfort those Christian spirits he saw in torment (*ibid*). Nor in such a dress did he follow Christ through martyrdom, but when he laid it aside and confessed the faith of Christ, he was despoiled of such clothing and slain for Christ.

Conclusion: If all that may be read concerning the lowly dress of the saints, namely of Martin, Peter, Paul, James, and the other apostles and saints, were written, an excessively lengthy work would be produced, and it would be still more prolix if all of their sayings, which on this subject are innumerable, were to be cited (*Jerome*). The wicked have told me fables, but not as your law (*Psa. cxviii, 85*).

After this there is a picture of Christ washing the feet of the disciples, and saying: Know you what I have done to you? You call me master and lord and you say well, for so I am. If I then, your lord and master, have washed your feet, you also ought to wash one another's feet. The servant is not greater than his lord; neither is he that is sent greater than he that sent him. If you know these things, happy are you, if you do them. I speak not of you all; I know whom I have chosen (*Joh. xiii, 12–18*). But be not you called Rabbi, for one is your master, even Christ; all you are brethren. Call no man your father upon the earth, for one is your father who is in heaven. He that is greatest among you shall be your servant. And whosoever shall exalt himself shall be abased; and he that shall humble himself shall be exalted (*Mat. xxiii, 8–9, 11–12*).

Then after this he washes [the feet], and this text is

B, SZ (*deest* dicit); humilem habitum dicit *Q*; *deest Ceteri* // 14 ferebat] gerebat *Z* // 15 Septimi] *deest QR*; Septimi est *S* // 15 Sed] hic *S* // 16 videbat] deficere videbat *R* // 18 et] in *R* // 19 confessa] confessor *R* // 19 habitu tali es] *deest R* // 19 et] *deest T* // 20 trucidatus] trucidatus. Ibidem *QV*; cruciatus *S* // 21–28 Conclusio . . . Psalmista] *deest V* // 22 Petri et] et *deest BKQST* // 23 apostolorum et] et *deest K* // 23 et sanctorum, leguntur] *deest Q* // 23 leguntur] legerentur et *S* // 24 scriberentur] *deest R* // 24 adhuc] ad hoc *S* // 25 innumera] inventa *B* // 27 michi] *deest K* // 29–30 Post hoc . . . dicit] sic *Z*; *deest K*; Curia Cristi *BPQV*; Hic arguunt papam quod pedes sibi osculari permittit. Et Cristus lavat pedes discipulorum *R*; Cristus lavit pedes discipulorum et dixit *S*; Hic dicit papam anticristum per hoc quod in persona vicariatus Cristi pedes sibi osculari permittit. Et Cristus lavat pedes discipulorum *T* // 30 vobis] *deest K* // 30–63 Scitis quid . . . manus rodens] Ordo alius in *RT*: Nota . . . Curia vult marcas . . . manus rodens; servus . . . pedum; Ihesus . . . discipulorum; Scitis . . . Mat. vi // 32 ego] *deest B* // 35 maior est] maior *B*; est maior *SZ* // 35 illo] *deest ST*; eo *BRZ* // 36 hec] hoc *RT* // 36 beati] bene *Q* // 36 feceritis] hoc feceritis *R*; facitis *S* // 37 ea] *deest RT* // 37 vobis] hoc *Z* // 39 enim est] est enim *QRSTV* // 40 estis] estis et *KRT* // 40 nolite vocare] nolite vobis vocare *QRSTZ*, *V* (vocari) // 41 super terram] vobis *B* // 41 pater] pater vester *BKRT* // 41–42 qui in celis est] qui est in celis *RT* // 42–43 Qui maior . . . vester] *deest V* // 43 omnis] *deest V* // 43 exaltat humiliabitur] humiliat exaltabitur *B* // 44 humiliaverit exaltabitur] exaltat humiliabitur *B*; humiliat exaltabitur *KRVZ* // 46 Tunc post hoc . . . ibi] sic *Z*; *deest Ceteri* // 46–63 Tunc . . . manus rodens] ordo alius in *Z*: Post hoc ponitur papa . . . rodens manus; Tunc post hoc lavit . . . petitur // 46–47 Ihesus . . . apostolorum] *deest V* // 47 apostolorum] discipulorum *BKRTWZO*, *Q* (dis-

---

³ *AA. SS. Boll., II, 629* (Acta S. Sebastiani, c. i, § 2): ". . . ad hoc tantum sub chlamyde terreni imperii Christi militem agebat absconditum, ut Christianorum animos, quos inter tormenta videbat deficere, confortaret. . . ."

⁴ *Loc. cit.*

⁵ *Non inventum.*

⁶ Psa. cxviii, 85.

⁷ Joh. xiii, 12–18.

⁸ Mat. xxiii, 8–9, 11–12.

⁹ *Cf.* Joh. xiii, 4–5; "surgit a coena, et ponit vestimenta sua, et cum accepisset . . . et coepit lavare pedes discipulorum . . ."

In opposito osculantur pedes pape et ponitur ibi:
Servus servorum dei ad oscula pedum beatorum.
50 *Respondet papa:* Fiat ut petitur.
Post hoc ponitur papa, et ponitur modus curie:
Curia vult marcas, bursas exhaurit et archas.
[V 185']
Si burse parcas, fuge papas et patriarchas.
55 Si dederis marcas, et eis impleveris archas,
Culpa solveris quacumque ligatus eris.
Item, Modus curie:
Intus quis! Tu quis? Ego sum. Quid queris?
Ut intrem. Fers aliquid? Non. Sta foris!
60 Fero. Quid? Satis. Intra!
Johannes Monachi dicit: Quod Roma fundata a predonibus adhuc de primordiis retinet, dicta "Roma" quasi manus rodens. *Versus:* Roma manus rodit, quem rodere non valet odit; dantes
65 exaudit non dantibus hostia claudit. Curia curarum genetrix nutrixque malorum. Ignotos notis inhonestos equat honestis.

Concordant: Johannes Andree, *in Novella, De statu regularium, c. unico, Libro sexto.*[10] Et de
70 malicia romanorum, Johannes Monachi, *in c. Fundamenta, De eleccione, Libro sexto, in Novella*[11] remittit ad primum capitulum Romanorum, ubi Paulus scribit specialiter de vicio contra naturam.[12] Et concordat Bernhardus, *in epistola ubi*
75 *scribit ad Eugenium Papam.*[13]

written there: Jesus rose from the table and began to wash the feet of the apostles (*Joh. xiii, 4–5*).

Opposite this the Pope's feet are being kissed and this title is written there: The Servant of the Servants of God, receiving kisses of his blessed feet. *The Pope responds:* Let it be done as it is asked. *After this there is a picture of the Pope and the system of his Curia is placed there, so:*

Money is what the Curia likes best,
It empties many a purse and chest.
If you are stingy with your marks,
Stay away from popes and patriarchs.
But give them marks, and once their chests are filled
You will be absolved from the bondage of all your guilt.

Again the system of the Curia:
Someone wishes to enter. Who are you? Me. What do you want? To enter. Do you bring anything? No. Stay out! I do bring something. What? Enough. Enter!

John the Monk says that Rome, founded by robbers, still preserves the traces of her origin, for she is called "Roma," as though to say "gnawing hands" (*manus rodens*). Truly, Rome gnaws hands, and whom she cannot gnaw she hates. She listens to those who give and closes her gates to those who do not give. The Curia is the mother of cares and the nurse of evils. She equates the ignoble to the noble, the base to the worthy.

For concordant authorities see: John Andree *in the Novella, on Liber Sextus,* III, xvi. And concerning the maliciousness of the Romans: John the Monk *in his gloss on Liber Sextus,* I, vi, 17, *in the Novella* refers to *Rom. i, 26–27,* where Paul writes especially on unnatural vice. And also Bernard, in a letter written to Pope Eugene.

---

cipulorum suorum); apostolorum. Sequitur alia tabula *S* // 48 In opposito ... ibi] *sic Z;* Papa *Q; deest Ceteri* // 49–50 Servus ... petitur] *deest in loco V (inclusum est ad finem Tabule Octave cum adumbracione intitulata:* Sedes) // 49 dei] *deest RT* // 49 beatorum] *deest RT* // 50 Respondet papa] *deest V;* papa *Q;* Et ipse respondet *Z* // 50 Respondet ... petitur] *deest RT* // 50–75 Respondet papa ... Eugenium Papam] *deest W* // 51 Post hoc ... modus curie] *sic Z;* Modus curie *B;* Modus Curie (*hec in margine*): Roma manus rodit, quos non potest rodere odit *K;* Modus Curie Seu Curia Pape *P;* Curia pape. Modus curie, versus *Q;* Nota (*T:* Nota bene), modus curie Romane *RT;* Modus Curie *S;* Modus Curie Romane *V* // 38 *sqq.* Curia vult ...] *Iuxta hec in margine:* Item: Lis est romanis de causis quottidianis. Si sonat ante fores, bona vita, sciencia, mores, non exauditur si nummus non repperitur. Audito nummo quasi viso principe summo. Exibunt valve non auditur nisi salve. Nummus procedit loquitur pater audit obedit. Singula concedit sine testibus omnia credit. *Q* // 52 bursas] *deest S* // fuge] fugias *B* // 56 eris] (fueris) *B* // 57 Item, Modus Curie] *sic Z; deest Ceteri* // 58 tu quis] *deest RT* // 59 foris] satis *R* // 60 satis] stas *RT* // 61 quod] *deest K* // 61 Roma] Roma quasi *K* // 61–62 fundata a predonibus] fundata est a predonibus et *RT* // 62 retinet] retinet nomine *V* // 63 manus rodens] rodens manus *RZ* // 63–75 Versus: Roma ... Eugenium Papam] *deest RSTZ* // 63 Versus] *deest BQZ;* unde *V* // 63 Roma] Romana *Z* // 67 inhonestos] inhonestis *BQV* // 67 honestis] *sic K;* honestos *Ceteri* // 68–73 Concordant ... naturam] Et de malicia romanorum Johannes Andree in omelia de statu regularium, c. unico, Libro sexto. *Q* // 70 Johannes] Johannes in omelia *B* // 70 Monachi] *deest B;* Monachus *V* // 73 scribit specialiter] specialiter scribit *KV* // 74–75 Et concordat ... Papam] *deest V* // 74–75 ubi scribit] *deest B*

---

[10] *Novella non ad manum; Liber Sextus,* III, xvi (Friedberg, II, 1053–54.).

[11] *Novella non ad manum; Liber Sextus,* I, vi, 17 (Friedberg, II, 957–59).

[12] Rom. i, 26–27.

[13] *De consideracione, Passim.*

Post hoc ponitur Anticristus cum meretricibus.

1 [Tabula Nona] **[W 66']**
Primus: O pastor et ydolum derelinquens gregem.
Zac. xi.[1]
Secundus: Nichil est ydolum in mundo. *I Cor.*
5 *viii.*[2] Quod autem nichil est, nullam **[Q 92]** inmundiciam **[P 239']** aut consecracionem facere potest. *Lira ibidem.*[2a]
Tercius: Et faciet iuxta voluntatem suam rex, terram dividet gratuite. *Dan. xi.*[3]
10 Quartus: Et erit in concupiscenciis feminarum. *Ibidem.*[3a] Tu ergo ille es de quo locutus sum in diebus antiquis. *Eze. xxxviii.*[4]
Quintus: Regnum anticristi pertinet quodammodo ad regnum romanum, de quo orietur. *Lira, Dan.*
15 *viii.*[5] **[R 261]**
Sextus: Non est potestas super terram que compararetur ei, nec quis dicere potest, cur ita facis? Quis arguet coram eo viam eius? *Iob, ix, xii, xli; Gregorius de anticristo.*[6]
20 Septimus: Erit tunc tribulacio magna qualis non fuit ab inicio mundi usque modo, neque fiet. *Mat. xxiiii.*[7]
Octavus: Et ruent in gladio et flamma et in captivitate [et in] rapina dierum. *Dan. xi.*[8]
25 **[B 303']**
Nonus: Et datum est illi facere bellum sanctis et vincere **[T 132']** illos. Et faciet ut quicumque ymaginem bestie, id est anticristum, hominem bestialem, non adoraverit, id est ei obedierit, occi-
30 detur. Et ne quis possit emere, id est **[K 118]**

(The Ninth Table)

(*After this there is a picture of the Antichrist, with whores. What is said of the Antichrist applies to the Pope.*)

1. Oh idol shepherd that leaveth the flock! (*Zech. xi, 17*).
2. An idol is nothing in the world (*I Cor. viii, 4*). And what is nothing cannot confer either impurity or consecration (*Lira*).
3. And the king shall do according to his will and shall divide the land for gain (*Dan. xi, 36, 39*).
4. And he shall be greedy for the enjoyment of women (*Dan. xi, 37*). You then are he of whom I have spoken in old time (*Eze. xxxviii, 17*).
5. The Kingdom of Antichrist refers in a certain sense to the Roman kingdom, from which he will arise (*Lira, on Dan. viii*).
6. There is no power on earth that is his like, nor anyone who can say to him, Why do you thus? Who shall expose his way to his face? (*Job xli, 24; ix, 12; xxi, 31. And cf. Gregory, on the Antichrist: Moralia, XXXII*).
7. Then shall be great tribulation, such as was not since the beginning of the world to this time, no, nor ever shall be (*Mat. xxiv, 21*).
8. They shall fall by the sword and by flame, by captivity and by spoil, many days (*Dan. xi, 33*).
9. And it was given unto him to make war with the saints, and to overcome them. And he shall cause whoever does not adore—that is, obey—the image of the beast—that is, Antichrist, the Beast-Man—to be killed. And he shall not allow any man to buy—that is, bring

---

Tabula Nona

Post ... meretricibus] *sic Z; deest Ceteri* // 1 [Tabula Nona]] *deest in codicibus; tituli varii habentur:* Videamus ergo utrum (?) dicta sanctorum loquentes (*sic!*) de anticristo conveniunt romano pontifici *Q*; Hic multa dicta de anticristo exponit de papa *R*; Sequitur tabula ultima (*in margine:* Tabula Decima, de anticristo) *S*; Hic multa que de anticristo dicta sunt exponit mendaciter de papa *T* // 2 ydolum] ydolo *Z* // 4 est] *deest R* // 5 inmundiciam] mundiciam *RW, S (forsan)* // 6 consecracionem] construccionem *S* // 6 facere] dare *QVW* // 6-7 facere potest] potest dare *RSTZO* // 7 Lira ibidem] *sic Ceteri; deest P* // 8 Et] *deest W* // 8 faciet] fecit *RT* // 8 iuxta] secundum *Z* // 9 dividet] diriget *V* // 9 gratuite] gratuito *STZO* // 10 erit] *deest Z* // 12 Eze. xxxviii] Eze. xxxviii. Et elevabitur et magnificabitur adversum vestrum deum et adversum deum deorum, et cetera *W* // 13 anticristi] autem Cristi *B* // 14 ad regnum] ad regem *Z* // 14 romanum] *sic BKQSTZO*; romani *P*; romanorum *RVW* // 16 que] *deest Q* // 16 compararetur] comparetur *KRSTWO*; comparetur *in* comparetur *correctum Q* // 18 arguet] arguit *Q* // 19 de anticristo] loquens de anticristo ibidem super Iob *Q*; de anticristo, xiiii Moralium *Z* // 20 Erit tunc] Et tunc erit *W* // 20-21 qualis ... fiet] *deest W* // 21 usque ... fiet] *deest V* // 21 fiet] fuit *Z* // 23-24 Octavus ... Dan. xi] *deest W* // 23 Et ruent] *ante hoc in Z habetur iterum paragrafus sextus:* Non est ... Iob ix. // 23 et flamma] et in flamma *BVO;* flamma *R* // 24 [et in]] *sic O;* in *B; deest Ceteri* // 24 rapina] ruina *R* // 26 illi] ei *W* // 27-28 faciet ... bestie] faciet ymaginem bestie, ut quicumque ymaginem bestie *W* // 27 ut] *sic Ceteri; deest KP* // 28 bestie] *deest B* // 28 id est] et *Z* // 28-29 anticristum, hominem bestialem] hominem bestialem, anticristum *RT* // 28 hominem] *deest W* // 29 id est] et *Z* // 29 obedierit] non obedierit *R;* obediet *W* // 30 possit] posset *W* // 30 id est] *deest W*

Nona Tabula

[1] Zac. xi, 17.
[2] I Cor. viii, 4.
[2a] *Est in loco, plenius;* Quod autem nihil est, nullam immundiciam aut consecracionem potest dare rei immolate.
[3] Dan. xi, 36, 39; *citacio composita.*
[3a] Dan. xi, 37.
[4] Eze. xxxviii, 17.
[5] Lyra *super* Dan. viii, 25, *in verba,* "et sine manu conteretur."
[6] Job xli, 24; ix, 12; xxi, 31; *citacio composita. Hic nichil, ut videtur e Gregorio sumptum est; cf. eius Moralia in Job, lib. XXXIV (super Job xli, 13-25), MPL, 76, 717 sqq., ubi lacius tractatur de anticristo.*
[7] Mat. xxiv, 21.
[8] Dan. xi, 33.

bonam vitam reportare vel servos dei acquirere vel veritatem studere, aut vendere, id est docere vel predicare, nisi qui habeat caracterem, id est vite et doctrine conformitatem, scilicet anticristi.
35 *Apo. xiii, et super hoc Gorram.*[9]
Decimus: Illa temptacio non per partes sed totum mundum examinabit.[10] Fideles vero illo tempore non predicabunt, **[V 186]** quia tamquam excommunicati habebuntur tunc boni. *Thomas in Com-*
40 *pendio, et Haymo super Apokalypsim.*[10a]
Undecimus: Et pedes eius sicut pedes ursi. **[Z 335']** *Apo. xiii.*[11] Pedes anticristi sunt predicatores per mundum ipsum ferentes; et sicut ursus est animal inmundum, conculcans pedibus et de-
45 vorans, amans mel et dulcia, sic illi erunt inmundi, per luxuriam, conculcabunt qui nolunt eis acquiescere, et dulcia, scilicet temporalia, amant. *Hec glosa.*[11a]
Duodecimus: Anticristus **[Q 92']** nascetur in
50 Babilone. Babilon est Roma. *Lira, I Pet. ultimo; et Mic. iiii, super verbo, "in Babilone."*[12]
Tredecimus: Impie agent impii, neque intelligent omnes impii; porro docti intelligent, id est devoti, exercentes se in scripturis. *Dan. xii.*[13]
55 Decimus Quartus: Sic patet quod intellectus huius prophecie non est interclusus bonis et devotis, sed tantum malivolis et impiis. **[S 35]** *Lira ibidem.*[14]

in a good life, or win servants for God, or seek after truth—or sell—that is, teach or preach—except him who has the mark of Antichrist—that is, who conforms to him in life and doctrine (*Apo. xiii, 7, 15, 17; and glosses*).

10. That trial will not be confined to certain regions but will examine the whole world (*Cf. Thomas Aquinas, Compendium Theologiae, I, ccxliii, sq.*). But in that time the faithful will not preach, for the good will be regarded as the excommunicate (*Cf. Haimo of Halberstadt, Enarratio in Apocalypsin, Bk. iv (on Apo. xiii, 17)*).

11. And his feet were as the feet of a bear (*Apo. xiii, 2*). The feet of the Antichrist are the preachers who carry him through the world; and just as the bear is a foul animal, who tramples with his feet and devours, who loves honey and sweet things, so they are foul, in their carnal lust, and they will trample those who refuse to consent to them, and they love sweet things—that is, temporal goods (*Gloss*).

12. The Antichrist will be born in Babylon. Babylon is Rome (*Lira, on I Pet. v, 13, and Mic. iv, 10, on the words, "in Babylon"*).

13. The wicked shall do wickedly, and none of the wicked shall understand; but the wise shall understand—that is, the devout, who are diligent in the study of Scripture (*Dan. xii, 10, and gloss*).

[*RT add:* But if our gospel be hid, it is hid to them

// 31 bonam vitam] *sic Ceteri*; vitam bonam *P* // 32 vel veritatem] et veritatem *K* // 32–33 docere vel] docere et *RW* // 33 habeat] habet *QVW* // 34 scilicet] *deest R;* id est *T* // 35 et super hoc Gorram] *sic W; deest Ceteri* // 36 Decimus] Decimus est *R* // 36 temptacio] temptaciones *R* // 36 totum] per totum *BQSW* // 37 examinabit] examinabit (?) *B;* inquit examinabit *S* // 38 quia] sed *V* // 42 predicatores] eius predicatores *W* // 44 et devorans] et *deest R* // 45 amans] animas *W* // 45 erunt] erant *Z* // 45 inmundi] in mundo *W* // 46 conculcabunt] *sic SV;* conculcabuntur *BKPZ;* et conculcabunt eos *Q;* et conculcabunt *R;* conculcabuntur et *T;* conculcabunt eos *W* // 46 nolunt] noluerint *BK* // 46 nolunt eis acquiescere] eis acquiescere nolunt *Q;* eis nolunt acquiescere *V* // 47 scilicet] id est *BR* // 47 temporalia] temporalia et carnalia *QZ* // 47 amant] ament *K;* amant et carnalia *V* // 48 Hec glosa] *sic RT; deest Ceteri* // 49 nascetur] nasceretur *B* // 51 et Mic. ... "in Babilone"] *deest RT* // 51 "in Babilone"] "erit in Babilone" *W* // 53 porro] pueri *Z* // 54 exercentes] exercitantes *RT* // 54 scripturis] scripturis sacris *Q* //54 Dan. xii] *post hoc habetur in RT:* Et II Cor. iv (*R:* xiiii): Quod si eciam apertum (*recte:* opertum) est ewangelium nostrum (*R:* nostrum *deest*) in hiis que per tunc (*recte:* pereunt); est apertum (*recte:* opertum), ut non fulgeat illuminacio ewangelii glorie Cristi qui est ymago invisibilis dei (*citacio confecta et corrupta; cf.* II Cor. iv, 3–4) // 55–57 Decimus Quartus . . . ibidem] *deest W* // 55 sic] sicut *K* // 55 quod] *deest Z* // 56 prophecie] tabule *B* // 56 non est] *deest Q* // 57 tantum]

---

[9] Apo. xiii, 7, 15, 17; *citacio composita; glose non sunt invente, forsan sunt de Gorran sumpte, ut habetur in W—non sunt, utique, de Lyra, cuius glose hic sunt litterales seu historice. Nota autem quod textus Vulgate apud Lyram citatus conformet aliquantum cum nostro: "faciet" et "adoraverit" loco "faciat" et "adoraverint," ut habetur in Vulgata modernis temporibus edita; nostrum "occidetur" tamen est "occidatur" in textu Lyrano, "occidantur" in moderno.*

[10] *Non inveni hec verba in Compendio Thome, nec potest eciam dici quod concordant in sensu, quia Thomas de iudicio ultimo, non de temptacione ab anticristo perficienda, loquitur; cf. Sancti Thome Aquinatis, Compendium theologie ad fratrem Reginaldum, I, ccxliii sq., Opera omni, XVI (Parmae, 1865).*

[10a] *Cf. Haymonis Halberstatensis, Enarrationem in Apocalypsin, lib. iv, super xiii, 17 (MPL. 117, 1102):* Tempore . . . Antichristi nemo . . . bonorum praedictatorum . . . poterit praedicare libere Christum, quia carceribus recludentur, et insuper interficientur. . . . *Hoc Nicolaus noster suo modo interpretatus est.*

[11] Apo. xiii, 2.

[11a] *Glosa non inventa; non est de Lyra.*

[12] Lyra *super* I Pet. v, 13: "'. . . ecclesia, quae est in Babylone . . .' Id est in Roma, quam figuraliter Babylonem vocavit, secundum quod dicit Hieronymus in libro illustrium virorum, quia sicut Babylon fuit civitas maxima idolatrie dedita, sicut patet in Daniele, sic Roma fuit postea ex simili opere, unde dicit Leo Papa, in sermone de sanctis Apostolis Petro et Paulo, de civitate romana, quod magnam credebant fecisse religionem si nullius respueret falsitatem, id est idolatriam." Mic. iv, 11: "et nunc congregatae sunt super": Lyra: "que est in Babilone collecta, id est Roma."

[13] Dan. xii, 10; Lyra, *glosa super* "porro docti intelligent."

[14] *Glosa eadem.*

Quindecimus: [P 240] Beatus qui vigilat et custodit vestimenta sua, ne nudus ambulet et videant turpitudinem eius. *Apo. xvi.*[15]

Sedecimus: Sedet in insidiis cum divitibus, in occultis ut interficiat innocentem. Insidiatur quasi leo in spelunca sua, rapere pauperem dum attrahit eum. *Ps. ix.*[16]

Decimus Septimus: Ita ut in templo dei sedeat, ostendens se tamquam sit deus. Cuius adventus in omni seduccione iniquitatis in hiis qui pereunt; eo quod caritatem veritatis non receperunt. *II Thes. ii.*[17] Reges humiliabit et putabit quod possit mutare leges et tempora. [B 304] *Dan. vii.*[18]

Decimus Octavus: Et tunc revelabitur ille iniquus quem dominus Ihesus interficiet spiritu oris sui. *II Thes. ii.*[19] Aggrediamur adversarium non fuste, non saxo, sed manswetudine et bonis operibus. Hec sunt arma fidei nostre. Precepta Cristi arma sunt cristiani. *Ambrosius, in libro de officiis.*[20]

Finis est novi et antiqui coloris.

that are lost, that the light of the glorious gospel of Christ, who is the image of the invisible God, not shine unto them (*II Cor. iv, 3–4*).]

14. Thus it is clear that the understanding of this prophecy is not hidden from the good and the devout, but only from the evil and impious (*Lira, on Dan. xii, 10*).

15. Blessed is he that watches and keeps his garments, lest he walk naked and they see his shame (*Apo. xvi, 15*).

16. He sits in ambush with the rich, in the hidden places, that he may murder the innocent. He lies in wait as a lion in his den, luring the poor man and seizing him (*Ps. x, 8*).

17. So that he sits in the temple of God, showing himself as God. Whose coming is with all the seduction of unrighteousness in them that perish; because they have not received the love of truth (*II Thes. ii, 4, 9–10*). He shall humble kings and think that he can change laws and times (*Dan. vii, 24–25*).

18. And then shall that wicked one be revealed whom the Lord Jesus shall consume with the spirit of his mouth (*II Thes. ii, 8*). Let us attack the enemy not with club, not with rocks, but with mildness and good works. These are the arms of our faith; the precepts of Christ are the arms of the Christian (*Ambrose, De officiis [?]*).

[RT add: For the mountains shall be thrown down—that is, many of the priests, prelates, and princes—and the fences shall fall—that is, the regulars and the doctors shall fall away from the faith of Christ, in the time of the Antichrist (*Lira, on Eze. xxxviii, 20, with Gloss*). Therefore the Antichrist shall not be revealed by such doctors, but by those who walk in sackcloth (*cf. Apo. xi, 3*).]

---

bene *RT* // 58 Beatus] Talis *R* // 58 custodit] custodiat *Q* // 59 et] ne *W* // 59 videant] videat *KZ*; videatur *RT* // 60 turpitudinem] turpitudo *RT* // 62 innocentem] innocentes *K* // 64 Ps. ix] *post hoc:* Confitebor tibi Domine *W* // 65–69 Decimus Septimus . . . II Thes. ii] *deest W* // 66 se] *deest S* // 66 sit] ipse sit *K* // 67 in hiis] in *deest Ceteri, O* // 69 Reges] *ante hoc:* Decimus Octavus *Q* // 70 leges et tempora] tempora et leges *BWO* // 72 Decimus Octavus] *deest in loco Q* // 72–74 Decimus Octavus . . . II Thes. ii] *deest W* // 72 iniquus] impius *Z* // 73 Ihesus] deus *V* // 74 adversarium] adversarium nostrum *Q*; ad sacrum nostrum *W* // 77 cristiani] cristiana *Z* // 77 Ambrosius] Hec Ieronimus et Ambrosius *R, T* (et *deest*) // 77–78 Ambrosius . . . officiis] *deest B* // 78 *in RT paragrafus decimus octavus sic productus est:* Quia subvertentur montes, id est multi de sacerdotibus, prelatis et principibus, et cadent sepes, id est religiosi, doctores, a fide Cristi, id est (id est *deest T*) tempore anticristi. Hec Lira, Eze. xxxviii, cum glosa. Ergo per tales doctores non revelatur anticristus sed per ambulantes in saccis. *Apo. xi* (*R:* ultimo) // 79 Finis . . . coloris] *deest QW*; Finitus est novus color et antiquus. Anno

---

[15] Apo. xvi, 15. *Ad quid pertinet nescio, nisi ad paragrafum sequentem, et hoc moraliter; cf. glosas Lyre:* "Beatus qui vigilat," attendendo divinam iusticiam. "Et custodit vestimenta sua," scil. virtutum," ne nudus ambulet," nam ipsis spoliatur per mortale peccatum. "Et videant turpitudinem eius," scil. deus et angeli eius.

[16] Psa. (x), 8.

[17] II Thes. ii, 4, 9–10.

[18] Dan. vii, 24–25.

[19] II Thes. ii, 8.

[20] *Non inveni in opere Ambrosii de officiis, sed alique verba similia habentur in Homilia XCII. S. Maximi Taurinensis (fl. prim. dimid. sec. V.), que homilia nonnullis in codicibus ascribitur Ambrosio (MPL, 57, 465):* Praecepta enim Christi arma sunt Christianis. . . . Arma autem haec nostra sunt quibus nos Salvator instruxit . . . adversarii meritis magis quam virtute vincuntur. . . . *Cf. autem dicta Ambrosii in Decreto, XXIII. q. viii, cc. 3, 21.*

The end of the new and the old color. [*S adds:* In this table and in all the others, the new color signifies the Jurists, who are better called pseudoprophets, and the old color signifies the humble imitators of Jesus Christ and his law.]

---

domini MCCCCXIIII, Dominico die post festum Sancti Bartholomei Apostoli, etc. *B* (*hoc omne post "Finitus," due quippe linee integre, deletum est*); Finitus est novus color et antiquus, sub anno domini MCCCCXIIII, Sabbato ante Esto michi, etc. *K;* Finitur blasphemia contra ecclesiam. Ista scripta, ad hunc sensum hereticum collecta, sunt redacta in hanc formam per Draznenses, qui de Drazna expulsi plurimos seduxerunt, qui eciam nec de purgatoria quod est, nec de suffragiis sanctorum, tenuerunt, oppositum docendo *R;* Et sic est finis supradictorum. In hac igitur tabula et aliis omnibus per novum colorem intelliguntur Iuriste qui dicuntur pocius pseudoprophete, per antiquum vero humiles Ihesu Cristi imitatores et sua lex, etc. *S;* Explicit blassphemia hussitarum contra ecclesiam romanam *T;* Explicit novus et antiquus color *V;* Amen si sunt omnia vera quod etc. *Z // in W habetur hec materia, forsan superaddita:* Si quis aliquando videt clericum cito penitenciam agentem et si deprehensus humiliaverit se, non ideo dolet quia peccavit sed confunditur quia perdit gloriam suam. *Hec Crisostomus, de pen. di. i, Quis aliquando (?).* (*Hoc habetur in Quinta tabula, ceteris in codicibus.*) Et disperdet dominus ab Israhel caput et caudam incurvantem et refrenantem die una. Longewus et honorabilis ipse caput, et propheta docens mendacium ipse est cauda. Et erunt qui beatificant populum istum seducentes, et qui beatificantur precipitati. *Isa. ix (14–16).* Robur autem datum est ei contra iuge sacrificium propter peccata, et prosternetur veritas in terra. Et prosperabitur et faciet et interficiet robustos et populum sanctum secundum voluntatem suam, et dirigetur dolus in manu sua, et cor suum magnificabit, et copia rerum omnium occidet plurimos, et contra principem principum consurget et sine manu conteretur. *Dan. viii (12, 24–25).*

CONSUETUDO ET RITUS PRIMITIVE ECCLESIE ET MODERNE

The text is transcribed from the single known manuscript copy, in MS. Prague, University and National Library, IV G 15, f. 240–249. It follows immediately after the *Tabule* in this codex (for which see the description of MS. *P*, above), is written in the same hand, and has the *explicit*, "Amen. Anno domini 1417." The date of composition was probably soon after that of the *Tabule*. The two works are similar in style, include some of the same material, and the *Consuetudo et ritus* seems clearly to be a sequel to the *Tabule*. The copy does not identify the author, but all the just-noted factors point to Nicholas of Dresden. There are a few marginal notes, in a contemporary hand; they are included as footnotes, with asterisks.

For this edition, the text has been corrected when necessary by comparison with the originals of its quotations; such corrections are noted in brackets. The ordinals "primus" etc. of the manuscript text have been replaced as paragraph numbers by numerals.

[f. 240]

Consuetudo et ritus primitive ecclesie et moderne, seu derivative.

[I]

1. Et cum complerentur dies penthecostis erant omnes discipuli pariter in eodem loco. Factus est repente de celo sonus advenientis tamquam spiritus vehementis et replevit totam domum ubi erant sedentes. Seditque supra singulos eorum et repleti sunt omnes spiritu sancto. *Act. ii.*[1]

2. Tempore apostolorum in primitiva ecclesia spiritus sanctus visibiliter operabatur; ideo tantum imponebant manus supra ordinandos et oracionem infundebant, et sic sufficiebat quod ordinator diceret ordinando: Sis presbiter, vel dyaconus, vel similia verba. Sic Cristus in confirmacione nulla fuit usus materia, nec apostoli, sed sola manus imposicione, nec aliqua forma. Nam manifesta spiritus sancti apparencia, que tunc temporis visibiliter operabatur, erat ipsis pro materia et forma; et apparicio spiritus sancti, que tempore primitive ecclesie duravit, postmodo fide debilitante defecit. Quare opus fuit quod aliqui rectores ecclesiarum certam materiam et formam invenirent. *Hec Innocens papa et Guilelmus doctor iuris.*[2]

3. Cottidie perdurantes unanimiter in templo et frangentes circa domos panem sumebant cibum cum exultacione. *Act. ii.*[3]

4. Innocencius constituit pacis osculum dari [f. 240'] loco communionis circa annos domini ccc. vii., *ut patet in Cronicis, Flores Temporum.*[4]

5. Multitudinis credencium erat cor unum et anima una; erant illis omnia comunia. *Act. iiii.*[5]

6. Iure nature omnia sunt communia omnibus, quod non solum inter eos servatum, de quibus legitur: Multitudinis credencium erat cor unum etc.; verum eciam ex precedenti tempore a philozophis traditum invenitur.

THE CUSTOMS AND RITES
OF THE
PRIMITIVE AND MODERN CHURCHES

1. And when the days of the Pentecost were accomplished, all the disciples were all together in one place. And suddenly there came a sound from heaven, as of a mighty spirit coming, and it filled the whole house where they were sitting, and it sat upon every one of them. And they were all filled with the Holy Spirit. (*Acts ii, 1–4*.)

2. During the lifetime of the apostles, in the Primitive Church, the Holy Spirit worked visibly. Therefore [in ordinations] they merely placed their hands upon the ones to be ordained and poured forth [only] a prayer; and it was enough that the ordainer would say to the one to be ordained: "Be a priest," or "deacon," or some similar words. Thus, Christ did not use any substance or special form in confirmation, nor did the apostles, but only the laying-on of hands. For the evident presence of the Holy Spirit, which at that time was working visibly, was both substance and form for them. But this presence of the Holy Spirit, which persisted throughout the time of the Primitive Church, afterwards ceased, with the weakening of faith. Whence it was necessary for certain rectors of churches to contrive some particular substance and form. (*Cf. Pope Innocent and William, Doctor of Law.*)

3. And continuing daily with one accord in the temple and breaking bread from house to house, they took their food with gladness (*Acts ii, 46*).

4. (Pope) Innocent around the year of our Lord 307, introduced the kiss of peace in place of communion (*see the chronicle, "Flores temporum"*).

5. The multitude of believers had but one heart and one soul; all things were common to them (*Acts iv, 32*).

---

[1] Act. ii, 1–4.
[2] *Sentencia Innocencii de ritu ordinacionis laudata est ab Johanne Andree,* Novella in quinque decretalium libros (*Venetiis, 1581; reimp. 1963*) **1**: p. 173 (ad I, xvi, 3).
[3] Act. ii, 46.
[4] *Edicio huius chronici materiam laudatam continens non est ad manum.*
[5] Act. iv, 32.

Unde apud Platonem illa civitas iustissime ordinata traditur, in qua quisque proprios nescit affectus.[6] Nam iure divino, domini est terra et plenitudo eius; pauperes et divites dominus de uno limo fecit, et pauperes et divites una terra supportat. Iure ergo humano dicitur: Hec villa mea est, hec domus mea est, hic servus meus est. Tolle iura imperatoris et quis audet dicere: Hec villa mea est, meus est iste servus, mea est hec domus? Per iura regum possidentur possessiones; dixisti: Quid michi et regi? Noli dicere possessiones tuas, quia ipsa iura renuncciasti humana, quibus possidentur possessiones.[7] *Hec VIII. di., I. pars, et c. Quo iure.*

7. Dilectissimis fratribus et condiscipulis Ierosolimis, cum karissimo fratre Iacobo et coepiscopo: Clemens episcopus. Communis vita omnibus est necessaria, fratres, et maxime hiis, qui deo irreprehensibiliter militare cupiunt et vitam apostolorum eorumque discipulorum imitari volunt. Communis enim usus omnium, que sunt in hoc mundo, omnibus esse hominibus debuit, sed per iniquitatem alius hoc dixit esse suum, et alius istud, et sic inter mortales facta est divisio. Quapropter hec vobis cavenda mandamus, et doctrinis et exemplis apostolorum obedire precipimus, quia hii qui eorum mandata postponunt non solum rei sed eciam extorres fiunt. Que non solum vobis cavenda, sed eciam omnibus predicanda sunt. *Hec XII. q. i, Dilectissimis.*[8]

8. "Precipimus": *glosa:* id est, "monemus." In primitiva ecclesia hoc potuit precipere qui[a] tunc renuncciaverunt propriis sed si hoc preciperet hodie deformaret status ecclesie universalis. *Hec glosa Bartholomei Brixiensis in c. Dilectissimis.*[9] *Et dicit idem, eadem causa et questione, in c. Videntes:* Episcopi tenent locum apostolorum quoad dignitatem, monachi quoad renuncciacionem propriorum et comunem vitam, omnes sacerdotes quoad sacramentorum disposicionem. *Hec. ille.*[10] Sed hoc nota **[f. 241]** quod in primitiva ecclesia omnes credentes, seu laici seu clerici, nichil possidebant, sed omnia erant eis comunia (*ut dicit idem ibidem, "Clericus"*), nunc autem intelligendum est de consilio vel secundum tempus primitive ecclesie vel de aliis qui renuncciaverunt propriis. *Hec ibi.*[11] Nam dicit lex quod solum inmensitas est mensura rerum donatarum in ecclesia, *ut Codex, de sacrosanctis ecclesiis, Au-*

6. By the law of nature all things are common to all, and not only was this principle maintained among them of whom it is read that "all who believed were of one accord" etc. (*Acts ii, 44–46*), but it is known to have been handed down from earlier times by the philosophers. Thus with Plato, that city is supposed to be most justly ordered in which no one has private ties. (*Decretum, VIII, di. Part I.*)

For by divine law the earth is the Lord's and the fullness thereof; he made rich and poor of one clay, and one earth supports both rich and poor. It is thus by human law that one says: "this estate is mine, this house is mine, this slave is mine." Take away the Emperor's laws and who will dare to say: "this estate is mine, mine is this slave, mine this house?" Possessions are possessed by the laws of kings; but you have said: "What do I have in common with the king?" Do not then call possessions yours, since you have renounced the very human laws by which possessions are possessed." (*Decretum, VIII. di., c. 11.*)

7. Clement, Bishop, to the most beloved brethren and fellow disciples of Jerusalem, and to James, dearest brother and fellow bishop. Brothers a common life is necessary for all, and especially for those who would serve God irreprehensibly and would imitate the life of the apostles and of their disciples. For the use of everything in this world was supposed to be common to all men, but iniquity has caused one to say this was his, another to say that was his, and so there came about division among mortals. We therefore command you to take care against these things, and we order you to obey the doctrines and the examples set by the apostles, for those who neglect their mandates are thereby not only guilty but also exiled (from the Church). Let these things not only be a caution for you but also preached to all. (*Decretum, XII. q. i, c. 2.*)

8. "We order." *The gloss:* That is, "we admonish." In the Primitive Church, he could order this because then they had renounced private property, but if he were to order it today, he would damage the estate of the universal Church. *The gloss of Bartholomew of Brescia, on XII. q. i., c. 2. And in his gloss on XII. q. i., c. 16, he says:* The bishops hold the place of the apostles with respect to dignity; the monks, with respect to renunciation of property and to a common life; and all the priests, with respect to the administration of the sacraments. *Thus far Bartholomew.* But note

---

[6] VIII. dist., I pars (Friedberg, I, 12).
[7] VIII. dist., c. 1 (Friedberg, I, 12–13).
[8] XII. q. i., c. 2 (Friedberg, I, 676–677).
[9] *Glosa ordinaria in verbum* "Precipimus," XII. q. i., c. 2 (Friedberg, I, 676–677; *Edit. Lugdun., col. 965*): id est, "monemus." simile XXVIII. q. i., Sic enim. Videtur tamen, quod hoc fuit preceptum, quia primitiva ecclesia hoc potuit precipere; sicut continentiam. Sed si hoc hodie preciperetur, deformaret statum ecclesie universalis. Quod non debet esse. I. q. ultima, Et si illa. Vel dic, quod preceptum erat eis, qui tunc renuntiaverant propriis, non aliis. XVII. q. i., c. i.
[10] *Glosa ordinaria in verbum* "Apostolorum," XII. q. i., c. 16 (Friedberg, I, 682–683; *Edit. Lugdun., col. 973*).
[11] *Recte, glosa ordinaria in verbum* "clericos," XII. q. i, *in principio* (*Edit. Lugdun., col. 963 f.*); *cf. Wyclif*, De civili dominio, III, 248.

*tem.*¹² Sed hodie nec una decima bene datur et ideo fame et penuria et aliis penis maledicti sumus, *ut XIII. q. i., Hüs ita, in glosa, et XVI. q. i., Revertimini.*¹³

9. Sanximus ut nullis [*MS:* nullos] nisi dignitate preditis, aut personatum obtin[en]tibus seu ecclesiarum kathedralium canonicis, cause auctoritate literarum sedis apostolice vel legatorum eiusdem de cetero committantur, *ut De rescriptis, Statutum, Libro VI.*¹⁴

10. Ne in obprobrium proprium cogantur episcopi et magni clerici coram iudicibus [*recte:* rudibus] et pannosis clericis litigare. Hoc non solum videtur inductum in favorem partis, sed eciam in favorem ipsius apostolice sedis, ne vilipendatur in tali ministerio. *Johannes Andree, ibidem.*¹⁵

11. Romanus pontifex non puri hominis sed veri dei vicem gerit in terris. *Extra de translacione prelatorum, Quanto.*¹⁶

12. Unde dicitur habere celeste arbitrium. *Codex, de summa trinitate, L. i., in fine.*¹⁷ Et ideo rerum naturam immutat. *Codex, comunia de legatis, L. ii.*¹⁸ Et de nichilo potest aliquid facere. *Codex, de rei uxorie accione, L. i., in principio.*¹⁹ Quia sentenciam que nulla est facit aliquam. *III. q. vi., Hec quippe.*²⁰ De iusticia potest facere iniusticiam, *Extra de iure naturali, Sed quod principi.*²¹ Nec est enim quis ei dicat, cur ita facis. *De penitencia, di. iii., Ex persona.*²² Et plenitudinem obtinet potestatis. *II. q. vi., Ut* [*sic*] *Decreto.*²³

13. Prohibentur non nulli accusare propter paupertatem, ut qui minus quam 50 aureos habent: *ut II. q. i., Prohibentur.*²⁴ Testes ad testimonium non admittendos esse censemus, qui nec ad accusacionem admitti iussi sunt: *ut IIII. q. iii., Testes.*²⁵ Unde generaliter colligitur quod quicumque sacerdotes non sunt vel sacerdotes esse non possunt in sacerdotes accusacionem vel testificacionem proferre non possunt: *ut II. q. vii., Penitentes.*²⁶ Sed non habens titulum beneficii vel patri-

that in the Primitive Church, none of the believers, neither laymen nor clerics, possessed anything, but all things were common to them (*as in the gloss on "Clericus"*); but now this is to be understood as a counsel, either according to the condition of the Primitive Church, or with regard to those who have renounced their property (*thus the gloss*). For the law says that only immeasurability is the measure of things offered in the church (*Codex*). But today not even one tenth is rightly given, and because of that we are cursed with hunger, need, and other punishments (*Glosa ordinaria on "Servis," Decretum, XIII. q. i., II. pars; and XVI. q. i, c. 65*).

9. We have decreed that judicial cases should moreover not be committed, neither by authority of letters of the Apostolic See nor by authority of her legates, to anyone except those possessing high rank or office or who are canons of cathedral churches (*Sext., I, iii, 11*).

10. Bishops and high-ranking clerics should not be forced, to their ignominy, to litigate before mean judges and clerics. This provision seems to have been introduced not only in favor of these litigants but also in favor of the Apostolic See, lest it be held in low esteem on account of such an official. (*John Andree, gloss on the preceding text.*)

11. The Roman pontiff holds the place on earth not of mere man but of very God (*Decretals, I, vii, 3*).

12. Whence his will is said to be celestial. And therefore he can change the nature of things. And out of nothing he can make something; for a sentence that is null he can make valid. Out of justice he can make injustice. Nor is there anyone who may say to him, "Why do you thus?" And he holds the fullness of power. (*Decretals, I, vii, 3, glosa ordinaria on "Veri Dei vicem."*)

13. Some are not allowed to make an accusation, because of their poverty, as for example those who have less than fifty *aurei*. (*See Decretum, II. q. i., c. 14*).

---

¹² *Non inventum.*
¹³ *Glosa ordinaria in verbum* "Servus," XIII. q. i, II pars. (Friedberg, I, 718–719; *Edit. Lugdun., col. 1024*). XVI. q. i, c. 65 (Friedberg, I, 783–784).
¹⁴ *Liber Sextus*, I, iii, 11 (Friedberg, II, 941–942).
¹⁵ *Glosa in verbum* "committantur," *Liber Sextus*, I, iii, 11 (Friedberg, II, 941–942; *Edit. Lugdun., col. 38*): "Dicebat Bernardus et omnes post eum quod tacite et expresse poterat pars huic iuri renunciare. Introductum est enim in ipsorum favorem, ne scilicet in opprobrium proprium cogantur episcopi et magni clerici coram rudibus et pannosis clericis litigare. . . . Sed hodie per finem istius decretalis, credo contrarium. . . .Quia hoc videbitur non solum in favorem partium inductum, sed etiam in favorem ipsius Apostolicae sedis, ne vilipendatur in tali ministro."
¹⁶ *Decretales*, I, vii, 3 (Friedberg, II, 98–99).
¹⁷ *Cod.* I, i, 1 (*q.v.*) *Totus hic XII. paragrafus desumptus est, pene ad literam, de glosa ordinaria in verbum* "Veri Dei vicem," *Decretales*, I, vii, 3 (*Edit. Lugdun., col. 217*).
¹⁸ *Cf. Cod.* VI, xliii, 2, §1–2.
¹⁹ *Cf. Cod.* V, xiii, 1.
²⁰ III. q. vi., c. 10 (Friedberg, I, 521–522).
²¹ *In glosa legitur, hoc loco*, "quia in his que vult ei est pro ratione voluntas. Instit., de iure naturali, Sed quod principi." *Verba*, "de iusticia potest facere iniusticiam" *intelligenda sunt ut corruptela, sine dubio tendenciose facta a Nicolao, horum verborum, que leguntur in glosa, paulo inferius:* "Idem de iniustitia potest facere iustitiam corrigendo iura et mutando. Infra, de appellationibus, c. Ut debitus; et Infra, de consanguinitate et affinitate, c. Non debet."
²² "Nec est . . . ita facis": *Cf. Job 9: 12; in De pen., dist. III,* § *Ex persona, c.* [22] *"Quamvis" (Friedberg, I), sunt alia verba, sed sensus idem.*
²³ II. q. vi., c. 11 (Friedberg, I, 458).
²⁴ II. q. i., c. 14 (Friedberg, I, 444), *q.v.!*
²⁵ IV. q. iii., c. 1 (Friedberg, I, 538).
²⁶ II. q. vii., par. Penitentes (*post c. 9*): *sed non videtur pertinere.*

monii unde possit congrue sustentari [**f. 241′**] non debet ad ordines promoveri: *Extra de prebendis, Episcopus.*[27] Ymmo expedit ecclesie plures habere divites clericos, ut eam possint melius defensare: *in Autentica, Ut iudices sine quoquo suffragio, I. Coll. ii.*[28]

14. Aurum et argentum non est michi. *Act. iii.*[29] Ecce nos reliquimus omnia, et secuti sumus te; quid ergo erit nobis?[30]

15. Ego sum lux mundi. Qui sequitur me non ambulat in tenebris, sed habebit lumen vite. *Joh. viii.*[31] Eritis michi testes in Ierosolymam et in omni Iudea et Samaria, usque ad ultimum terre. *Act. i.*[32] Quecumque audivi a patre meo nota feci vobis. Et vos testimonium perhibebitis quia ab inicio mecum estis. *Joh. xv.*[33] Data est michi omnis potestas in celo et in terra. Euntes ergo docete omnes gentes baptizantes eos in nomine patris et filii et spiritus sancti, docentes eos servare omnia quecumque mandavi vobis. *Mat. ult.*[34] Euntes in mundum universum, predicate ewangelium omni creature. *Mar. ult.*[35] Si mundus vos odit, scitote quia me priorem vobis odio habuit. Si de mundo fuissetis, mundus quod suum erat diligeret; quia vero de mundo non estis, sed ego elegi vos de mundo, propterea odit vos mundus. Si me persecuti sunt, et vos persequentur; si sermonem meum servaverint [*sic*], et vestrum servabunt. Sed hec omnia facient vobis propter nomen meum quia nesciunt eum qui misit me. *Joh. xv.*[36]

16. Quicumque tecum non colligit, spargit, hoc est, qui Cristus non est anticristus [est]: *Jeronimus, XXIIII. q. i., Quoniam, in fine.*[37] Piscatori Petro, fabri filio, successorem querimus, non Augusto. Nobilitas fastum, fastus litem parit; armat lis odium; capiunt hec tria mortis iter.[38] Unde dominus Ihesus mittens ad ewangelizandum discipulos misit eos sine auro, sine argento, sine pecunia, sine virga, ut incentiva litis et instrumenta eriperet ulcionis.[39] *Hec XXIIII. q. i, in glosa; et Ambrosius, XI. q. iii., Ira.*

17. *Bernhardus, in persona Cristi loquens, dicit:* In vita mea poteris cognoscere vitam tuam, ut sicut ego paupertatis, humilitatis, caritatis, obediencie, et paciencie, indeclinabiles semitas tenui, et tu eisdem vestigiis incedas, non declines ad dextram neque ad sinistram.[40]

We do not think witnesses should be allowed to testify who have not been allowed to accuse (*see Decretum, IV. q. iii., c. 1*).

Thus in general it seems to be the rule that those who are not priests, and those who cannot become priests, cannot make an accusation or offer testimony against priests (*see Decretum, II. q. vii., Par. Penitents (after c. 9)*). But he who has no title to a church benefice or a patrimony sufficient for his proper support should not be promoted to holy orders (*Decretals, III, v, 4*). Indeed it is to the advantage of the church to have many rich clerics, who can defend her better (*Authentica, I. Coll. ii (see note 28)*).

14. Gold and silver have I none (*Acts iii, 6*). Behold, we have forsaken all, and followed thee; what shall we have therefore? (*Mat. xix, 27*).

15. I am the light of the world. He that followeth me does not walk in darkness, but shall have the light of life (*Joh. viii, 12*). You shall be witnesses unto me both in Jerusalem and in all Judea, and in Samaria, and unto the uttermost part of the earth (*Acts i, 8*). All things that I have heard of my Father I have made known unto you (*Joh. xv, 15*). And you also shall bear witness, because you have been with me from the beginning (*Joh. xv, 27*). All power is given unto me in heaven and in earth. Go you therefore, and teach all nations, baptizing them in the name of the Father, and of the Son, and of the Holy Spirit: teaching them to observe all things whatsoever I have commanded you (*Mat. xxviii, 18–20*). Go you into all the world, and preach the gospel to every creature (*Mar. xvi, 15*). If the world hate you, know that it hated me before it hated you. If you were of the world, the world would love his own: but because you are not of the world, but I have chosen you out of the world, therefore the world hates you. If they have persecuted me they will also persecute you; if they shall have kept my saying, they will keep yours also. But all these things will they do unto you for my name's sake, because they know not him that sent me (*Joh. xv, 18–21*).

16. Whoever is not working with you to gather is working to scatter: that is, whoever is not a Christ is an Antichrist (*Jerome in Decretum, XXIV. q. i., c. 25*). We seek a successor to Peter the fisher and to the son of a carpenter, not to Augustus. Nobility breeds arrogance, arrogance controversy, and contro-

---

[27] *Decretales*, III, v, 4 (Friedberg, II, 465).
[28] *Non inventum.*
[29] Act. iii, 6.
[30] Mat. xix, 27.
[31] Joh. viii, 12.
[32] Act. i, 8.
[33] Joh. xv, 15, 27.
[34] Mat. xxviii, 18–20.
[35] Mar. xvi, 15.
[36] Joh. xv, 18–21.

[37] XXIV. q. i., 25 (Friedberg, I, 975–976); *ubi legitur*, "... qui Christi non est antichristi est."
[38] *Glosa ordinaria in verbum* "invidia," XXIV. q. i., c. 25 (Friedberg, I, 975–976; *Edit. Lugdun., col. 1396*): "Id est, extollentia: unde invidia saepe nascitur: unde cum duo certarent de electione, et unus allegaret ignobilitatem alterius, alius ex adverso respondit: Piscatori Petro fabri filio successorem querimus, non Augusto. Nobilitas fastum; fastus litem parit; armat lis odium; capiunt hac tria mortis iter."
[39] XI. q. iii., c. 68 (Friedberg, I, 662).
[40] *Non inventum.*

18. Mundus [f. 242] clamat, ego deficio; caro, ego inficio; dyabolus, ego interficio; Cristus, ego reficio. Quem ergo sequeris, miser homo? Ego me convertam ad Ihesum nudum pendentem in cruce. Putas michi requies erit. Utique non negabit michi auxilium qui latroni obtulit paradisum. *Hec S. Bernhardus.*[41]

19. Quia Cristus paupertatem laudavit, divitibus maledixit, contumelias honoribus pretulit, gaudio et quieti tristiciam preposuit et laborem, ideo Romani carnales avari et superbi dicebant cultores paucos habebit, quia omnino stultus esset qui in se vel in proximo paupertatem aut contumelias vel tristiciam diligeret aut laborem; dicebant eciam Ihesum immundum, eo quod honorem divinitatis cum diis nollet habere comunem. *Hec in Cronicis, Flores temporum.*[42]

20. Ecclesias singulas singulis presbiteris dedimus, parrochias et cymiteria eis divisimus, et unicuique ius proprium habere statuimus; ita videlicet ut nullus alterius parrochie terminos aut ius invadat, sed unusquisque terminis suis sit contentus: *ut XIII. q. i., Ecclesias.*[43]

21. *Ieronimus:* Olim idem presbiter, qui et episcopus, et antequam dyaboli instinctu studia in religione fierent, et diceretur in populis: ego Pauli, ego Appollo, ego autem Cephe, comuni presbiterorum concilio ecclesie gubernabantur. Postquam autem unusquisque eos, quos baptizaverat, suos esse putabat, non Cristi, in toto orbe decretum est, ut unus de presbiteris superponeretur et scismatum semina tollerentur. Sicut ergo presbiteri sciunt se, ecclesie conswetudine, ei qui sibi prepositus fuerit esse subiectos, ita episcopi noverint se, magis conswetudine quam dispensacionis dominice veritate, presbiteris esse maiores, et in comuni debere ecclesia[m] regi. *XCV. di., Olim.*[44]

22. Dicunt quidam quod tunc omnes apostoli erant simplices sacerdotes et tamen [*MS:* tunc] consecrare poterant; nam Moises simplex sacerdos erat, et tamen consecravit Aaron, nec tunc differencia erat inter episcopum et sacerdotem. *Hec invenies LXVI. di., Archiepiscopus, in glosa.*[45]

23. Non amplius quam duos ordines inter discipulos domini esse cognovimus, id est, xii apostolorum et lxxii discipulorum. Unde iste tercius, scilicet corepiscopi, processerit [f. 242'] ignoramus. Et quod racione caret extirpandum est: *Ut LXVIII. di., Cur episcopi.*[46]

24. Inter hos quedam discrecio servata est, ut alii appellentur simpliciter sacerdotes, alii archipresbiteri,

versy nourishes hate: these three include the path of death. (*Decretum XXIV. q. i., c. 25, glosa ordinaria on "invidia."*) Whence Lord Jesus, sending his disciples out to preach the gospel, sent them without gold, without silver, without money, without staffs, in order to remove the incentives to controversy and the instruments of vengeance (*Decretum, XI. q. iii., c. 68*).

17. *Bernard, speaking in the person of Christ, says:* In my life you can come to know your own: just as I have held to the undeviating path of poverty, humility, love, obedience, and suffering, so may you follow in those very traces, and turn neither to left nor to right.

18. The world cries, "I pass away." The flesh, "I corrupt." The Devil, "I kill." Christ, "I restore." Whom then will you follow, wretched man? For my part, I shall turn to the naked Jesus hanging on the cross. You think I shall be at peace? At least he who offered paradise to a thief will not refuse help to me. (*St. Bernard.*)

19. Because Christ praised poverty, cursed the rich, and preferred scorn to honor, because he set sorrow and toil before joy and repose—therefore, the carnal, greedy, proud Romans said, he had few worshipers. For a man would be an utter fool who loved poverty, scorn, sorrow, or toil, for himself or for his neighbor. And they said that Jesus was base because he would not share divine honor with the gods. (*In the chronicle, "Flores temporum."*)

20. We have given particular churches to particular priests, and have distributed parishes and churchyards to them, and have decreed that each should have his own right; and we have done so in order that none should infringe on the boundaries or rights of another's parish, but that each should be content with his own boundaries (*Decretum, XIII. q. i., c. 1*).

21. *Jerome:* Once priest and bishop were one, and before rivalries incited by the Devil had arisen in religion and before it had used to be said among the people, "I am Paul's," "I am Apollo's," "But I am Cephas's"—before this, the churches were governed by the common council of the priests. But after each had come to regard those whom he had baptized as his own, not as Christ's, it was decreed everywhere that one of the priests should be set over the others, that the seeds of schism be removed. Therefore, just as the priests know they are subject, by custom of the church, to him placed over them, so the bishops may know it is more by custom than by the truth of the Lord's dispensation that they are greater than the priests and that the church is to be governed in matters of common concern. (*Decretum, XCV. dist., c. 5.*)

---

[41] *Non inventum.*
[42] *Non ad manum.*
[43] XIII. q. i., c. 1 (Friedberg, I, 717–718).
[44] XCV. dist., c. 5 (Friedberg, I, 332–333); ultima particula legitur: ". . . et in commune debere ecclesiam regere."

[45] (*Recte:* LXVI. di., Porro.) *Glosa ordinaria in verbum* "Ordinatus," LXVI. dist., c. 2 (Friedberg, I, 253; *Edit. Lugdun., col. 341*).
[46] LXVIII. dist., c. 5 (Friedberg, I, 255); *recte:* "Corepiscopi."

alii corepiscopi, alii episcopi, alii archiepiscopi seu metropolite, alii primates, alii patriarche, alii summi pontifices. Horum discrecio a gentibus maxime introducta est, qui suos [*MS:* servos] flammines alios simpliciter flamines, alios archiflammines, alios prothoflammines appellabant: Simpliciter vero maiorum et minorum sacerdotum in novo testamento discrecio ab ipso Cristo sumpsit exordium. *XXI. di., Decretis.*[47]

25. Crisostomus super Mattheum, de imperfecto: In novissimo populi cristiani quasi tempore Roboam, habundante iniquitate et refrigescente caritate, plenius conscissus est populus cristianus, ita ut maxima pars cristianorum divideretur in hereses et faceret sibi populus [*recte:* proprios] episcopos quasi proprios [reges] et vix paucissimi cristiani remanerent in ecclesia Cristi sub Cristo. Et sicut tunc Roboam, abiciens consilia seniorum, et coetaneorum suorum sequens, occasionem prebuit dissidionis, sic et circa finem episcopi relinquentes consilia seniorum apostolorum et prophetarum, secundum quod consiliati fuerant, episcopos conversari debere vel episcopatum suum tractare, et secuti consilia coetanorum suorum iuvenum, consiliancium episcopum opportere divitem fieri et hospitalitatem [*recte:* inhospitalem] et timorem abicere, et talia quedam alloqui que moveant plausum, dederunt occasionem dyabolo faciendarum precisionum. Et vide quia quomodo tunc in regno Iude quidam reges extiterunt peccatores, quidam autem mediocriter peccatores, in regno autem Israhel nemo regum inventus est iustus: sic et in ecclesia Cristi inveniuntur quidam episcopi [boni] et peccatores, in heresibus autem nemo invenitur rectus omnino, sed omnes perversi.[48] Quoniam et symea omnia membra hominis habet, et per omnia hominem imitatur; numquid propter ea dicenda est homo? Sic et hereses omnia signa ecclesie habent et imitantur, sed non sunt ecclesie.[49] Isti sunt quasi fundati cristiani et ecclesias suas habentes. Et quid dicam? Ecclesias eciam palam regentes cum libertate subvertunt,[50] qui putant se sicut in hoc seculo homines deceperunt, sic et ibi deum fallere posse dicentes, [f. 243] Domine, domine, in nomine tuo hoc et hoc fecimus, mencientes eciam post mortem.[51] Qui ergo secundum deum vocem humilitatis et confessionis emittit, ovis est; qui autem adversus veritatem turpiter blasphemiis ululat contra deum, lupus est.[52] Quem videris de prato scripturarum herbas floridas iusticie colligentem, ovis est; quem videris autem in sanguine persecucionis gaudentem, lupus est.[53]

22. Some say that in that time all the apostles were simple priests, yet they could consecrate [i.e., ordain]; for Moses was a simple priest and yet he consecrated Aaron, nor was there any difference then between a bishop and a priest. (*This you will find in the gloss to Decretum, LXVI. dist., c. 2.*)

23. We know that there were no more than two orders among the disciples of our Lord, namely, the orders of twelve apostles and seventy-two disciples. Whence the third group originated, that of the assistant-bishops, we do not know. And what is void of reason should be rooted out. (*According to the Decretum, LXVIII. dist., c. 5.*)

24. A certain distinction has been maintained among these, that some be called simply priests; some, archpriests; some, assistant-bishops; some, bishops; some, archbishops or metropolitans; some, primates; some, patriarchs; some, supreme pontiffs. This distinction has been taken over mainly from the heathen, who used to call some of their flamens simply flamens; others, archflamens; and still others, protoflamens. But the simple distinction between major and minor priests in the New Testament took its origin from Christ himself. (*Decretum, XXI. dist., I pars.*)

25. [*Pseudo-*] *Chrysostom, in the Opus imperfectum on Matthew:* In this age of the Christian people, as in the time of Rehoboam, iniquity overflows and charity grows cold, and the Christian people have been fragmented even more. Most of them are divided among several heresies and each group sets up its own bishops, almost as kings, so that hardly any Christians remain in Christ's church under Christ. And just as Rehoboam then rejected the advice of the elders and followed the counsels of men his own age, thereby provoking dissension, so now, towards the end, the bishops have given the Devil his opportunity for making schisms; for they have abandoned the counsels of the seniors—the apostles and the prophets—which had told them what kind of a life bishops should lead and how they should handle their episcopal office, and have followed the counsels of young men their own age, who told them that a bishop should grow rich, not be hospitable, put aside fear, and by his discourse court applause. Similarly, then in the Kingdom of Judah some kings were sinners, others not quite so bad, while in the Kingdom of Israel there was no king who was just: so also in the church of Christ some bishops are good, some are sinners, but among the heretics no one is righteous at all, all are perverted.

An ape has all the limbs of a man and imitates men in everything: should he then be called a man? So

---

[47] XXI. dist., I. pars (Friedberg, I, 66–67).
[48] PseudoChrysostomi, *Opus imperfectum in Matthaeum*, Homilia I. (*MPG*, 56, col. 622); *citacio leviter corrupta et compressa.*
[49] *Non inventum.*

[50] *MPG,* 56, col. 738.
[51] *Ibid.,* col. 743.
[52] *Ibid.,* col. 739.
[53] *Loc. cit.*

quia qui vult esse verus cristianus non solum non occidit sed nec irascitur sine causa; non solum non periuret, sed nec iuret, et sic de aliis mandatis Cristi.[54] *Mat. v.*

26. Pater noster monet ut nobilis et dives non superbire[nt] contra minores; non enim vere possunt dicere "pater noster" nisi fratres sint: *ut dicit glosa ordinaria, Mat. vi.*[55] Omnes enim vos fratres estis. *Mat. xxiii.*[56]

27. Caveant tamen clerici ne cum scribunt episcopo vocent eum fratrem, prout dicit dominus imperator, quod iudices superioribus debent honorem facere in salutacione. *Codex, De officio [diversorum] iudicum, l. ii., et in glosa, c. Esto, XCV. di.*[57] Concordat *Extra de crimine falsi, Quam gravi:*[58] ubi vult papa solum episcopos et supra sibi esse fratres.

28. Consecrare presbiter altare non presumat. Benediccionem super plebem fundere aut penitentem in ecclesia benedicere presbitero non liceat. *XXVI. q. vi., Ministrare.*[59]

heresies bear all the signs of the church and imitate her, but they are not churches. They seem to be solid Christians, who even have their own churches; indeed I may say that they openly and freely rule their churches, subverting them—those heretics who think that as they have deceived men in this world, so they can deceive God, when they say, "Lord, Lord, in thy name we have done" this or that, lying even after death! He then who speaks with the voice of humility and confession, according to God, is of the sheep; but he who opposes the truth and howls in foul blasphemies against God, he is a wolf. Of the sheep is he whom you see gathering the flowering plants of justice in the meadow of Scripture; a wolf is he whom you see rejoicing in the blood of persecution. For the man who would be a true Christian not only does not kill but does not even anger; not only may he not perjure himself without cause, but may not swear at all; and so it is with Christ's other mandates.

26. Our Father admonishes the rich and noble not to be arrogant to those below them; for they cannot truly say "Our Father" unless they be brothers (*the Glossa Ordinaria on Mat. vi*). For all of you are brethren (*Mat. xxiii, 8*).

27. Let clerics take care not to call a bishop "brother" when writing to him; for as the Lord Emperor says, judges should do honor to their superiors in their salutations (*Codex, cited in gloss on Decretum, XCV. dist., c. 7*). In the same sense is the passage in *Decretals, V, xx, 6*, where the pope would have only bishops and above as his brothers.

28. A priest may not presume to consecrate an altar. Nor may it be permitted to a priest to pronounce benedictions over the people or to bless a penitent in church. (*Decretum, XXVI. q. vi, c. 3.*)

[II]

1. Nullum, absque formata, peregrinorum clericorum suscipi opportet.[60] Hortamur cristianitatem vestram, iuxta sanctorum canonum instituta, [ut] in ecclesiis a vobis fundatis aliunde veniens presbiter non suscipiatur nisi [*MS: nec*] aut fuerit a vestre ecclesie episcopo consecratus, aut ab eo per commendaticias literas suscipiatur.[61] *LXXI. di, Extraneo [recte: Hortamur], et c. sequente.*

2. Numquid egemus, sicut quidam, commendaticiis epistolis ad vos, aut ex vobis? Epistola nostra vos estis, scripta in cordibus nostris, que scitur et legitur ab omnibus hominibus; manifestati quoniam epistola

(II)

1. No wandering cleric should be received without credentials. We exhort your Christianity that, according to the regulations of the holy canons, a priest coming from elsewhere not be received in churches that you have founded, unless he has been consecrated by the bishop of your church or unless he be received by him on the basis of letters of commendation. (*Decretum, LXXI. dist., c. 9, c. 8.*)

2. Do we need, as some do, epistles of commendation to you or from you? You are our epistle, written in our hearts, known and read by all men. For you are manifested to be the epistle of Christ, ministered by us, written not with ink, but with the spirit of the

---

[54] *Non inventum; cf.* Mat. v, 21–22, 33–34.
[55] *Non ad manum.*
[56] Mat. xxiii, 8.
[57] *Glosa in verba,* "quasi clericos," *XCV. dist., c. 7 (Friedberg, I, 334; Edit. Lugdun., col. 460); allegacio Codicis habetur in hac glosa.*

[58] *Decretales,* V, xx, 6 (Friedberg, II, 819–820).
[59] XXVI. q. vi., c. 3 (Friedberg, I, 1036).
[60] LXXI. dist., c. 9 (Friedberg, I, 259).
[61] LXXI. dist., c. 8 (Friedberg, I, 259).

estis Cristi, ministrata a nobis, et scripta non attramento, sed spiritu dei vivi, non in tabulis lapideis sed in tabulis cordis carnalibus. *II Cor. iii.*[62]

3. Ex fructibus eorum cognoscetis eos. *Mat. vii.*[63] Venite ad me omnes qui laboratis, et onerati estis, et ego reficiam vos. Tollite iugum meum super vos, et invenietis requiem animabus vestris, et discite a me quia mitis sum [f. 243'] et humilis corde. Iugum enim meum suave est et onus meum leve.[64]

4. Peccatum paganitatis incurrit quis dum cristianum se esse asserit, sedi apostolice obedire contempnit. *LXXXI. di., Si qui.*[65] Et licet quid vix ferendum ab illa sancta sede imponatur, iugum tamen feramus et pia devocione tolleremus. *XIX. di., In memoriam.*[66]

5. Canon, *Si qui* dicit quod nullus presumat audire officium eorum qui in fornicacionis crimine iacent, et qui huic saluberrimo precepto obedire noluerint, ydolatrie peccatum incurrunt.[67]

6. In hoc quod Cristus in altum tolli se permittit [*sic*] sed monenti [*MS: monere*] cadere non obedivit, ostendit ut cuicumque bona et alta imperanti obediamus, sed precipitare volenti contraeamus. *Hec glosa ordinaria, Mat. iiii, super isto, "Et statui eum super pynnaculum templi," etc.*[68] Sic obediendum est, non solum probis sed et discolis.

7. In dubiis humanior et tucior est via eligenda, *ut XIIII. di., c. ult., ubi dicitur:* In hiis que vel dubia fuerint aut obscura, id noverimus sequendum quod nec preceptis ewangelicis contrarium est, nec decretis sanctorum patrum inveniatur adversum. *Hec ibi.*[69] Qui omnipotentem deum metuit, nec contra ewangelium, nec contra apostolos, nec contra prophetas vel sanctorum patrum instituta agere nullo modo consentit. *XI. q. iii., Qui omnipotentem.*[70]

8. *Ysyderus* [*sic*]: Si is qui preest fecerit aut cuiquam quod a domino prohibitum est facere iusserit, vel quod scriptum est preterierit aut preterire mandaverit; Sancti Pauli sentencia ingerenda est, dicentis: Eciam si nos aut angelus de celo ewangelizaverit vobis preter quam quod ewangelizavimus vobis, anathema sit. Idem: Si quis prohibet nobis quod a domino preceptum est, vel rursus imperat fieri quod dominus prohibet fieri, execrabilis sit omnibus qui diligunt deum. Idem: Is qui preest, si preter voluntatem dei vel preter quod in sanctis scripturis evidenter precipitur, vel dicit aliquid vel imperat, tamquam falsus testis dei aut sacrilegus habeatur. *Hec XI. q. iii., Si is.*[71]

living God; not in tables of stone, but in the fleshy tables of the heart. (*II. Cor. iii, 1–3.*)

3. By their fruits you shall know them (*Mat. vii, 20*). Come to me all you that labor and are heavy laden, and I will give you strength. Take my yoke upon you and you will find rest for your souls; and learn of me, for I am meek, and lowly in heart. For my yoke is sweet and my burden is light. (*Mat. xi, 28–30.*)

4. He incurs the sin of paganism who while asserting himself a Christian, scorns to obey the Apostolic See (*Decretum, LXXXI. dist., c. 15*). And although something hardly to be borne may be imposed by the Holy See, let us nevertheless bear the yoke and support it with pious devotion (*Decretum, XIX. dist., c. 3*).

5. The canon "Si qui" states that no one should presume to listen to the divine offices of those who are guilty of fornication, and whoever will not obey this most salutary command incurs the sin of idolatry (*Decretum, LXXX. dist., c. 15*).

6. By the fact that Christ allowed himself to be carried on high, but did not obey the admonition to fall down [and worship], he showed that we should obey anyone commanding good and lofty things, but resist those who would thrust us down. (*The Glosa ordinaria on Mat. iv, 5ff., "And set him upon the pinnacle of the temple," etc.*) It is in this sense that obedience should be shown not only to the upright, but also to the wayward (*Cf. I Pet. ii, 18*).

7. In doubtful cases, the more humane and surer road should be chosen, *as is said in the Decretum, XIV. dist., c. 2:* "In dubious or obscure cases, we know that the course to be followed is one that neither contradicts evangelical precepts nor goes against the decrees of the holy Fathers." He who fears the omnipotent God will in no way consent to act against the gospel, against the apostles, or against the prophets, or the institutes of the holy Fathers (*Decretum, XI. q. iii, c. 95*).

8. *Isidore:* If one who is in command does, or orders someone to do, what the Lord has forbidden, or if he oversteps or orders someone to overstep what has been written, then St. Paul's judgment should be applied, which says: "Even if we or an angel from heaven preach any other gospel to you than that which we have preached to you, let him be accursed" (*Gal. i, 8*). *Again Isidore:* If anyone forbids us what has been ordered by the Lord, or conversely, if he orders us to do what the Lord forbids to be done, let him be held accursed by all who love God. *The Same:* If one in command either says or orders something against the will of God or against what has been clearly set down in the Holy Scriptures, he should be considered as a

---

[62] II Cor. iii, 1–3.
[63] Mat. vii, 20.
[64] Mat. xi, 28–30.
[65] LXXXI. dist., c. 15 (Friedberg, I, 285).
[66] XIX. dist., c. 3 (Friedberg, I, 60).
[67] LXXXI. dist., c. 15 (Friedberg, I, 284–285); *citacio composita*.
[68] Mat. iv, 5; *glosa non ad manum*.
[69] XIV. dist., c. 2 (Friedberg, I, 33).
[70] XI. q. iii., c. 95 (Friedberg, I, 669).
[71] XI. q. iii., c. 101 (Friedberg, I, 671).

9. Maledicti qui declinant a mandatis tuis. *Psa. cxviii.*⁷² Ve vobis viri impii qui dereliquistis legem domini altissimi, et si nati fueritis in maledicione nascimini, et si mortui fueritis in maledicione erit pars vestra. *Ecclus. xli.*⁷³

10. Si peccaverit in te frater tuus, vade et corripe [f. 244] eum inter te et ipsum solum. Si te audierit, lucratus eris fratrem tuum; si autem te non audierit, adhibe tecum unum vel duos testes, ut in ore duorum vel trium testium stet omne verbum; quod si non audierit eos, dic ecclesie; si autem et ecclesiam non audierit, sit tibi sicut ethnicus et publicanus. Amen dico vobis, quecumque alligaveritis super terram erunt ligata et in celo, et quecumque solveritis super terram erunt soluta et in celo. *Mat. xviii.*⁷⁴

11. Si quis venit ad vos et hanc doctrinam non affert, nolite recipere eum in domum nec ave ei dixeritis; qui enim dicit illi ave comunicat operibus illius malignis. *II Joh. i.*⁷⁵ Quod si quis non obedierit verbo nostro per epistolam, hunc notate et ne conmisceamini cum illo ut confundatur. *II Thess. ult.*⁷⁶ Multi enim ambulant quos sepe dicebam vobis, nunc autem et flens dico, inimicos crucis Cristi, quorum finis interitus, quorum deus venter est, et gloria in confusione eorum qui terrena sapiunt. *Phil. iii.*⁷⁷ Ne conmisceamini fornicariis aut avaris, aut rapacibus, aut ydolis servientibus; si is qui frater nominatur inter vos est fornicator aut avarus aut ydolis serviens aut maledicus aut ebriosus aut rapax, cum huiusmodi nec cibum sumere. *I. Cor. v.*⁷⁸ Unde *Ozee iiii* ⁷⁹ dicitur: Quia tu Israhel fornicaris, non delinquas saltem tu Iuda; dimitte eum ne consorcio eius corrumparis; convivium eorum est separatum. *Lira:* id est, excomunicatum.⁸⁰ Nolite errare; neque fornicarii neque ydolis servientes neque adulteri neque molles neque masculorum concubitores neque fures neque avari neque ebriosi neque maledici neque rapaces, regnum dei possidebunt. *I Cor. vi.*⁸¹ Quoniam qui talia agunt digni sunt morte, non solum qui faciunt ea sed et qui consenciunt facientibus. *Rom. i.*⁸² Nunc iniusta sentencia bene est timenda ex facti occurrencia, quia sepe fertur; iusta autem rarissime, quia regulariter non excomunicantur symoniaci, fornicatores, adulteri, prevaricatores, cupidi, elati, blasphemi, raptores, invidi, percussores, ypochrite, nigromantici, sortilegi, mendaces, et alii de quibus supra, sed pauperes pannosi, simplices devoti, legem Cristi zelantes et verbo false witness of God and as sacrilegious. (*Decretum, XI. q. iii, c. 101.*)

9. Cursed are they who err from your commandments (*Psalm cxviii, 21; King James cxix*). Woe to you, ungodly men, who have forsaken the law of the Lord most high. And if you be born, you are born in malediction, and if you die, in malediction shall be your portion. (*Ecclus. xli, 11–12.*)

10. If your brother shall sin against you, go and tell him his fault between you and him alone. If he shall hear you, you have gained your brother; but if he will not hear you, then take with you one or two witnesses, that in the mouth of two or three witnesses every word may be established. But if he shall neglect to hear them, tell it to the church; but if he neglect to hear the church, let him be to you as a heathen and a publican. Verily, I say unto you, whatsoever you shall bind on earth shall be bound in heaven; and whatsoever you shall loose on earth shall be loosed in heaven. (*Mat. xviii, 15–18.*)

11. If there come any unto you, and bring not this doctrine, receive him not into your house, neither bid him God speed. For he that bids him God speed is a partaker of his evil deeds. (*II Joh. i, 10–11.*) And if any man obey not our word by this epistle, note that man and have no company with him, that he may be ashamed (*II Thess. iii, 14*). For many walk of whom I have told you often, and now tell you even weeping, that they are the enemies of the cross of Christ, whose end is destruction, whose God is their belly, and whose glory is in their shame, who mind earthy things (*Phil. iii, 18–19*).

Do not keep company with fornicators or with the covetous or extortioners or with idolators; if any man that is called a brother among you be a fornicator, or covetous, or an idolator, or a reviler, or a drunkard, or an extortioner, with such a one do not eat (*I Cor. v, 9–11*). Thus in *Hosea, iv, 15, 17–18*, it is said: Though you, Israel, play the harlot, at least you, Judah, should not fall away; leave him, lest you be corrupted by his friendship: Their fellowship has been severed. *Lira:* That is, excommunicated. Be not deceived; neither fornicators nor idolators nor effeminates, nor abusers of themselves with other men, nor thieves nor covetous, nor drunkards nor revilers nor extortioners shall possess the kingdom of God (*I. Cor. vi, 9–10*). For they who commit such things are worthy of death, and not only they who do them, but also they who consent to them that do them (*Rom. i, 32*).

Nowadays it is well to fear an injust sentence on

---

⁷² Psa. cxviii, 21.
⁷³ Ecclus. xli, 11–12.
⁷⁴ Mat. xviii, 15–18.
⁷⁵ II Joh. i, 10–11.
⁷⁶ II Thess. iii, 14.
⁷⁷ Phil. iii, 18–19.
⁷⁸ I Cor. v, 9–11.
⁷⁹ Hos. iv, 15, 17–18.
⁸⁰ Lyra, *glosa, in loco.*
⁸¹ I Cor. vi, 9–10.
⁸² Rom. i, 32.

et opere ipsam confitentes, et non mirum quia boni temporibus novissimis habebuntur tamquam excomunicati; *ut dicit Hay[mo] super Apok., et Thomas in compendio.*[83]

12. *In Meldensi concilio:* Nemo episcoporum quemlibet sine certa et manifesta peccati causa communione privet ecclesiastica; [f. 244'] sub anathemata autem nullum presumat ponere nisi pro mortali crimine, et illis qui aliter non potuerint corrigi. *XI. q. ii., Nemo.*[84] Anathema * dicitur sentencia qua quis separatur a consorcio fidelium, ibi ad mensam. Nullus sacerdotum quemquam recte fidei hominem pro parvis et levibus causis a comunione suspendat; *ibi in c. Nullus.*[85] Unde reprehenditur quidam episcopus qui pro iniuria propria quemdam excomunicavit: *XXIII. q. iiii., Inter, ubi dicitur:* Que res nos vehementer afflixit, quia si ita est, nil cogitare te de celestibus ostendis, sed terrenam te habere conversacionem significas, dum pro vindicta proprie iniurie, quod sacris regulis prohibetur, maledictionem anathematis invexisti. Unde de cetero omnino esto circumspectus atque sollicitus, et talia cuiquam pro defensione proprie iniurie inferre denuo non presumas. Nam si tale aliquid feceris, in te scias postea esse vindicandum.[86]

13. Sentencia pastoris, seu iusta seu iniusta fuerit, cave, timenda est. *XI. q. iii., Sentencia. (per Gregorium).*[87]

14. Nisi in duobus casibus, scilicet cum post appellacionem lata et cum continet intollerabilem errorem, *ut Extra de sentencia excommunicacionis, Per tuas.*[88] Ubi dicit Bernhardus in glosa: Error intollerabilis potest dici quodlibet peccatum, vel si precipiat aliquid impossibile, vel turpe.[89] *Unde dicit idem Gregorius, XI. q. iii:* Non debet is penam sustinere canonicam in cuius dampnacione non est canonica prolata sentencia.[90] Ipse ligandi ac solvendi potestate se privat, qui hanc pro suis voluntatibus et non subditorum moribus exercet; *hec ille.*[91] *Unde dicitur, ibidem, in Par. Ex hiis:* Non ergo ab eius comunione abstinendum est, nec ab eius officio cessandum, in quem cognoscitur prolata iniqua sentencia.[92] Tercium casum apponunt, cum pro indebitis exaccionibus aliquis excomunicatur: *Hec in glosa., c. Sentencia.*[93] Item, sentencia si contra ius scriptum fera-

the basis of experience, because such are often passed; but a just one most rarely. For normally symoniacs, fornicators, adulterers, falsifiers, covetors, people full of vanity, blasphemers, robbers, haters, murderers, hypocrites, sorcerers, soothsayers, liars and others mentioned above—these are not excommunicated, but rather the ragged and poor, the devout simple people, those zealous of the law of Christ and confessing it in word and deed. And no wonder, for in the last days the good will be regarded as the excommunicate, *as Haymo says in his commentary on Apocalypse, and Thomas in his Compendium.*

12. *In the Synod of Meaux:* No bishop may deprive anyone of communion with the church, except by clear-cut reason of obvious sin; and he should not presume to put anyone under anathema, unless for mortal crimes and those that could not be otherwise corrected (*Decretum, XI. q. iii, c. 41*). (Anathema is the sentence by which someone is separated from the fellowship of the faithful, there at the table.) No priest should suspend a man of the right faith from communion for minor unimportant causes (*Decretum, XI. q. iii, c. 42*). For this reason a bishop was reprimanded who, because of personal injury, excommunicated someone: *Decretum, XXIII. q. iv, c. 27, which says:* This matter has distressed us greatly, because, if it is so, you show that you think nothing of heavenly things; rather you indicate that you follow an earthly way of life, when for the vindication of your own injury you have inflicted a curse of anathema—which is prohibited by the holy rules. In the future, therefore, be most circumspect and careful, and do not again presume to pass such sentences on anyone to make good a personal injury. For if you do something like that, know that later you will be punished for it.

13. Take care: the sentence of a pastor, be it just or unjust, must be feared (*Gregory, Decretum, XI. q. iii, c. 1*).

14. Except in two cases, namely when pronounced after an appeal or when it contains an intolerable error; *cf. Decretum, XI. q. iii, c. 1 (Glosa ordinaria); and Decretals, V, xxxix, 40, gloss:* There, in the Gloss, *Bernard [of Parma] says:* An intolerable error can be any sin: or if the sentence orders something which is either impossible or base. *Whence the same Gregory says, XI. q. iii, c. 64:* He should not suffer a canonical penalty in whose condemnation no canonical sentence

---

[83] *Nichil ad propositum in* Compendio Theologie *Sancti Thome videtur stare, ubi loquitur de iudicio ultimo (cf. I, ccxliii sq., Opera omnia, XVI (Parmae, 1865)). In opere Haymonis Halberstatensis,* Enarratio in Apocalypsin, *lib. iv, super xiii, 17 (MPL, 117, 1102), hoc legitur:* "Tempore . . . Antichristi nemo . . . bonorum praedicatorum . . . poterit praedicare libere Christum, quia carceribus recludentur, et insuper interficientur. . . ."

[84] XI. q. iii., c. 41 (Friedberg, I, 655).

* Anathema.

[85] XI. q. iii., c. 42 (Friedberg, I, 655).

[86] XXIII. q. iv., c. 27 (Friedberg, I, 912).

[87] XI. q. iii., c. 1 (Friedberg, I, 642).

[88] *Glosa ordinaria in verba* "timenda est," XI, q. iii., c. 1 (*Edit. Lugdun., col. 920*).

[89] Bernardi Parmensis, *Glosa in verba* "intollerabilem errorem," Decretales V, xxxix, 40 (*Edit. Lugdun., col. 1912*).

[90] XI. q. iii., c. 64 (Friedberg, I, 660).

[91] XI. q. iii., c. 60 (Friedberg, I, 660).

[92] XI. q. iii., *post* c. 64 (Friedberg, I, 661) (*Gracianus*).

[93] *Glosa ordinaria in verba* "timenda est," XI. q. iii., c. 1 (*Edit. Lugdun., col. 920*).

tur, nullas vires obtinet; nec contra eam est necessarium auxilium provocacionis. Venales quoque sentencias, que in mercede a corruptis iudicibus proferuntur, et citra interposite provocacionis auxilium, infirmas esse decretum est. *Ut II. q. vi., Par. Si sentencia.*[94] Talis sentencia nulla est, nec aliquam obligacionem inducit de facto vel de iure. Nam et iuxta legitimas sanxiones pactum turpe, vel rei turpis aut impossibilis, de iure vel de facto nullam obligacionem inducit. *Ut Extra de pactis, c. ult.,*[95] *et in glosa, c. Per tuas.*[96]

Pysanus in summa sua[97] *dicit:* In quibus [f. 245] casibus sentencia excomunicacionis nulla est ipso iure? Respondit in questionem: *Primus est:* Si ille qui tulit eam non habebat de hoc potestatem, ut quia non erat eius iudex, vel erat excomunicatus, et huiusmodi, *ut XXIIII. q. i., Audivimus, dicitur:*[98] Ligandi namque vel solvendi potestas veris non falsis sacerdotibus a domino tradita est, apostolis enim * dicturus, "quorum remiseritis peccata," etc., premisit: "accipite spiritum sanctum"; ut evidenter cunctis ostenderet, eum qui spiritum sanctum non habet peccata non posse tenere vel remittere. *Et sequitur:*[98a] Cum ergo peccata dimittere vel tenere, excomunicare vel reconciliare, opus sit spiritus sancti et virtus Cristi, apparet quod hii qui extra ecclesiam sunt nec ligare possunt nec solvere, nec reconciliando ecclesiastice comunioni reddere nec excomunicando eius societati privare. Qua ipsi heresi vel scismate polluti sive sentencia notati penitus probantur carere. Unde cum omnibus discipulis parem ligandi atque solvendi potestatem dominus daret, Petro pre omnibus et pro omnibus claves regni celorum se daturum promisit, dicens: Tibi dabo claves regni celorum; quicumque ergo ab unitate ecclesie que per Petrum intelligitur fuerit alienus, execrare potest, consecrare non valet, excomunicacionis vel reconciliacionis potestatem non habet, etc. *Ut ibi.* Extra enim unitatem ecclesie spiritus sanctus non accipitur, *ut dicit Ciprianus ibi, in c. Loquitur:*[99] Sic loquitur dominus ad Petrum: Ego dico tibi quia tu es Petrus et super hanc petram edificabo ecclesiam meam. Super unum edificat ecclesiam, et quamvis apostolis omnibus post resurreccionem suam potestatem tribuat: "Sicut pater me misit et ego mitto vos, accipite spiritum sanctum"; [tamen] ut unitatem manifestaret, unitatis eiusdem originem ab uno incipientem sua auctoritate disposuit. Hoc erant utique ceteri apostoli, quod Petrus fuit, pari consorcio prediti et honoris et potestatis. Sed exor-

was pronounced. *And:* He deprives himself of the power of binding and loosing who exercises it not for the morals of those under him, but for his own desires (*Decretum, XI. q. iii, c. 60*). *Whence it is said* [*by Gratian*], *in Par. "Ex hiis" (after c. 64):* Therefore when it is known that the sentence pronounced on a man is unjust, there should be no abstention from his communion or suspension of his office. A third case is added, when someone is excommunicated for not having paid what has been unduly exacted of him (*Glosa ordinaria, Decretum, XI. q. iii, c. 1*). Further (*Decretum, II. q. vi, VIII. pars, 5*), if a sentence be pronounced against the written law, it has no force, and there is no need to resort to an appeal against it. *And (ibid., Par. 9):* It has also been decreed that purchasable sentences, pronounced by corrupt judges for a bribe are invalid, even if there has been no resort to an appeal. Such a sentence is of no value and carries no obligation *de facto* or *de iure;* for according to lawful decrees, a dishonorable agreement or one made for either a dishonorable or impossible thing, carries no obligation *de iure* or *de facto* (*Decretales, I, xxv, 8, and the Gloss*).

Pisanus says, in his Summa: In what cases is a sentence of excommunication void according to the law itself? *And he answers this question: First:* If the one who has pronounced it had no power to do so; for instance, because he was not a judge in the matter, or he had been excommunicated, and so forth. *Thus it is said in the Decretum, XXIV, q. i, after c. 4:* The authority to bind and loose has been given by the Lord to true and not to false priests. For when he was about to say to the apostles (*John xx, 22–23*): "Whosesoever sins you remit" etc., he first said: "Receive ye the Holy Spirit," so as clearly to show all that he who has not the Holy Spirit cannot retain or remit sins. *And* [*Gratian*] *continues:* Since, therefore, to remit or retain sins, to excommunicate or to reconcile is the work of the Holy Spirit and the virtue of Christ, it is evident that those who are outside the church can neither bind nor loose, neither restore to the church's communion by reconciling, nor exclude from the church's society by excommunicating. For they themselves are proven to be entirely destitute of this society, who are polluted by heresy or schism, or branded with judicial sentence.

Therefore, when the Lord was giving all the disciples the equal power of binding and loosing, he promised to give Peter before all others and on behalf of all others the keys of the kingdom of heaven, saying (*Mat. xvi, 19*): "I will give unto you the keys of the kingdom of heaven." Whoever, therefore, has been estranged

---

[94] II. q. vi., c. 41 (Friedberg, I, 482).
[95] *Decretales,* I, xxv, 8 (Friedberg, II, 206).
[96] *Glosa ordinaria in verba* "In Sardicensi autem concilio," *Decretales,* V, xxxix, 40 (*Edit. Lugdun., col. 1912*).
[97] *Non ad manum.*

[98] XXIV, q. i., *post* c. 4 (Friedberg, I, 967–968) (*Gracianus*).
* *Absolucio.*
[98a] *Ibidem.*
[99] XXIV. q. i., c. 18 (Friedberg, I, 971–972); "Extra . . . accipitur" *est titulus capituli.*

dium ab unitate proficiscitur, ut ecclesia Cristi una monstretur. *Hec ibi.* Que scilicet ecclesia Cristi non consistit in hominibus racione potestatis vel dignitatis, ecclesiastice vel secularis, quia multi principes et summi pontifices et alii inferiores inventi sunt apostatasse a fide, propter * quod ecclesia consistit in illis personis in quibus est noticia et vera confessio fidei et veritatis. *Hec Lira, Mat. xvi.*[100] *Secundus:* Quando est lata post appellacionem legittimam. *Tercius casus:* Quando continet intollerabilem [f. 245′] errorem. *Quartus casus est,* quando alius excomunicaret maiori excomunicacione illos qui excomunicato participarent; non in crimine sed in locucione et aliis casibus in quibus incurritur minor. Nam talis sentencia non valet nisi trina amonicione premissa vel una pro tribus. Et nisi exprimantur nominatim ipsi admonendi. *Ut De sentencia excomunicacionis, Statutum, et c. Constitucionem, Libro Sexto.*[101] *Quintus:* Quando prelati interdicerent suis subditis ne exponant suis superioribus vel legatis, aut inquisitoribus, statum ecclesiarum suarum seu monasteriorum suorum, et de hoc ferrent sentenciam excomunicacionis. *Ut De officio ordinarii, Quia plerique, Libro Sexto.*[102]

from the unity of the church, which is represented by Peter, can curse, but does not avail to consecrate, and has no power of excommunication or of reconciliation, etc. *Thus far [Gratian].* For outside the unity of the church the Holy Spirit is not received, *as Cyprian says in the Decretum, XXIV. q. i, c. 18:* Thus the Lord speaks to Peter: I say to you that you are Peter and upon this rock I will build my church (*Mat. xvi, 78*). He builds his church upon one man, and although he will bestow power upon all the apostles after his resurrection—As my Father has sent me, even so I send you. Receive the Holy Spirit (*John xx, 21–22*)— nevertheless, in order to show unity, he ordered the origin of that unity by his authority as beginning from one person. Certainly, the other apostles were what Peter was: furnished with equal fellowship of dignity and power. But the origin springs from unity, in order that the church of Christ may present itself as one. (*Thus far Cyprian.*) And this church of Christ does not consist in men by reason of their power or office, whether ecclesiastic or secular, because many princes and supreme pontiffs and others, subordinates, have been known to have abandoned the faith; therefore the church consists in those persons in whom are knowledge and true confession of faith and of truth (*So Lira, on Mat. xvi, 18*).

Secondly [*i.e., in Pisanus's cases: supra*]: When the sentence has been pronounced after a legitimate appeal.

The third case: When the sentence includes an intolerable error.

A fourth case is when someone else excommunicates through a major excommunication those who are associated with the excommunicated, not in crime, but in speech, and in the other cases in which a lesser excommunication is incurred. For such a sentence is invalid unless preceded by three admonitions or by one for the three, and unless those to be admonished are cited by name. (*Sext., V, xi, 13; 9.*)

A fifth case: When prelates forbid their subordinates to disclose the state of affairs of their churches or monasteries to their superiors, or to legates, or to inquisitors, and when on account of this the prelates pronounce a sentence of excommunication (*Sext., I, xvi, 4*).

[III]

1. Clemens Quintus, *De statu monachorum, Ne in agro, Clementinis,*** de habitu monachorum nigrorum dicit:[103] Statuimus ut superior vestis ipsorum habitui proxima, nigri, bruni, aut albi coloris existat. Sit eciam vestis ipsa rotunda per circuitum et non fissa

(III)

1. *Clement V, in the Clementines, III, x, 1,* says of the habit of the black monks: We have decreed that their upper garment, directly over their habit, should be black, brown, or white in color; it should be a round, undivided garment. And let them have full sleeves,

---

* In quibus consistit ecclesia.
[100] Lyra *super Mattheum, xvi, 18, in verba* "et porte inferi."
[101] *Liber Sextus,* V, xi, 13, 9 (Friedberg, II, 1103, 1101); *periphrasis.*

[102] *Liber Sextus,* I, xvi, 4 (Friedberg, II, 987); *periphrasis.*
** De monachis.
[103] *Clementine,* III, x, 1 (Friedberg, II, 1166–1168); *citacio composita.*

[*recte:* scissa]; largas eciam manicas habeant usque ad pugnum protensas; almuciis de panno nigro vel pellibus capuciorum loco cum capuciis habitus quem gestaverint sint contenti: iuxta tamen disposicionem abbatis, fissis [*recte:* scissis] super humeros et honestis capuciis uti possunt. Estivalibus largis aut botis altis pro calciamentis utantur. Nullus zonam, cultellum, calcaria cum ornatu deferre audeat, aut cum sella clavorum ornatu superfluo decorata, vel nimis sumptuosa seu cum freno ferraturam [*MS:* fracturam] ad ornatum habente equitare presumat. Rursus in locis in quibus fuerit congregacio duodecim monachorum aut supra, infra septa monasterii abbas, prior, aut alius presidens portet flocum aut kucullam etc. Extra monasterium flocum, kucullam, aut cappam clausam habeant, et subtus cappam kukullam, aut si maluerint, scapulare. Kukulle nomine habitum longum et amplum sed manicas non habentem; nomine vero floci habitum qui longas et amplas habet manicas, nos intelligere declaramus.

A venacionibus aut aucupacionibus [*MS:* occupacionibus] semper abstineant, nisi saltus (et est nomen loci bestiarum saltancium), vivaria (nomen loci piscium), vel garenas (locus tubi aves habitant), proprias, vel ius venandi in alienis haberent, in quibus cuniculi vel fere alie forsan essent, quo casu hoc eis permittitur, dum nec venacioni presenciam exhibent personalem etc.

Glosa: nigredo habitus [**f. 246**] in mortificacione carnis fuit inventa; utinam meritorum [nigredo?] et virtutum per illa[m] hodie non signetur. *Estivalibus:* et sunt calciamenta corii quibus in estate utor, et optima fiunt aput Sanctum Severinum. *Botis altis,* que capiunt supra talos et ligantur, id est, sokulares [*recte:* sotulares] corrigiatos [*sic!*]. *Ad ornatum:* patet quod quando non ad ornatum, sed propter ingruentem necessitatem, talibus uterentur, essent excusabiles. *Cappam:* tondelli [*recte:* rondelli] qui nunc sunt in usu, non sunt proprie cappe, seu cappa dicatur a capite seu a "capio-capis," quia totum hominem capiat; non enim habent capucium appensum. *Glosa Johannis Andree.*[104]

2. "Ecce ego mitto vos sicut agnos inter lupos. Nolite portare sacculum neque peram neque calciamenta,"[105] "neque virgam,"[106] id est baculi auxilium. *Sic ponitur secundum Mat. et Luc., decimis capitulis, sed secundum Mar. vi. dicitur:* "nisi virgam tantum"[107] —id est potestatem vivendi de ewangelio: *secundum Bedam.*[108] "Sed calciatos sandaliis"[109]—*Augustinus:* vel soleis, ut neque pes sit tectus neque ad terram nu-

reaching down to the fist. In place of an [outer] hood they should be content with an almuce of black cloth or of leather, together with the hood of the habit that they have on. By disposition of the abbot, however, they may use finer hoods, divided over their shoulders. For shoes let them use roomy summer-shoes or high boots. Let no monk venture to wear a belt, carry a dagger, or wear ornamented spurs, and let him not presume to rise on a saddle superfluously studded with ornamental nails, or on one excessively sumptuous, or with reins ornamented by iron-work. Back in places where twelve or more monks are grouped, the abbot, prior, or other chief may wear a coat or cowl, etc., within the monastery enclosure. Outside the monastery they may have a coat or cowl; or they may have a fastened cape, and under the cape a cowl or, if they prefer, a scapular. By "cowl" we understand a habit that is long and full but does not have sleeves; by "coat" [*flocus*] a habit that has long and full sleeves.

Let them always abstain from hunting or falconry unless they have their own forests [*saltus*] (the name of a place where there are beasts that jump [*saltancium*]), fish-ponds [*vivaria*], (the name of a place where there are fish), or warrens [*garenas*] (a place where birds live), or the right of hunting on others' property where there may perhaps be rabbits or other game. In this case hunting is allowed to them, provided that they are not personally present at the hunt.

John Andree's gloss: Blackness of habit, was designed for mortification of the flesh—would that blackness of merits and virtues were not signified by it today. *Summer-shoes:* these are shoes of hide that I use in the summer—the best ones are made near St. Severin's. *High boots* are those that come up above the ankles and are bound—that is, laced shoes. *Ornamented:* It would of course be excusable if they used these not for the sake of ornament but in case of unforeseen necessity. *Cape:* the round mantles that are now in use are not properly capes—whether cape [*cappa*] be so called from "head" [*caput*] or from "to cover" [*capio*], because it covers the whole man—for they do not have an attached hood.

2. "Behold, I send you forth as lambs among wolves, Carry neither purse, nor scrip, nor shoes"; "nor a staff," that is, the help of a stick. This is what is written in the tenth chapters of *Luke* (*x, 3–4*) and *Matthew* (*x, 10*), but according to Mark vi, 8, it says "Save a staff only"—that is, the power of living from preaching the gospel (*this according to Bede*). "But be shod with sandals" (*Mark vi, 9*)——*Augustine:* Or-with strapped-on soles, so that the foot be neither cov-

---

[104] Johannis Andree, *Glose in verba citata, Clementine, III, x, 1 (Edit. Lugdun., col. 206). Sed glosa alia invenitur in verbum* "nigredo.")

[105] Luc. x, 3–4; *cf.* Mat. x, 16, 10.

[106] Mat. x, 10.

[107] Mar. vi, 8.

[108] *Non inventum.*

[109] Mar. vi, 9.

dus;¹¹⁰ *et secundum Liram,* non dicuntur calciamenta proprie.¹¹¹ "Non panem neque in zona es," *secundum Mar.;*¹¹² *sed secundum Mat.:* "nolite possidere aurum neque argentum neque pecuniam in zonis vestris," "neque duas tunicas."¹¹³ *Secundum Luc.:* * "Et neminem per viam salutaveritis." "Nolite transire de domo in domum," etc.¹¹⁴

Veniet hora ut omnis qui interficit vos arbitretur se obsequium prestare deo. Absque sinagogis facient vos. *Joh. xvi.*¹¹⁵ Non est discipulus super magistrum suum neque servus supra dominum suum. Si patrem familias Belzebup vocaverunt, quanto magis et domesticos eius. Cavete ergo ab hominibus; tradent enim vos in conciliis. Nolite timere eos qui occidunt corpus, etc.; capilli capitis vestri omnes numerati sunt, etc. *Mat. x.*¹¹⁶ Beati estis cum maledixerint vobis homines et persecuti vos fuerint, etc. *Mat. v.*¹¹⁷ *Translacio antiqua habet:* et expulerint.¹¹⁸ Non veni mittere pacem in terram, etc. *Mat. x.*¹¹⁹ Hec locutus sum vobis ut in me pacem habeatis; sed confidite, quia ego vici mundum. *Joh. xvi, in fine.*¹²⁰ Qui non accipit crucem suam et sequitur me non est me dignus. *Mat. x.*¹²¹ Qui animam suam perdiderit propter me et ewangelium salvam faciet eam. *Mar. viii.*¹²² Et accipiat cencies tantum cum persecucionibus. *Mar. x.*¹²³ Ponite in cordibus vestris non premeditari quemadmodum respondeatis. Ego **[f. 246']** enim dabo os et sapienciam cui non poterint [*recte:* poterunt] resistere et contradicere omnes adversarii vestri. Trademini autem a parentibus, fratribus, et cognatis et amicis, et morte afficient ex vobis; et eritis odio omnibus propter nomen meum. Et capillus de capite vestro non peribit. In paciencia vestra possidebitis animas vestras. *Luc. xx[i], et Mat. x.*¹²⁴ Iam conspiraverunt iudei ut si quis confiteretur eum Cristum, extra synogogam fieret. Ideo maledixerunt ceco nato et dixerunt: Tu discipulus illius sis. In peccatis natus es totus et tu doces nos? Et eiecerunt eum foras. Et audivit Ihesus et cum invenisset eum dixit ei: Tu credis in filium dei? *Joh.*

ered nor bare on the ground; *and according to Nicholas of Lira,* sandals are not properly called shoes. "No bread, no brass in their belts," *according to Mark vi, 8;* but *according to Matthew x, 9, 10:* "Do not possess gold, or silver, or money in your belts, "nor two coats." *According to Luke x, 4, 7:* "And salute no man by the way." "Go not from house to house," etc.

The time will come, that whosoever kills you will think that he does God service. They shall put you out of the synagogues. (*John xvi, 2.*) The disciple is not above his master, nor the servant above his lord. If they have called the master of the house Beelzebub, how much more shall they call them of his household. So beware of men; for they will deliver you up in their councils. Fear not them which kill the body, etc. The hairs of your head are all numbered, etc. (*Mat. x, 24, 25, 17, 28, 30.*) Blessed are you when men shall revile you and persecute you, etc. (*Mat. v, 11.*) *The old translation says:* "and shall drive you out." I have not come to send peace on earth, etc. (*Mat. x, 34.*) These things I have spoken unto you, that in me you might have peace; but be of good cheer—I have overcome the world. (*John xvi, 33.*) He that takes not his cross and follows after me, is not worthy of me. (*Mat. x, 39.*) Whosoever shall lose his life for my sake and the gospel's, the same shall save it. (*Mark viii, 35.*) And he shall receive a hundredfold, with persecutions. (*Mark x, 30.*) Put it in your hearts, not to premeditate how you shall answer. For I will give a mouth and wisdom, which all your adversaries shall not be able to gainsay nor resist. And you shall be betrayed both by parents, and brethren, and kinsfolk, and friends; and some of you shall they cause to be put to death; and you shall be hated of all men for my name's sake. But there shall not a hair of your head perish. In your patience possess you your souls. (*Luke xxi, 14–19; cf. Mat. x, 19, 53, 22, 30.*)

The Jews had plotted already that if any man did confess that he was Christ, he should be put out of the synagogue. Therefore they reviled the man who had been born blind, and said, "You are his disciple. You were altogether born in sins, and do you teach us?"

---

¹¹⁰ *Glosa super Mar. vi, ut fertur Augustini, invenitur apud Bedam: In Marci Evangelium Expositio, Lib. II (MPL, vol. 99, col. 187):* "Proinde Marcus dicendo calceari eos sandaliis vel soleis aliquid hoc calceamentum mysticae significationis habere admonet, ut pes neque tectus sit, neque nudus ad terram; id est, nec occultetur Evangelium nec terrenis commodis invitatur."

¹¹¹ Lira, *glosa super Mar. vi, in verba* "Sed calciatos sandaliis": "Ex quo patet quod sandalia non dicuntur calciamenta proprie quia illis poterant uti apostoli ut hic dicitur."

¹¹² Mar. vi, 8.

¹¹³ Mat. x, 9, 10.

* Persecucio.

¹¹⁴ Luc. x, 4, 7.

¹¹⁵ Joh. xvi, 2.

¹¹⁶ Mat. x, 24, 25, 17, 28, 30.

¹¹⁷ Mat. v, 11.

¹¹⁸ *Non ad manum.*

¹¹⁹ Mat. x, 34.

¹²⁰ Joh. xvi, 33.

¹²¹ Mat. x, 38.

¹²² Mar. viii, 35.

¹²³ Mar. x, 30: *In contextu:* (29) "Respondens Jesus ait: Amen, dico vobis, nemo est, qui reliquerit domum aut fratres aut sorores aut patrem aut matrem aut filios aut agros propter me et propter evangelium, (30) qui non accipiat centies tantum nunc in tempore hoc, domos et fratres et sorores et matres et filios et agros cum persecutionibus, et in saeculo futuro vitam aeternam."

¹²⁴ Luc. xxi, 14–19; *cf.* Mat. x, 19, 53, 22, 30.

ix.[125] Ideo et Nicodemus venit ad eum nocte. *Joh. Joh. iii.*[126] Ex principibus multi crediderunt in eum sed propter pharizeos non confitebantur, ut de sinagoga non eicerentur. Dilexerunt enim gloriam hominum magis quam gloriam dei. *Joh. xii.*[127] Quomodo potestis vos credere qui gloriam ab invicem accipitis? *Joh. v. [MS: vi].*[128]

3. Ampla kuculla nimis, nigra vestis, bucca [*recte:* botta?] rotunda, non faciunt monachum, sed mens a crimine munda.[129] Si cupis hoc esse quod diceris, monachus, id est solus, quid facis in urbibus que utique non sunt solorum habitacula sed multorum?*[130] Monasteria non sunt construenda in urbibus.[131] *Ut Jeronimus, XVI. q. i., Si cupis, et in glosa; c. Placuit, ii.*[132]

4. Loquitur secundum ea tempora, cum monachi fuerunt laici; *ut XVIII. q. ii, Quidam, in glosa.*[133] Sed nunc, proch dolor, in multis deficiunt verborum exemplorum documenta; et ad instar filii prodigi dissipate sunt patrum substancie, et quandoque cupiunt implere [*MS:* cupiunt debere implere] de siliquis ventrem suum. *Johannes Andree, De statu monachorum, Ne in agro, in Clementinis.*[134]

5. "Monus" grece, latine "unus"; "achus" grece, latine "tristis"; unde dicitur "monachus": id est, unus tristis. Sedeat igitur tristis, et officio suo vacet. Quia sicut piscis sine aqua caret vita, ita sine monasterio monachus. Sedeat itaque solitarius, et taceat, quia mundo est mortuus. *Ut in Decreto, c. Placuit.*[135]

6. Licet monachus dicatur mortuus mundo, tamen ad hoc generare potest; *ut in Speculo, de testibus, par. i, versu, "Item excipitur."*[136] Concordat Extra de homicidio, "Sicut ex literarum," ubi quedam mulier lesam dicit se a quodam kartuziensis ordinis,** prius monachus niger, que eciam asserebat se concepisse ex eo.[137] Caute ergo puer quidem in cunabulis fuit sectus et postea monachus factus; *ut Extra de corpore viciatis, Ex parte, primo.*[138]

7. "Monachus" grece, latine "singularis." Unde monachum [f. 247] per omnia singulariter agere oportet. Quamobrem firmiter et indissolubiliter omnes precipimus ut aliquis monachus penitenciam nemini tribuat,

And they cast him out. And Jesus heard of this and when he had found him, he said to him: "Do you believe in the son of God?" (*John ix, 22, 28, 34, 35.*) Therefore even Nicodemus came to him by night (*cf. John iii, 1–2*). Among the chief rulers many believed in him; but because of the Pharisees they did not confess him, lest they should be put out of the synagogue. For they loved the praise of men more than the praise of God. (*John xii, 42–43.*) How can you believe, who receive honor one of another? (*John v, 44.*)

3. A full-cut cowl, garments that are all too black, a plump cheek—not these make a monk, but rather a mind pure of guilt. Do you wish to be that which you are called, a monk—that is, a man alone? Then what are you doing in towns, which are not indeed the dwelling-places of solitaries, but of the many? (*Jerome, in Decretum, XVI. q. i, c. 5.*) *The gloss:* Monasteries are not to be built in towns.

4. He speaks according to those times, when monks were laymen (*Decretum, XVIII. q. ii, c. 10, in the gloss*). But now, alas, many lack the credentials of words and deeds, and, like the prodigal son, they have wasted their fathers' substance, and sometimes are eager to fill their bellies with husks. (*John Andree gloss on "sacra," Clementines, III, x, 1.*)

5. "Monus" in Greek, "unus" in Latin; "Achus" in Greek, "tristis" in Latin: whence the name "monachus" (monk)—that is, "unus tristis" (a sorrowful one). Let him therefore sorrowful reside, and let him tend to his duty. For as a fish without water lacks life, so does a monk without a monastery. And so he should remain solitary and keep silence, for he is dead to the world. (*Decretum, XVI. q. i, c. 8.*)

6. Even though a monk is said to be dead to the world, still he can procreate thereto, as is said in the *Speculum [iudiciale]*, "On witnesses." And the *Decretals agree, V, xii, 20*, where a certain woman says she had been violated by a member of the Carthusian order, formerly a black monk, and also said she had conceived from him. The boy was therefore cautiously castrated in the cradle, and was afterwards made a monk (*Decretals, I, xx, 3*).

7. "Monachus" in Greek; "singularis" in Latin. Whence a monk must hold himself apart in all things. We therefore impose this firm and indissoluble com-

---

[125] Joh. ix, 22, 28, 34, 35.
[126] Joh. iii, 1–2.
[127] Joh. xii, 42–43.
[128] Joh. v, 44.
[129] *Versus ab auctore anonymo; inveniuntur eciam in tractatu Johannis Wyclif, De religione privata II, Polemical Works,* ed. R. Buddensieg, II (London, 1883), 535.
* *Interpretacio monachi.*
[130] XVI. q. i., c. 5 (Friedberg, I, 762).
[131] *Glosa ordinaria in verbum "solorum," Decretum,* XVI. q. i., c. 5 (*Edit. Lugdun., col. 1093*).
[132] *Id est, capitulum "Placuit" secundum (c. 8), XVI. q. i.; sed de hoc nichil hic desumptum est.*

[133] *Glosa ordinaria in verba "vel monachi," Decretum,* XVIII, q. ii., c. 10 (*Edit. Lugdun., col. 1201*).
[134] *Glosa ordinaria in verbum "sacra," Clementine,* III, x, 1 (*Edit. Lugdun., coll. 204–205*). *Hic legitur:* ". . . *quandoque nostri* cupiunt. . . ."
[135] XVI. q. i., c. 8 (Friedberg, I, 763).
[136] *Speculum iudiciale Guillelmi Durantis non ad manum.*
** *Cisterciensis.*
[137] *Decretales,* V, xii, c. 20 (Friedberg, II, 802).
[138] *Decretales,* I, xx, c. 3 (Friedberg, II, 145); *non verbatim; insuper, verba* "Caute ergo" *sunt addita a Nicolao.*

nisi invicem, mortuum non sepeliat, nisi monachum in monasterio secum commorantem. *Ut XVI. q. i., Placuit. Et est sancta Nicena synodus.*[139] *Et ibi in c. Placuit, ii, dicitur:* Neque penitenciam dare neque baptizare neque infirmum visitare neque mortuum sepelire, sit claustro suo contentus.[140]

8. Religio munda et inmaculata aput deum patrem, hec est: Visitare pupillos et viduas in tribulacionibus eorum, et inmaculatum se custodire ab hoc seculo. *Jacobi primo.*[141] Infirmus fui et non visitastis me, etc. *Mat. xxv.*[142] Ille egregius predicator qui dissolvi cupit et esse cum Cristo, fortis preliator, detineri intra claustra noluit sed certaminis campum quesivit; *ut XXIII. q. v., Ibi adunati.*[143]

9. Religiosus enim velle vel nolle non habet, quia arbitrium voluntatis religiosi dependet ex imperio sui superioris, quem vice dei super caput suum posuit; *ut De eleccione, Si religiosus, Libro VI.*[144]

10. *Dicitur autem Sap. xv.,* Quod deus constituit hominem ab inicio et reliquit eum in manu consiliarii sui; *dicit Lira:* id est, in potestate sui liberi arbitrii.[145] Ipsi autem non habent velle neque nolle. Qui autem perspexerit in lege perfecte libertatis et permanserit in ea, non auditor obliviosus factus sed factor operis, hic beatus in facto suo erit. *Jac. i.*[146]

11.* Nimia religionum diversitas gravem in ecclesia dei confusionem inducit; *Extra De religiosis domibus, c. ult., et est concilium generale.*[147]

12. *Secundum Jeronimum in c. Olym. supra:* Huiusmodi studia in religione instinctu dyaboli sunt facta, ut diceretur in populis; ego sum Pauli, ego sum Appollo, ego autem Cephe, etc.[148] *Nonne hodie dicitur, ille est Benedictinus, ille Celestinus, iste Cisterciensis, ille Premonstratensis, et sic de aliis.* Nec nomen aliud est sub celo datum hominibus in quo opporteat salvos fieri, et non in aliquo alio salus quam in nomine Cristi Nazareni. *Act. iiii.*[149]

13. Favore religiosis multa contra racionem statuuntur; *ut Digestum, De religiosis et sumptibus, Sunt persone.*** [150]

14. Spiritus manifeste dicit, *I. Thim. iiii.* Quia in novissimus temporibus discedent quidam a fide, attendentes spiritibus erroris et doctrinis demoniorum in ypocrisi loquencium **[f. 247']** mendacium et cauteriatam

mand upon all, that no monks assign penance to anyone, except to each other, that they not bury the dead, except if it be a monk living with them in the monastery. (*The Holy Synod of Nicea, in Decretum, XVI. q. i, c. 1.*) *And in XVI. q. i, c. 8, it says:* He should neither give penance, nor baptize, nor visit the sick, nor bury the dead, but let him be content with his cloister.

8. Pure religion and undefiled before God the Father is this, to visit the fatherless and widows in their affliction, and to keep himself unspotted from this world (*Ias. i, 27*). I was sick and you visited me not (*Mat. xxv, 43*). That most outstanding preacher who desired to be dissolved and to be with Christ, that strenuous warrior refused to be shut up behind walls, but sought the field of battle (*Decretum, VII. q. i, c. 49 [St. Gregory writing about Paul]*).

9. The religious have not to say yes or no, for the will of the religious depends on the rule of his superior, whom he has set over himself to hold the place of God (*Sext, I, vi, 27*).

10. It was God who made man in the beginning, and left him in the hands of his own counsel (*Ecclus. xv, 14*). That is, in the power of his own free will (*Nicholas of Lira*). But the religious "have not to say yes or no"! But who so looketh into the law of perfect liberty, and continues therein, he being not a forgetful hearer, but a doer of the work, this man shall be blessed in his deed (*Ias. i, 25*).

11. An excessive diversity of religious orders causes grave confusion in the church of God (*Decretals, III, xxxvi, 9: Fourth Lateran Council*).

12. According to St. Jerome (*Decretum, XCV. dist., c. 5*), as quoted above, such "rivalries arose in religion at the Devil's incitement" so that it was "said among the people, 'I am Paul's,' 'I am Apollo's,' 'But I am Cephas's,' etc." But is it not said today, "He is a Benedictine," "He is a Celestine," "That one is a Cistercian," "He is a Premonstratensian," and so on? "There is none other name under heaven given to men whereby they must be saved," and "there is no salvation in any other" than in the name of Christ the Nazarene (*Acts iv, 10, 12*).

13. Many things contrary to reason have been decreed to favor the religious (*cf. Digest, XI, vii, 43*).

14. *The Spirit says expressly,* that in the latter times some shall depart from the faith, giving heed to the spirits of error, and to doctrines of demons that speak lies in hypocrisy and have their consciences seared with

---

[139] XVI, q. i, c. 1 (Friedberg, I, 763).
[140] XVI, q. i, c. 8 (Friedberg, I, 763).
[141] Jac. i, 27.
[142] Mat. xxv, 43.
[143] *Recte:* VII, q. i., c. 49 (Friedberg, I, 587).
[144] *Liber Sextus*, I, vi, 27 (Friedberg, II, 962).
[145] *Recte:* Ecclus. xv, 14; *ubi legitur* "in manu consilii sui." *Glosa est in loco, sed interlinearis, non Lyrana.*
[146] Jac. i, 25.

* Religiosis domibus.
[147] *Decretales*, III, xxxvi, 9 (Friedberg, II, 607); *canon Concilii Lateranensis quarti.*
[148] XCV. dist., c. 5 (Friedberg, I, 332–333); *cf.* I Cor. i, 12.
[149] Act. iv, 10, 12.
** Reliquiis et sumptibus funerum.
[150] *Cf. Codicem* Lib. III, xliv, *et Digestum* Lib. XI, vii, 43 (*Corpus Juris Civilis (Lipsiae 1720)*: Cod., col. 147–148 et Dig., col. 273).

habencium conscienciam prohibencium nubere et abstinere a cibis quos deus creavit.[151] *Et II Tym. iiii:* Erit enim tempus, cum sanam doctrinam non sustinebunt, sed ad sua desideria coacervabunt sibi magistros *** prurientes auribus, et a veritate quidem auditum avertent, ad fabulas autem convertantur.[152] *Et ibi, iii:* Hoc autem scito, quod in novissimis diebus instabunt tempora periculosa, et erunt homines se ipsos amantes, cupidi, elati, superbi, blasphemi, parentibus non obedientes, ingrati, scelesti, sine affeccione, sine pace, criminatores, incontinentes, immites, sine benignitate, proditores, protervi, tumidi, ceci, voluptatum amatores magis quam dei, habentes speciem quidem pietatis, virtutem autem eius denegantes; et hos devita. *Concordant: Rom. i, Gal. v, Eph. ii.*[153]

15. Opportet deo magis obedire quam hominibus, non enim possumus que audivimus et vidimus non loqui. *Act. iiii, et v.*[154] Illi ergo profecti predicaverunt ubique, domino cooperante, et sermonem confirmante sequentibus signis. *Mar. ult.*[155] In omnem terram exivit sonus eorum. *Psa. xvii.*[156]

16. *Crisostomus:* Totus mundus mirabatur Cristum per apostolos mundum convertisse; huius autem quadruplex causa fuit: pecunie contemptus, glorie despectus, secularium occupacionum segregacio, et terribilium perpessio.* Eicere demonia comune opus est inter ministros dei et dyaboli; veritatem confiteri et iusticiam facere privatum est opus tantummodo sanctorum; ideo quem videris demonia eicientem, si non sit confessio veritatis in ore eius, nec iusticia in manibus eius, non est homo dei. Si autem videris veritatem confitentem et facientem iusticiam, etsi demonia non eicit, homo est dei.[157]

17. Mendicantes sunt qui certas possessiones, vel redditus non habent sed per questum publicum eis victum prebet incerta mendicitas, ut Predicatores, Minores, Heremite Sancti Augustini, et Carmelite; *ut De eleccione, Quorundam; De religiosis domibus, c. unico Libr. VI., et in glosa.*[158]

18. Beatus qui excutit manus suas ab omni munere. *Gregorius, I. q. i., Sunt nonnulli.*[159] *Jeronimus, ad rusticum monachum de cottidianis operibus monachorum, et ponitur, De consecracione, Di. V., Nunquam:* Facito aliquid operis ut semper [f. 248] dyabolus te inveniat occupatum. Si apostoli habentes potestatem de

---

a hot iron, forbidding to many and commanding to abstain from foods which God has created (*I Tim. iv, 1–3*). *And II Tim. iv, 3–4:* For the time will come when they will not endure sound doctrine; but after their own lusts shall they heap to themselves teachers, having itching ears; and they shall turn away their ears from the truth, and shall be turned to fables. *And II Tim. iii, 1–5:* This also know, that in the last days perilous times shall come. For men shall be lovers of their own selves, covetous, puffed up, arrogant, blasphemers, disobedient to parents, unthankful, unholy, without natural affection, without peace, false accusers, incontinent, fierce, unkindly, traitors, impudent, pompous, blind, lovers of pleasures more than lovers of God, having indeed an appearance of piety but denying its true virtue. From such turn away. (*And to the same sense are: Rom. i, 24–32; Gal. v, 19–21; Eph. v, 3–5.*)

15. We ought to obey God rather than men; for we cannot but speak the things which we have seen and heard (*Acts v, 29; iv, 20*). Therefore they went forth and preached everywhere, the Lord working with them and confirming the word with signs following (*Mark xvi, 20*). Their sound has gone out into every land (*Psa. xviii, 5 [King James xix, 4]*).

16. *Chrysostom:* The whole world was amazed that Christ had converted the world through the apostles. But there were four reasons why this was possible: contempt of money, scorn of praise, exclusion of worldly concerns, and endurance of dreadful things. To cast out demons is work common to ministers both of God and of the Devil, but to confess the truth and do justice is the peculiar work of the saints alone; whom therefore you see casting out demons, if there be no confession of truth in his mouth nor justice in his hands, he is not a man of God. But if you see one confessing the truth and doing justice, even if he not cast out demons, he is a man of God.

17. Mendicants are those who do not have definite possessions or incomes, but a loose sort of mendicancy provides them with a livelihood, at public expense. Such are the Preachers, Minorites, Hermits of St. Augustine, and the Carmelites. (*Sext., I, vi, 24 and gloss; and III, xvii, 1.*)

18. Blessed is he that shakes his hands free from every gift (*St. Gregory, in the Decretum, I. q. i, c. 114; cf. Isa. xxxiii, 15*). *And St. Jerome, writing to a country monk about the daily work of monks; in the Decretum, De cons., V. dist., c. 33:* Always be doing

---

[151] I Tim. iv, 1–3.
*** Blandientes magistri.
[152] II Tim. iv, 3–4.
[153] II Tim. iii, 1–5; cf. Rom. i, 24–32; Gal. v, 19–21; Eph. v, 3–5.
[154] Act. v, 29; iv, 20.
[155] Mar. xvi, 20.
[156] *Recte:* Psa. xviii, 5.
* Condiciones veri predicatoris.
[157] *Non inventum.*
[158] *Glosa ordinaria in verbum* "mendicantium," *Liber Sextus,* I, vi, 24 (*Edit. Lugdun., col. 146*): cf. *Sext.,* I, vi, 24 et III, xvii, 1 (Friedberg, II, 961–962, 1054–1055).
[159] I. q. i., c. 114 (Friedberg, I, 402–403); cf. Isa. xxxxiii, 15.

ewangelio vivere laborabant manibus suis, ne quemquam gravarent et aliis tribuebant refrigeria, pro quorum spiritualibus debebant metere carnalia, cur tu non prepares in usus tuos successura? Vel fiscellam texe iuncco, vel canistrum plecte, seratur humus, inserantur fructuose arbores; apum fabricare alvearia. Texantur et lina capiendis piscibus. Scribentur [sic] et libri ut manus operetur cibos, et anima leccione saturetur. In desideriis est omnis ociosus. Egiptiorum monasteria hunc morem tenent ut nullum absque opere et labore suscipiant, non tam propter victus necessaria quam propter anime salutem, ne vagentur perniciosis cogitacionibus, et instar fornicantibus Israhel omni transeunti diffaricent pedes suos. Questio: Quid? Ergo peribunt omnes, qui in urbibus habitant? Ecce illi fruuntur rebus suis, adeunt balnea, unguenta non respuunt, et in omnium flore versantur. Ad quod nunc breviter respondeo, me in presenti opusculo non disputare, sed monachum instruere. *Hec ille*.[160]

19. Nec existimat abbas quod super habenda proprietate possit cum aliquo monacho dispensare; quia abdicacio proprietatis, sicut et custodia castitatis adeo est annexa regule monachali, ut contra eam nec summus pontifex possit licenciam indulgere, ut [*recte*: quod] si proprietas aput quemquam inventa fuerit in morte, ipsa cum eo in signum perdicionis, extra monasterium in sterquilino substernetur: secundum quod Beatus Gregorius narrat in Dyallogo hoc fecisse. *Ut Extra de statu monachorum, Cum ad monasterium, par. Tales, et par. Quod si.*[161] *Et dicitur in glosa:* Quod abdicacio proprietatis et custodia castitatis sunt de substancia monachatus. Et ideo dixerunt Vincencius et Johannes quod papa non potest dispensare ut monachus habeat proprium existendo monachus.[162]

20. *Illud Mar. x*, "Nemo est qui reliquerit domum aut fratres aut sorores aut patrem aut matrem aut filios aut agros propter me et ewangelium, qui non accipiat cencies tantum, nunc in hoc tempore,"[163] *secundum Liram*, potest exponi de reliogiosis qui pro uno patre carnali vel fratre dimisso habent spirituales patres et fratres multos et eciam possessiones et agros in quantum ex possessionibus omnium fidelium sufficienter sustentantur. *Secundum illud Apostoli, II Cor. vi.:* Tamquam nichil [f. 248'] habentes et omnia possidentes.[164] *Hec ille*.[165] Ypochritas multos sub habitu monachorum usque quaque dispersit callidissimus hostis, circum-

some sort of work, so that the Devil may always find you busy. If the apostles who had the power of living from the Gospel worked with their hands, so as not to be a burden to any, and indeed gave help to others from whom they had a right to ask material support in exchange for spiritual benefits—why should you not provide things for your own use? Weave baskets of rushes or wicker-work; let the soil be sown and fruitful trees be planted; make beehives; let lines be braided for catching fish. Let books be written that the hand may earn food and the mind filled by reading. A man who is idle is always in want. The monasteries of Egypt hold to this practice, that they receive no one who will not work and toil—not so much on account of the necessary means of life as for the sake of the soul's salvation, lest the brethren drift into deadly thoughts and, like the whores of Israel, spread their legs for everyone passing by (*cf. Ezek. xvi, 25*).

A question: What, will everyone perish who lives in a town? For see, they enjoy their goods, they go to the baths, they do not refuse to be anointed, and they are surrounded by the best of everything. To this point I answer, briefly, that in the present tract I am not engaged in disputation but am instructing a monk. (*Thus far St. Jerome.*)

19. No abbot will suppose that he can give a monk a dispensation to have property; for abdication of property, like the preservation of chastity, is so much a part of the monastic rule that not even the Supreme Pontiff can license an exemption from it. So much, indeed, that if property be found with any monk at his death, then it and he are thrown in a dung-pit outside the monastery, as a symbol of his damnation: and this according to what St. Gregory in his *Dialogue* says he had done. (*Decretals, III, xxxv, 6.*) *And it says in the gloss* [*ibid.*]: Abdication of property and preservation of chastity are of the substance of monasticism. It is for this reason that Vincent [Hispanus] and John [Teutonicus] have said that the pope cannot grant a dispensation allowing a monk to have private property while he remains a monk.

20. "There is no man that has left house, or brethren, or sisters, or father, or mother, or children, or lands, for my sake and the gospel's, but he shall receive a hundredfold now in this time"—this text of *Mark x, 29–30* can, *according to Lira*, be applied to the religious, who have given up one fleshly father or brother and have many spiritual fathers and brothers in exchange, and also possessions and lands inasmuch as they are adequately supported from the possessions of all the

---

[160] De cons., V. dist., c. 33 (Friedberg, I, 1420–1421); *ubi ultima particula legitur:* "me in praesenti opusculo non de clericis disputare, sed monachum instruere."

[161] *Decretales*, III, xxxv, 6 (Friedberg, II, 599–600); *loco* "par. Tales" *deberet poni* "par. ultimo."

[162] *Glosa ordinaria in verba* "Abdicatio proprietatis," *Decretales*, III, xxxv, c. 6 (*Edit. Lugdun., col. 1297*).

[163] Mar. x, 29–30.

[164] II Cor. vi, 10. Cf. Augustini, *De Civitate Dei*, XX, c. xix (*MPL*, vol. 41, col. 685–687).

[165] Lira, *glosa, in loco*.

venientes omnes provincias petunt omnes, exigunt aut sumptus lucrose egestatis aut precium simulate sanctitatis. *Hec Augustinus.*[166]

21. Pseudopropheta qui predicabit anticristum erit simulacio paupertatis quo ad se. *Sicut enim secundum Augustinum, De civitate dei,* per aliquos pontifices ydolorum castissimos [*MS:* castissimus] multa impudica circa culturam ydolorum decens [*sic*] fieri consulebant, ut sic sub specie honestatis pontificum plebs ad ipsam traheretur:[167] Sic fiet, et tunc anticristus sic consulet et laudabit divicias, qui tamen ad maiorem fraudem in aliquibus casibus ac temporibus et personis quendam ypochritalem paupertatem fovebit. *Hec glosa, Mat. xxiiii, super isto, "Ecce in deserto est Cristus."*[168]

22. Rogo autem vos fratres, ut observatis eos qui dissensiones et offendicula, preter doctrinam, quam vos didicistis, faciunt, et declinate ab illis. Huiusmodi enim Cristo domino nostro non serviunt, sed suo ventri, et per dulces sermones et benedicciones seducunt corda innocencium. *Rom. ult.*[169] Ex hiis enim sunt qui penetrant domos, et captivas ducunt mulierculas oneratas peccatis que ducuntur variis desideriis, semper discentes et numquam ad scienciam veritatis pervenientes, etc. *II Tym. iii.*[170] Et ego gloriabor, ego: in laboribus plurimis, in carceribus habundancius, in plagis supra modum, in mortibus frequenter. A Iudeis quinquies quadragenas una minus, accepi. Ter virgis cesus sum, semel lapidatus sum. *II Cor. xi.**[171]

23. Triumphale martirium nomen letis obsequiis complectamur, qui per diversa tormentorum genera Cristi passionem non lacessentibus precordiorum mentibus imitabantur, alii fero perempti, alii flammis exusti, alii plagis verberati, alii ictibus perforati, alii vivi excoreati, alii lapidibus obruti, alii ligwis [*sic*] privati, alii vero truncis manibus sive ceteris membris spectaculum contumelie inter populos nudi pro nomine domini portaverunt. Sancti "per fidem vicerunt regna, operati sunt iusticiam. Alii distenti sunt; alii ludibria et verbera experti, insuper et vincula et carceres: lapidati sunt, secti sunt, temptati sunt, in occisione gladii mortui sunt, circuierunt in melotis, in pellibus caprinis, egentes, angustiati, afflicti, quibus dignus non erat mundus: **[f. 249]** in solitudinibus errantes et montibus, et in speluncis, et cavernis terre. Et hii omnes testimonio fidei probati sunt." *Heb. xi.*[172] *Prophecia Beate Hildegardis, ultimo, In diebus illis.*[173]

faithful. Thus according to the Apostle, *II Cor. vi, 10:* "As having nothing, and yet possessing all things." (*Thus far Lira.*)

The most cunning of enemies has scattered many hypocrites far and wide, under monastic garb, and they go through every province, all of them asking or demanding the costs of their profitable indigence, the price of their simulated holiness. (*Augustine, De opere monachorum, ch. xxviii.*)

21. The false prophet who will preach the Antichrist will himself present a false appearance of poverty. For just as, according to Augustine's *The City of God,* many shameless things used to be done in connection with the cult of idols, by priests of those idols, themselves most chaste, in order that the people might be attracted to the cult by the apparent worthiness of the pontiffs—so it will happen then, when the Antichrist will commend and praise riches but, in certain cases, times, and persons, to improve his deception, will foster a hypocritical poverty. (*The gloss on Mat. xxiv, 26.*)

22. Now I beseech you, brethren, mark them who cause divisions and offenses contrary to the doctrine which you have learned; and avoid them. For they that are such serve not our Lord Christ but their own belly, and by sweet words and benedictions seduce the hearts of the innocent. (*Rom. xvi, 17–18.*) For of this sort are they who creep into houses, and lead captive silly women laden with sins, led away with divers lusts, ever learning, and never arriving at knowledge of the truth (*II Tim. iii, 6–7*). I too will glory, I too: in labors more abundant, in prisons more frequent, in stripes above measure, in deaths often. Of the Jews five times received I forty stripes save one. Thrice was I beaten with rods, once was I stoned. (*II Cor. xi, 18, 23–25.*)

23. Let us embrace the triumphal name of martyrdom with joyous homage—martyrs who imitated the passion of Christ in divers kinds of torments, which they had not provoked in mind or heart. Some were killed by the sword, others burned in flames, scourged with stripes, run through with thrusts, flayed alive, or buried under stones; others had their tongues cut out, while yet others, their hands or other members cut off, a spectacle of shame among men, naked have begged for the sake of the Lord's name. The saints "through faith have subdued kingdoms and wrought righteousness. Some were tortured on the rack, others had trial of mockings and scourgings, and moreover of bonds and imprisonment; they were stoned, they were sawn

---

[166] Augustinus, "De opere monachorum" c. xxviii (*MPL* vol. 40, col. 575–576); "O servi Dei, itane dissimulatis callidissimi hostis insidias . . . tam multos hypocritas sub habitu monachorum usquequaque dispersit, circumeuntes provincias, . . . et omnes petunt, omnes exigunt, aut sumptus lucrosae egestatis, aut simulate pretium sanctitatis."
[167] *Non inventum.*

[168] Cf. Mat. xxiv, 26 (*Glosa non ad manum*).
[169] Rom. xvi, 17–18.
[170] II Tim. iii, 6–7.
* De corea ecclesie primitive.
[171] II Cor. xi, 18, 23–25.
[172] Heb. xi, 33–39.
[173] *Non inventum.*

24. *Jeronimus:* Nemo hinc episcoporum invidia dyabolice temptacionis infletur, vel irascatur, si plebem interdum exhortentur presbiteri. Si [non vult presbiteros facere] que iubentur a deo, dicat, quid maius Cristo? Aut quid poterit corpori aut sanguini eius anteponi? Si presbiter Cristum consecrat, cum in altario dei sacramenta benedicit, benedicere populum non debet, qui Cristum consecrare non metuit? Circa laicos ac mulieres, iubentibus vobis, iniustissimi sacerdotes, presbiter dei benediccionis perdit officia, amittit ligwe [sic] opus, non habet confiduciam predicandi, truncatus est omni parte virtutum, solum presbiteri habet [MS: habent] nomen, plenitudinem ac perfeccionem, que consecracioni eius competit, non retenta[t]. Quis ergo hic, rogo, sacerdotes, honor vester est, ut dampnum gibbi inferatis? (*Glosa:* Quia non predicantibus presbiteris incurvatur populus in delictis, et quasi gibbosus efficitur.) *Unde sequitur:* Quoniam ipsi presbiteri, ut legimus, episcopi nominantur: "qui vos posuit episcopos regere ecclesiam suam." Sed oderunt hoc superbi sacerdotes in presbiterii nomine, qui nolunt hoc esse, quod Cristus, qui discipulorum pedes lavit, qui baptizatus est a Iohanne, etc. *Ut XCV. di., Ecce ego.*[174] *Et in capitulo sequente dicitur:* Pessime conswetudinis est in quibusdam ecclesiis, tacere presbiteros et presentibus episcopis non loqui, quasi eis invideant, aut eos dedignantur audire. "Et si aliquid," inquit Paulus, "fuerit revelatum sedenti, prior taceat." Gloria patris est filius sapiens. Gaudeat episcopus in iudicio suo, cum tales elegit sacerdotes. Episcopi sacerdotes sciant se esse, non dominos. Unus dominus, unum baptisma, unum templum, unum sit ministerium. Recordemur semper, quod apostolus Petrus precipit sacerdotibus:* "Pascite eum, qui in vobis est, gregem domini, neque turpis lucri gracia, neque ut sitis dominantes in clero."[175]

Amen, anno domini 1417.

asunder, were put to the test, were slain with the sword; they wandered about in sheepskins and goatskins, being destitute, afflicted, tormented; of whom the world was not worthy. They wandered in deserts and in mountains, and in dens and caves of the earth. And all of them have been proven by the witness of faith." (Heb. xi, 33–39.) (*The prophecy of St. Hildegard.*)

24. *St. Jerome:* Let no bishop henceforth be angry or succumb to the diabolical temptation of arrogant envy if presbyters sometimes exhort the people. If the bishop would not have the presbyters do what God has ordered, let him then say, what is greater than Christ? Or what may be set above Christ's body and blood? If the presbyter consecrates Christ when he blesses the sacraments on the altar of God, should he then not bless the people—he who has not feared to consecrate Christ? At your orders, most unjust of priests [*sacerdotes*], God's presbyter loses his functions of benediction over the laity; he loses the work of his tongue, he is not trusted to preach, every one of his powers is cut away from him: he has only the name of presbyter, but does not retain the fullness and perfection that belong to his own consecration. I ask you, oh priests [*sacerdotes*], is this then your office, to impose a crippling hump? (*the gloss:* For when presbyters do not preach, the people are crooked in their misdeeds, and are like hunchbacks.) *And he continues:* For we read that these very presbyters are called bishops: "[the Holy Spirit] has made you overseers [*episcopos*], to rule his church" (*Acts xx, 28*). But arrogant priests [*sacerdotes*] hate this aspect of the presbyter's title; they do not want to be what Christ was, who washed the disciples' feet, who was baptized by John, etc." (*Decretum, XCV. dist., c. 6.*)

And in the following chapter (XCV. dist., c. 7) it says: It is the worst sort of practice that in some churches the presbyters remain silent and do not speak when the bishops are present, as if the latter were jealous of them or disdained to hear them. But Paul says: "If anything be revealed to another who sits by, let the first hold his peace" (*I Cor. xiv, 30*). A wise son is his father's glory. Let the bishop rejoice in his judgment which has chosen such priests [*sacerdotes*]. Let the bishops know that they are priests [*sacerdotes*], not lords. There is one Lord, one baptism, and one temple: let the ministry also be one. Let us always remember what the Apostle Peter enjoined upon priests [*sacerdotibus*]: "Feed the flock of God which is among you, not for filthy lucre and not as lords over the clergy" (*I Pet. v, 2–3*).

Amen, A. D. 1417

---

[174] XCV. dist., c. 6, pars. 2–6 (Friedberg, I, 333). *Glosa ordinaria in verbum* "damnum gibbi inferatis" (*Edit. Lugdun., col. 459*). "Qui vos posuit . . .": Act. xx, 28.
* Preceptum sacerdotibus predicare.

[175] XCV. dist., c. 7, pars. 6, 1, 4, 5 (Friedberg, I, 334); "Et si aliquid . . .": I Cor. xiv, 30; "Pascite . . .": I Pet. v, 2–3, *imprecise.*

INDICES

An Index of References in the Tabule

Each entry is followed by its Tabula number and Explanatory Note number.

1. THE BIBLE

Genesis: iii, 7 (VI, 3); iii, 21 (VI, 1).
Exodus: xx, 17 (IV, 17).
Numbers: xi, 29 (IV, 26).
Deuteronomy: iv, 2 (III, 11); xxvii, 26 (III, 11); xxxii, 15 (VI, 17).
I Samuel: xv, 23 (V, 30).
Job: ix, 12 (III, 8 and IX, 6); xxi, 31 (IX, 6); xli, 24 (IX, 6).
Psalms: x, 8 (IX, 16); cxviii, 85 (VIII, 6).
Isaiah: i, 5–6 (III, 3); liii, 2–3 (I, 1).
Ezekiel: xxxviii, 17 (IX, 4).
Daniel: vii, 24–25 (III, 14 and IX, 18); xi, 33 (IX, 8), 36 (IX, 3), 37 (IX, 3a), 39 (IX, 3); xii, 10 (IX, 13); xiii, 20–21 (V, 17), 22–24, 28 (V, 18); 52–53 (V, 19), 56–57 (V, 20).
Zachariah: xi, 17 (IX, 1).
Matthew: iii, 4 (VII, 2, 5); v, 13 (IV, 6), 17 (III, 12), 26 (IV, 16), 32 (IV, 18), 44 (III, 5); vii, 15 (VII, 8), 16 (IV, 24); viii, 20 (I, 8); x, 8 (V, 11), 9 (II, 2); xi, 11 (VII, 3); xii, 37 (IV, 11); xvi, 4 (IV, 23), 24 (I, 2); xviii, 15 (IV, 5); 17 (V, 28); xix, 6 (IV, 18), 27 (II, 7), 28 (IV, 7); xxiii, 4 (III, 10), 8–9, 11–12 (VIII, 8); xxiv, 21 (IX, 7).
Mark: ix, 39 (IV, 25); xv, 17 (I, 11).
Luke: ii, 7 (VI, 6), 15, 16 (II, 9); ix, 55–56 (III, 4); x, 5, 7 (II, 3); xi, 45 (IV, 28), 52 (IV, 27), 53–54 (IV, 28); xii, 14, 15 (I, 10); xiv, 35 (V, 28); xvi, 19, 20, 22 (VII, 1), 24–26 (VII, 7), 25 (VII, 6); xxiii, 11 (VI, 22a).
John: ii, 13–15 (V, 15); vi, 15 (I, 9); viii, 28 (III, 13), 44 (VIII, 2), 46 (IV, 4); xiii, 4–5 (VIII, 9), 12–18 (VIII, 7), xix, 2 (VI, 19), 23 (VII, 17), 23–24 (VII, 18); xxi, 18, 22 (I, 14).
Acts: iii, 6 (II, 5); vii, 51 (IV, 29), 54 (IV, 30); viii, 21 (V, 16).
Romans: i, 26–27 (VIII, 12).
I Corinthians: i, 26, 27 (II, 14); v, 11 (V, 28); viii, 4 (IX, 2).
Galatians: i, 8–9 (V, 29).
II Thessalonicans: ii, 4 (IX, 17); 9–10 (IV, 22 and IX, 17), 8 (IX, 19).
I Timothy: vi, 8 (VI, 24).
Hebrews: xi, 37, 38 (VI, 14); xiii, 14 (II, 10).
James: ii, 5 (II, 13).
I Peter: i, 18–19 (I, 13).
II John: 10 (V, 28).
Apocalypse: vi, 5 (V, 1); xiii, 2 (IX, 11), 7, 15, 17 (IX, 9); xvi, 15 (IX, 15).

2. CANON LAW

The Decretum

X. dist., c. 4 (IV, 19).
XI. dist., c. 7 (V, 10).
XII. dist., c. 12 (III, 6).
XXVII. dist., I pars. (V, 27).
XXXII. dist., c. 5 (V, 25).
XXXII. dist., c. 6, III pars (V, 26, 31).
XXXV. dist., c. 4 (VI, 27).
XL. dist., c. 5 (V, 12).
XLI. dist., c. 1 (VII, 16).
LXIII. dist., c. 30 (I, 12).
LXX. dist., c. 2 (II, 1).
LXXX. dist., c. 3 (II, 8).
XCVI. dist., c. 14 (I, 7 and VI, 5).
I. q. i, c. 5 (V, 13).
I. q. i, c. 14 (V, 14).
I. q. i, c. 21, par. 1 (V, 6).
I. q. i, c. 108 (V, 22).
I. q. i, c. 117 (V, 7).
I. q. ii, c. 9 (II, 12).
I. q. iii, c. 8 (V, 9).
I. q. iii, c. 13 (V, 3).
I. q. vii, c. 27 (V, 5).
II. q. vii, c. 1 (IV, 1).
II. q. vii, c. 2 (IV, 2).
IX. q. iii, c. 17 (IV, 3).
XVII. q. iv, c. 29 (III, 2).
XXI. q. iv, c. 1 (VI, 26).
XXIV. q. iii, c. 27 (V, 2).
XXIV. q. iii, c. 30 (V, 2).
XXIV. q. iii, c. 33 (V, 2).
XXV. q. i, c. 16 (III, 15).
XXVII. q. ii, c. 19 (IV, 19).
XXXIII. q. iii (de Pen.) I. dist., c. 87 (V, 4).

The Decretals

I, viii, 2, 3 (VI, 11).
I, viii, 4 (VI, 8).
I, xxix, 28 (IV, 9).
II, xxvi, 12 (V, 23).
III, i, 13 (V, 24).
III, v, 2 (II, 6).
III, v, 4 (II, 4).
III, v, 16 (II, 11).
III, v, 28 (II, 16).
III, viii, 4 (III, 9).
IV, i, 16 (IV, 15).
V, iii, 1 (V, 8).
V, iii, 9 (V, 8).
V, iii, 39 (V, 8).
V, vii, 12 (IV, 21).
V, xxxiii, 23 (I, 3 and VI, 9).
V, xl, 27 (III, 1).

3. OTHERS

Andree, Johannes: *Glosa super Librum Sextum:* (IV, 8); (VI, 10, 16); *Novella super Librum Sextum:* (VIII, 10, 11); *Glosa super Prohemium Clementinarum:* (I, 6). (See also under *Glosa ordinaria.*)
Ambrosius: *de officus* (IX, 20).
de Aquino, Thomas: *Compendium Theologie ad Fratrem Reginaldum* (IX, 10); (VII, 9).
Sanctus Augustinus: *De Doctrina Christiana* (VII, 16); *De Sermone Domini in Monte* (VII, 10); *Epistola ad Inquisitiones Ianuarii* (III, 6); (VII, 14); (IV, 12).
Sancti Bartholomei, *Passionale* (VIII, 1).
Bartholomeus Brixiensis: (V, 21); (VI, 18). (See under *Glosa Ordinaria.*)
Bernardus Clarevallensis: *De Consideracione* (I, 5); (VIII, 13); *Apologia ad Guillelmum* (VI, 13); (VII, 13); *Sermo, In Nativitate Domini* (VI, 7).
Chrysostomus, Johannes: *In Joannem Homilia* (VII, 21); (VII, 19, 20).

Corpus Iuris Civilis: Authentica, II, ii, Praefacio, Par. i (II, 15); *Digestum,* XI, vii, 43 (IV, 20); (IV, 14); *Institutiones,* I, ii, 6 (III, 7).

Glosa Ordinaria: super Decretum [Johannes Teutonicus, Bartholomeus Brixiensis]; XXXII dist., c. 5, "Audiet" (V, 21); II, q. iv, c. 2 "Presule" (III, 17); IX. q. iii, c. 14 "aliorum" (III, 17); XXI. q. iv, c. 1, "quod vero" (VI, 18); XXXII. q. v, 1 pars "Vis" (II, 18).

Super Decretales [Bernardus Parmensis]: I, xxix, 28 "Tenetur Eadem" (IV, 10); III, xxxiv, 5, "adimplere" (II, 17); *super Librum Sextum* [Johannes Andree]: I, iii, 11 "committantur" (IV, 8); V, vii, 6 (VI, 10, 16); *Glosa super Prohemium Clementinarum* [Johannes Andree]: "Papa" (I, 6).

Sanctus Gregorius: *Moralia in Job* (IX, 6); *XL Homiliarum in Evangelia* (VII, 4, 5); (IV, 13).

Haymo Halberstatensis: *Enarratio in Apocalypsin,* lib. iv (IX, 10a).

Huguccio: (IV, 10); (VI, 15).

Sanctus Jeronimus: *Epistola* (VII, 15); (V, 2); (VIII, 5).

de Lyra, Nicolaus: *Glosa super Biblia:* Gen. iii (VI, 2, 4); Dan. viii (IX, 5); Dan. xii (IX, 14); Mat. xxiii, 4 (III, 6, 16); Joh. xix (VI, 20, 21, 22, 23); I Cor. viii, 4 (IX, 2a); Tim. vi (VI, 25); I Pet. v, 13 (IX, 12); Mic. iv, 10 (IX, 12).

Sancti Martini, Passionale (VI, 12).

Maximus Taurinensis: *Homilia XCII* (IX, 20).

Monachus, Johannes: (VIII, 11).

Sancti Sebastiani, Passionale (VIII, 3, 4).

An index of references in the Consuetudo et Ritus

Each of the following entries is followed by its footnote number.

1. THE BIBLE

Job: ix, 12 (22).
Psalms: xviii, 5 (156); cxviii, 21 (72).
Ecclesiastes: xli, 11–12 (73).
Isaiah: xxxiii, 15 (159).
Ecclesiasticus: xv, 14 (145).
Hosea: iv, 15, 17–18 (79).
Matthew: iv, 5 (68); v, 11 (117); vi, 16 (63); x, 9 (113); 9, 10 (106, 113); 19, 53, 22, 30 (124); 24, 25, 17, 28, 30 (116); 34 (119); 38 (121); xi, 28–30 (64); xvi, 18 (100); xviii, 15–18 (74); xix, 27 (30); xxiii, 8 (56); xxiv, 26 (168); xxv, 43 (142); xxviii, 18–20 (34).
Mark: vi, 8 (107, 112); 9 (108); viii, 35 (122); x, 29 (163); 30 (123, 163); xvi, 20 (155); 15 (35).
Luke: x, 3–4 (105); 4, 7 (114); xxi, 14–19 (124).
John: ii, 1–2 (126); v, 44 (128); viii, 12 (31); ix, 22, 28, 34, 35 (125); xii, 42–43 (127); xv, 15, 27 (33); 18–21 (36); xvi, 2 (115); 33 (120).
Acts: i, 8 (32); ii, 1–4 (1); 46 (3); iii, 6 (29); iv, 10, 12 (149); 19 (154); 32 (5); v, 29 (154); xx, 28 (174).
Romans: i, 24–32 (153); 32 (82); xvi, 17–18 (169).
I Corinthians: i, 12 (148); v, 9–11 (78); vi, 9–10 (81); xiv, 30 (175).
II Corinthians: iii, 1–3 (62); xi, 18, 23–25 (171).
Galatians: v, 19–21 (153).
Ephesians: v, 3–5 (153).
Philippians: iii, 18–19 (77).
II Thessalonicans: iii, 14 (76).
I Timothy: iv, 1–3 (151).
II Timothy: iii, 1–5 (153); 6–7 (170); iv, 3–4 (152).
Hebrews: xi, 33–39 (172).
James: i, 25 (146); 27 (141).
I Peter: v, 2–3 (175).
II John: i, 10–11 (75).

2. CANON LAW

The Decretum.

VIII. dist., c. 1 (7).
VIII. dist., I pars. (6).
XIV. dist., c. 2 (69).
XIX. dist., c. 3 (66).
XXI. dist., I pars. (47).
LXVIII. dist., c. 5 (46).
LXXI. dist., c. 8 (61).
LXXI. dist., c. 9 (60).
LXXX. dist., c. 15 (67).
LXXXI. dist., c. 15 (65).
XCV. dist., c. 5 (148).
XCV. dist., c. 7, pars. 6, 1, 4, 5 **(175)**.
I. q. i, c. 114 (159).
II. q. i, c. 14 (24).
II. q. vi, c. 11 (23).
II. q. vi, c. 41 (94).
II. q. vii, par. Penitentes (26).
III. q. vi, c. 10 (20).
IV. q. iii, c. 1 (25).
VII. q. i, c. 49 (143).
XI. q. iii, c. 1 (87).
XI. q. iii, c. 41 (84).
XI. q. iii, c. 42 (85).
XI. q. iii, c. 60 (91).
XI. q. iii, c. 64 (92).
XI. q. iii, c. 64 (90).
XI. q. iii, c. 68 (39).
XI. q. iii, c. 95 (70).
XI. q. iii, c. 101 (71).
XII. q. i, c. 2 (8).
XII. q. i, c. 5 (11).
XIII. q. i, c. 1 (43).
XVI. q. i, c. 1 (139).
XVI. q. i, c. 5 (130).
XVI. q. i, c. 8 (135).
XVI. q. i, c. 8 (140).
XXIII. q. iv, c. 27 (86).
XXIV. q. i, c. 4 (98).
XXIV. q. i, c. 18 (99).
XXIV. q. i, c. 25 (37).
XXVI. q. vi, c. 3 (59).
De Cons. V. c. 33 (160).

The Decretals.

I, vii, 3 (16).
I, xvi, 3 (2).
I, xx, 3 (138).
I, xxv, 8 (95).
III, v, 4 (27).
III, xxxv, 6 (161).
III, xxxvi, 9 **(147)**.
V, xii, 20 (137).
V, xx, 6 (58).

The Sext.

I, iii, 11 (14).
I, vi, 24 (158).
I, xvi, 4 (102).
III, xvii, 1 (158).
V, xi, 13 (101).
X, vi, 27 (144).
X, xvi, 4 (102).

Clementines.

III, x, 1 (103).

3. Others

Andree, Johannes: *Glosa super Librum Sextum:* I, vi, 11 "committantur" (15); *Glosa super Clementinas:* (104); (134). (See also under *Glosa Ordinaria*.)

de Aquino, Thomas: *Compendium Theologie* (83).

Sanctus Augustinus: *De Civitate Dei* (164); (167); *De Opera Monachorum* (166); (110).

Beda: *In Marci Evangelium Expositio* (110).

Bartholomeus Brixiensis: (9); (10). (See also under *Glosa Ordinaria*.)

Sanctus Bernhardus: (40); (41).

Chrysostomus, Johannes: (157).

Chrysostomus (Pseudo): *Opus imperfectum in Matthaeum* (48, 50, 51, 52, 53).

Ciprianus: (99).

Clemens V: (103).

Corpus Iuris Civilis: Codex, III, xliv (150); (12); (17, 18, 19); *Institutiones,* I, ii, 6 (21); *Digest,* XI, vii, 43 (150); *Autentica* (28).

Flores Temporum: (4); (42).

Glosa Ordinaria: super Decretum, XCV. dist., c. 6, pars. 2–6 "Damnum gibbi inferatis" (174); XCV. dist., c. 7 "quasi clericos" (57); LXVI. dist., c. 1 "Ordinatur" (45); XI. q. iii, c. 1 "timenda est" (88); (93; XII. q. i, c. 2 "Precipimus" (9); XIII. q. i, c. 16 "apostolorum" (10); XII. q. i, II pars. "Hiis ita" (13); XVI. q. i, c. 5 "solorum" (131); XVI. q. i, c. 65 "Revertimini" (13); XVIII. q. ii, c. 10 "vel monachi" (133); XXIV. q. i, c. 25 "invidia" (38). *Super Decretales:* I, vii, 3 "Veri Dei Vicem": (17); III, xxxv, 6 "Abdicatio proprietatis" (162); V, xxxix, 40 "In Sardicensi autem concilio" (96); V, xxxix, 40 "intollerabilem errorem" (89). *Super Librum Sextum:* I, iii, 11 "committantur" (15); I, vi, 24 "Mendicantium" (158). *Super Clementinas:* III, x, 1 "nigredo," "Estivalibus," "Botis albis," "adornatura," "Cappam" (104); III, x, 1 "Sacra" (134).

Glosa Ordinaria super Biblia: Mat. iv, 5 (68); Mat. vi (55); Mat. xxiv, 26 (168).

Guiellelmus Durantis: (See under *Speculum iudiciale*.)

Haymo Halberstatensis: *Enarratio in Apocalypsin* (83).

Hildegardis: (173).

Sanctus Jeronimus: (132).

de Lyra, Nicolaus: *Glosa super Biblia:* Ecclus. xv, 14 (145); Hos. iv, 15, 17–18 (80); Mat. xvi, 18 (100); Mar. vi (111).

Parmensis, Bernardus: (89). (See also under *Glosa Ordinaria*.)

Pysanus: Summa (97).

Speculum iudiciale: (2), (136).

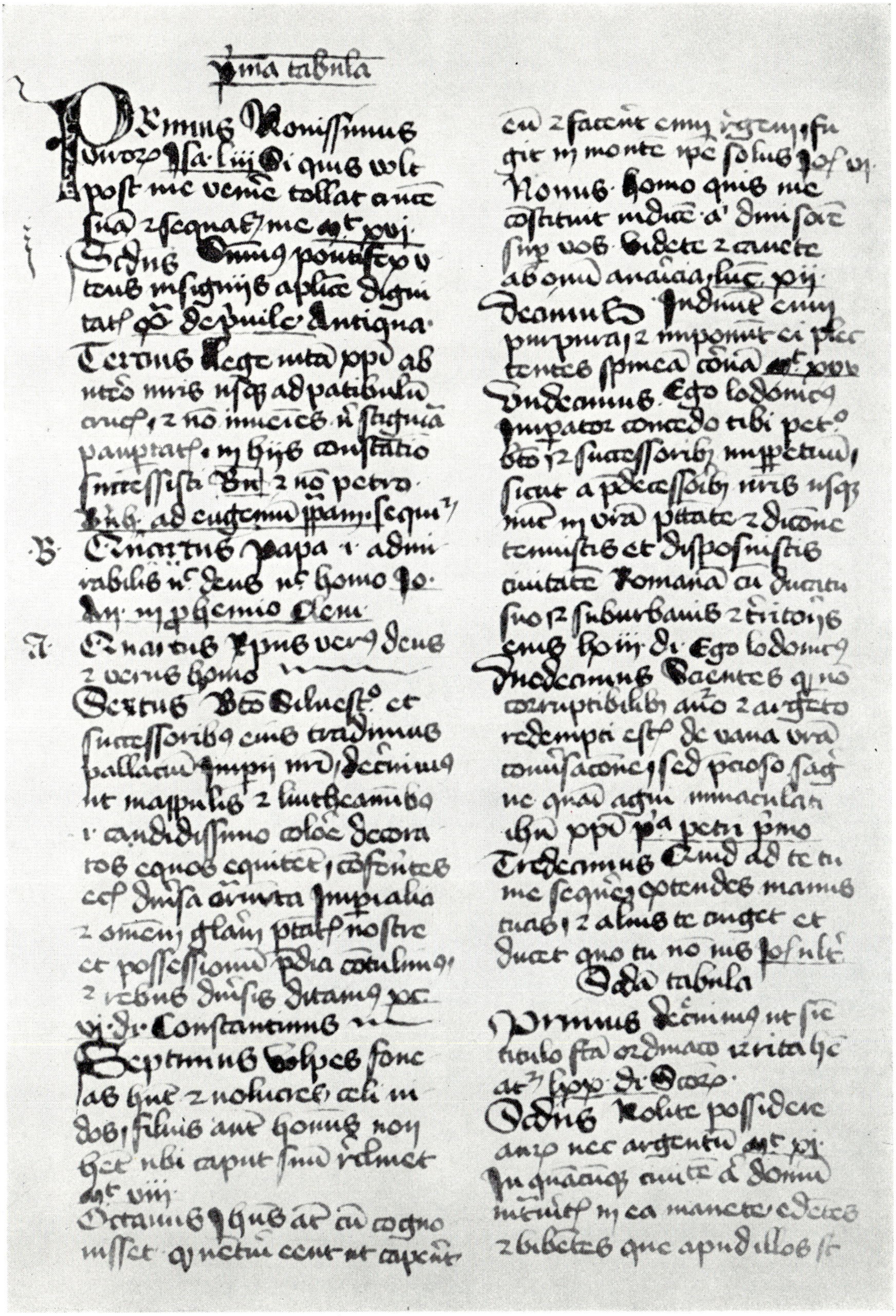

Fig. 1. MS. Prague University and National Library, IV G 15 ("P"), f. 232′.

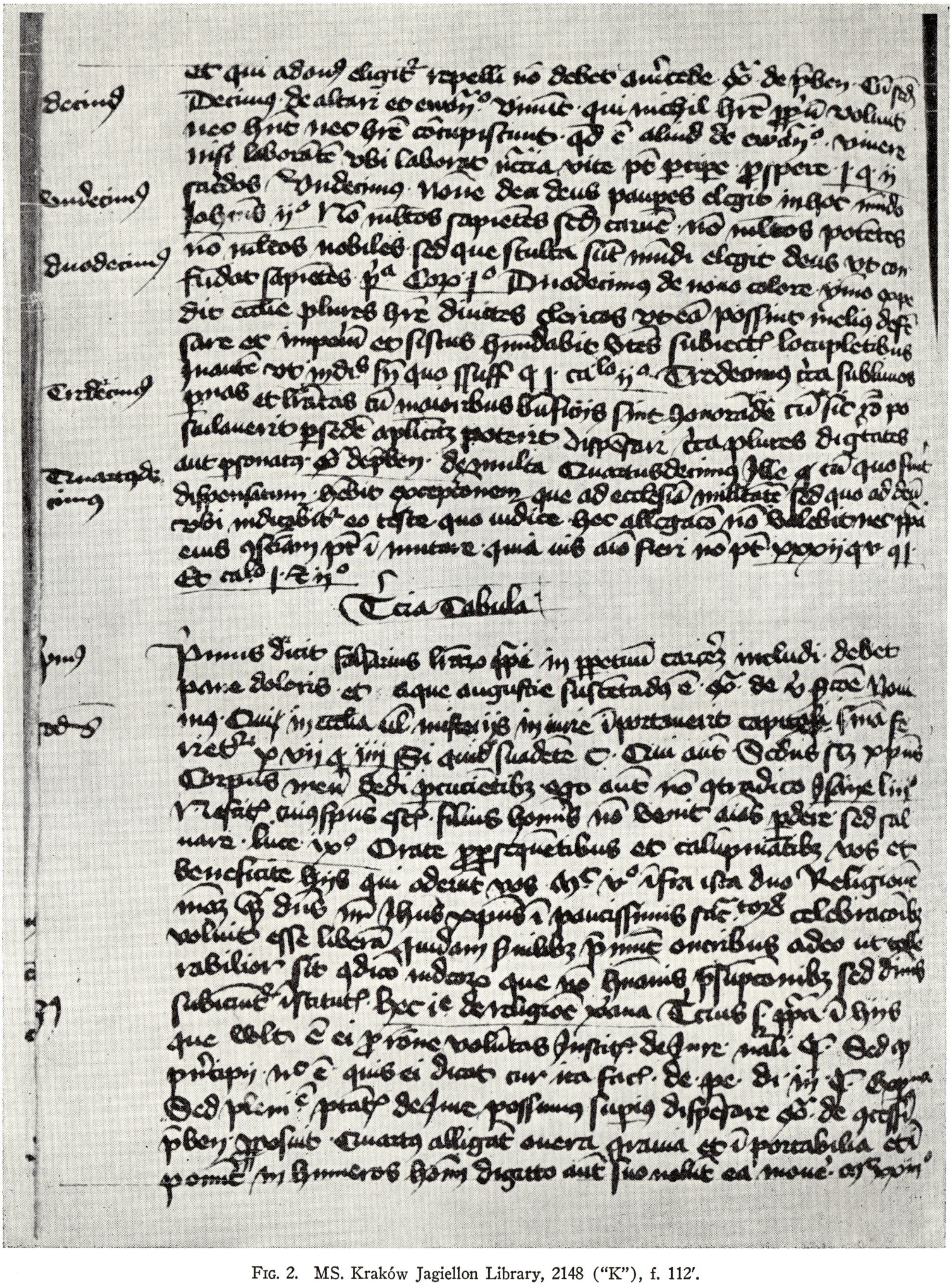

Fig. 2. MS. Kraków Jagiellon Library, 2148 ("K"), f. 112'.

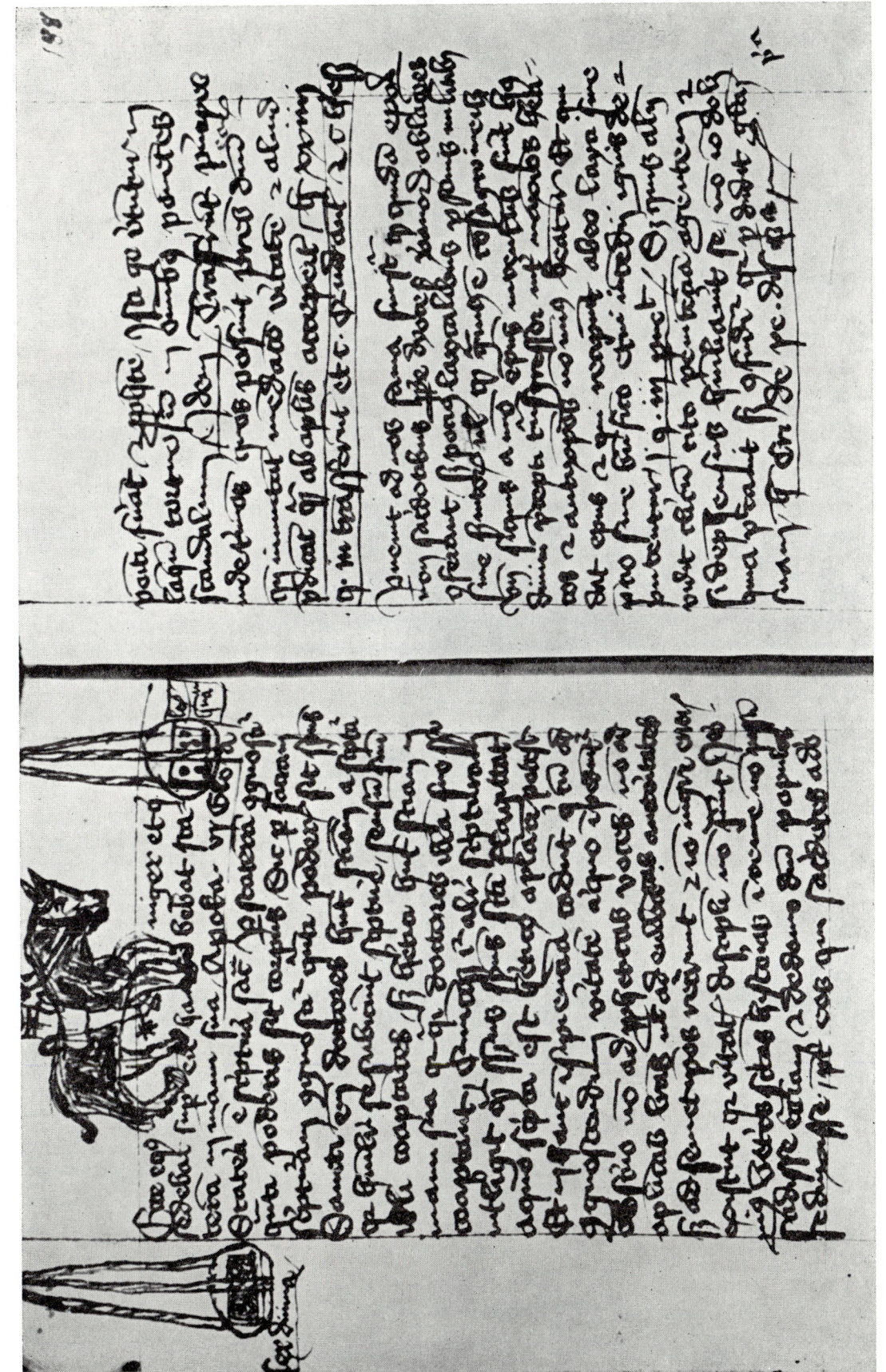

FIG. 3. MS. Vienna Nationalbibliothek, 4343 ("Y"), f. 187ʳ–188.

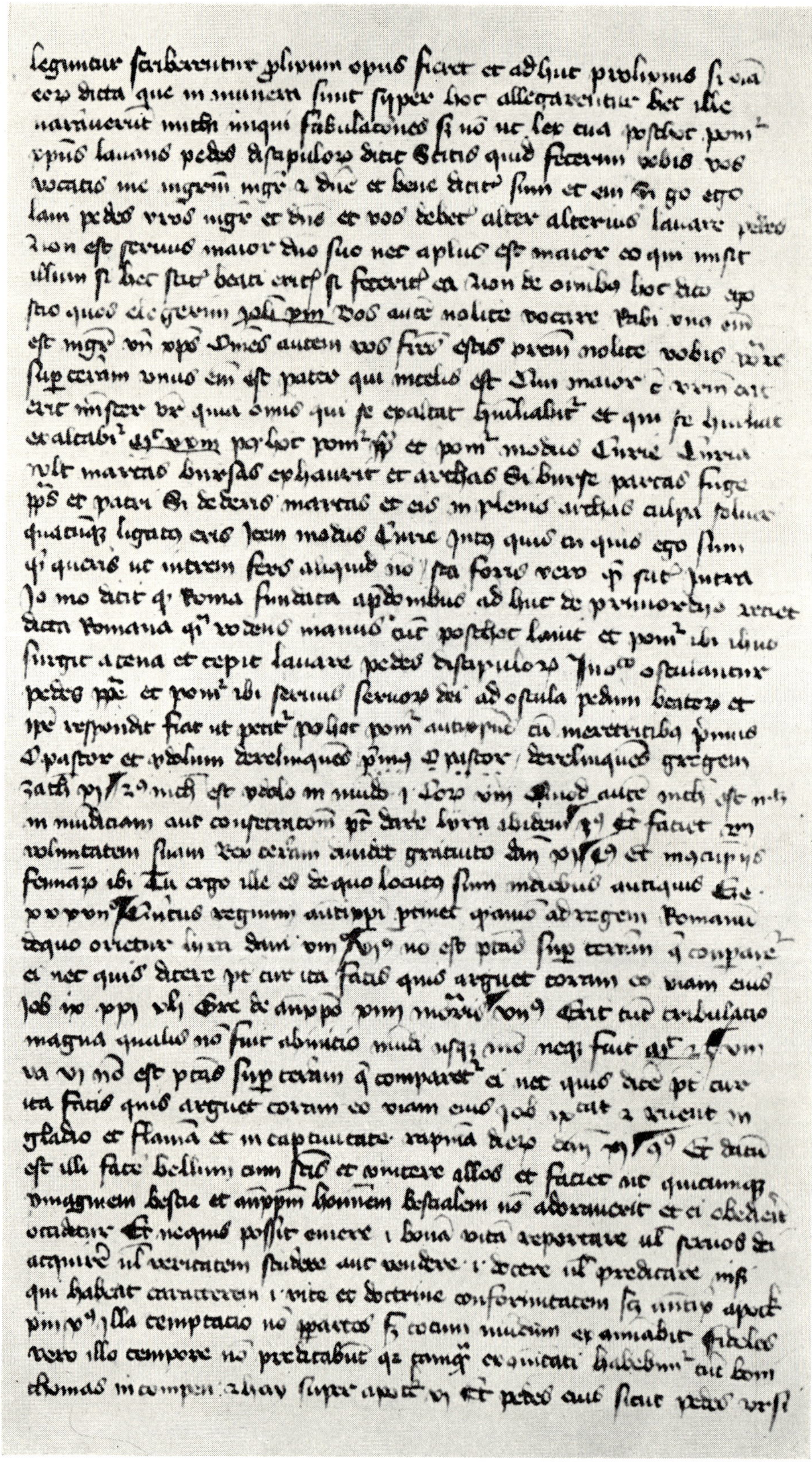

FIG. 4. MS. Vienna Nationalbibliothek, 4875* ("Z"), f. 335.

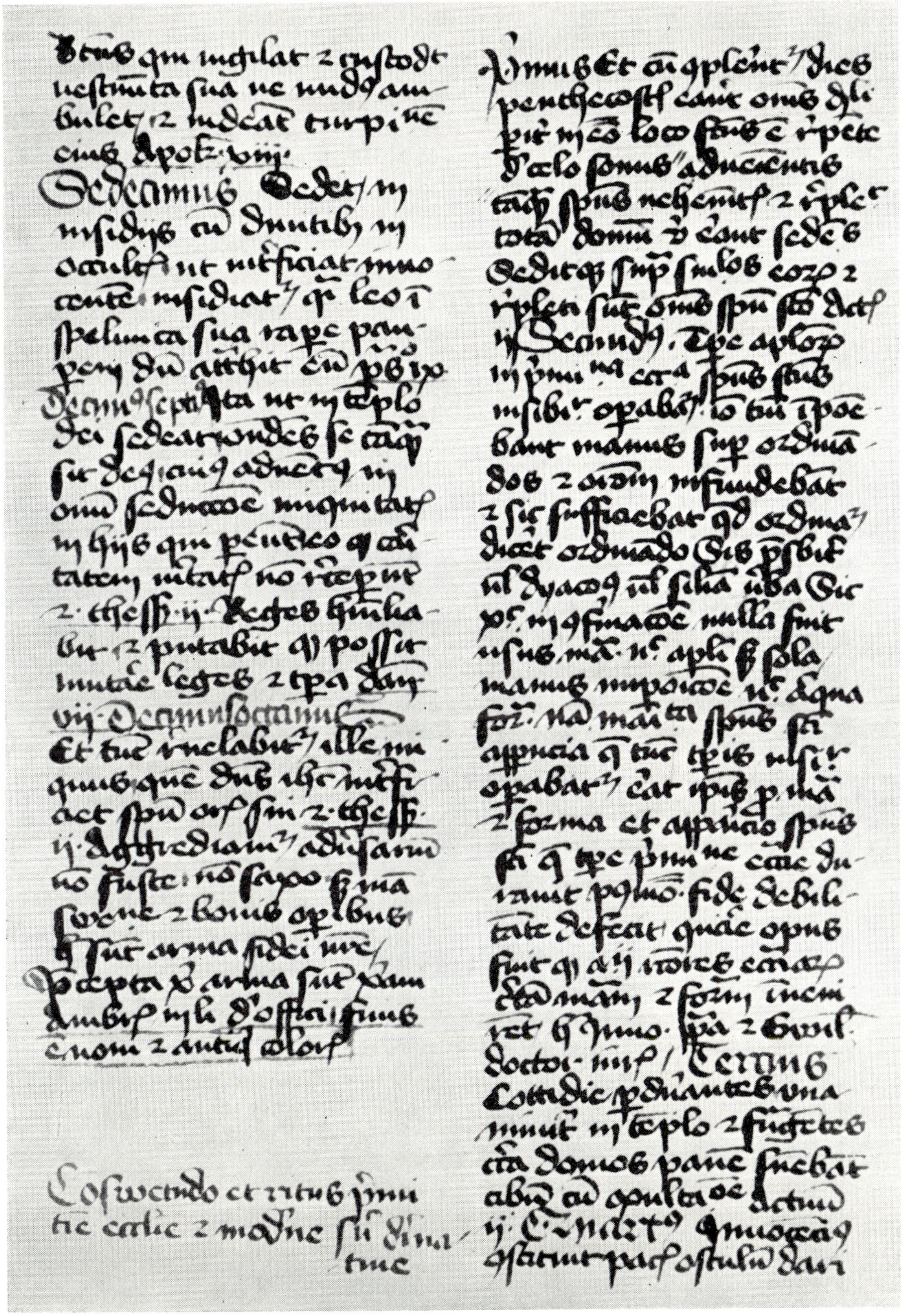

Fig. 5. MS. Prague University and National Library, IV G 15 ("P"), f. 240.

2

Bound by
DESS & TALAN
New York, N.Y.

SEP 1966